Lies, Damn Lies and Documentaries

Brian Winston

' "There are three kinds of lies – lies, damned lies and statistics." Mark Twain, *Autobiography* (1924)'

The International Thesaurus of Quotations, 1976

'As Disraeli said, "There are three kinds of lies – lies, damned lies and statistics." Attributed. Mark Twain, *Autobiography*'

Oxford Dictionary of Quotations, 1979

'(This phrase has also been attributed to Henry Labouchère, Abraham Hewitt and Commander Holloway R. Frost)'

Stevenson's Book of Quotations, Ninth Edition

bfi Publishing

For Charles Cooper in whose front room I discovered there was more to
cinema than could be seen at the Ritz, Neasden

and

in memory of Philip Donnellen

First published in 2000 by the
British Film Institute
21 Stephen Street, London W1P 2LN

The British Film Institute promotes greater understanding of,
and access to, film and moving image culture in the UK.

Cover design: Mark Swan

Set in Minion by Ketchup, London
Printed in Great Britain by Cromwell Press, Trowbridge, Wiltshire

British Library Cataloguing-in-Publication Data
A catalogue record for this book is available from the British Library
ISBN 0–85170–797–1 pbk
ISBN 0–85170–796–3 hbk

Contents

Acknowledgments

This book was sparked by the public row about documentaries that began in earnest in the UK in 1998. I have to thank my colleagues at Stirling University for giving me a first opportunity to outline my disquiet at the way the debate about documentary was developing; although (as can be seen below) I regret that we now seem to have reached very different views on this topic.

The book is much changed because of the careful advice of David Elstein and Peter Goodwin, but I fear there are still points I will not have carried with them. I am also grateful to Roger Laughton for his overview and to Roger James, a model of how 'no prior constraint' should work.

Thanks too to Terry Canon, John Downing (of Austin), Peter Hughes, Steve Knowlton, Vincent Porter, Wyke Rowland and Matthew Winston for help on various points; and Ian MacBride for permission to quote his 1999 Sheffield International Documentary Festival paper. John Merrill and Patti Zimmer-mann allowed me sight of their manuscripts prior to publication, which was of great help to me. Some parts of this argument have previously appeared in various guises and I am grateful to Peter Fiddick, John Izod and Richard Kilborn, Jon Prosser and Mike Wayne for editing these. I am also indebted to the Getty Institute where I explored nineteenth-century photographic 'fakery'.

Finally, thanks to Andrew Lockett for suggesting that I take another look at documentary, Adèle for her usual care and another person for keeping her A levels out of the way.

Argument

This is an argument about documentary film- and video-makers and those who regulate them and it takes an evenhanded approach to these parties in that, regretfully, it wishes something of a plague on both their houses:

– a plague on documentarists who abuse their position as public communicators, less for lying to their audiences and more for duping those whom they involve in their projects

– and a plague on regulators who abridge the documentarists' fundamental right of free expression in the name of preserving some amorphous notion of public trust.

If documentarists are be castigated for their unethical behaviour and regulators for authoritarianism, the argument is bound to become somewhat complex. *Lies, Damn Lies and Documentaries* looks for a way through this maze of legally and ethically dubious behaviours by examining in turn the 'Regulators' (in Part Two) and the 'Documentarists' (in Part Three) within the context of 'The State of Documentary' (in Part One).

It argues that, while documentarists ought to be exposed and pilloried if they lie about the status of their footage, nevertheless such exposure must depend on a proper acknowledgment of the complexities of filming. It cannot rest on the basis of a naïve belief that screen truth equates with non-mediation or that the latter is even possible in any meaningful way. The real difficulties of ethical documentary production turn on the degree and nature of intervention not on its absence or presence; and they rest far more on the relationship between documentarist and participant than between documentarist and audience.

Lies, Damn Lies and Documentaries also maintains that, in a free society where no legal offence has been committed, there is no place for the sort of draconian regulation increasingly seen in the UK. This is especially the case since the particular values of documentary expression are threatened because the form is no longer a discrete and valued genre. Despite a growth in its popularity, paradoxically its very continued existence is under threat because it has been subsumed by a new amorphous category, 'factual programming'. Much of its own distinct established grammar and procedures are no longer either fully understood nor considered legitimate.

We are confusing documentary programming with factual programming (including news), responsibilities to the audience with responsibilities to participants, regulation of media structures with regulation of programme content and image with reality. These confusions in total are chilling the concept of free documentary expression.

Part One, 'The State of Documentary', offers an overview of the current situation and especially the scandals that beset the form in the last years of the twentieth century.

Chapter One, 'Fakery', outlines (1.1) 'The Great British Documentary Scandal' which began at that time with the film *The Connection*. By the 1990s, the public mind apparently considered (1.2) 'Documentary as Journalism' and documentarists were therefore being held strictly to standards of behaviour that traditionally they treated with greater flexibility. The dominance of one particular style of Direct Cinema – commonly called Cinéma Vérité – limited the possibilities for documentary film-making originally envisaged in the 1920s. Instead expectations that the documentary could take various forms of personal expression were downgraded in the name of increasing a journalistic claim to be depersonalised witness. Direct Cinema's dominance over the last forty years established a clear vision of what the documentary was in the mind of print journalists, television's regulators and even many in broadcasting itself – hand-held, available-light and sound filming of actual unmediated events in long takes, minimally edited.

All the older techniques of reconstruction, pictorially pleasing shots, skilful editing, effective commentary and so on were now suspect – 'unsafe', like a conviction in a miscarriage of justice case. A lot of these techniques were even seen as belonging to a quite different and opposing form, docudrama. Now it was (1.3) 'Documentary v. Docudrama', with the latter alone being permitted to use the older styles of the former.

Because of these background factors, (1.4) 'The UK Scandal Acquires "Legs"'. More and more documentaries, some transmitted as many as four years before, were revealed as having 'faked' sequences.

There is a worldwide context for these British embarrassments since in a number of countries documentary is at the centre of similar storms. A dangerously expanded notion of 'fakery' embracing far more than deliberate mendacity is now the basis of (1.5) 'A Global Scandal' with major instances occurring in the rest of Europe, the United States and New Zealand. Documentary is at the centre of the debate about broadcasting ethics in particular and the quality of TV output in general.

Chapter Two, 'Public Service', suggests that this crisis about documentary authenticity has significance for the whole of broadcasting because the debate positions (2.1) 'Documentary as Public Service'. The concept of public service broadcasting in the UK offers a crucial justification for levels of content regulation above those traditionally imposed on the written Press. The same is true of (2.2) 'The American Tradition of Documentary Public Service' within a more commercialised environment.

The rationale behind broadcasting content regulation can be questioned; but, as (2.3) 'British Documentary Popularity' was first truly achieved in the 1990s in the form of docusoaps, the traditional importance of documentary to broadcasting culture is highlighted. Although docusoaps have been less tainted by the 'fakery' scandals (which have largely centred on 'investigative' crime stories), their success in the ratings in the late 1990s ensured a great deal of attention was paid to the regulation of documentary content overall.

In Part Two, 'Regulators', *Lies, Damn Lies and Documentaries* looks at the legal background of this regulation. The central issue is where the point of balance lies between socially necessary controls and the demands of freedom.

Chapter Three, 'Law', outlines the concept of (3.1) ' "Breach of Public Trust" ' which UK regulators have in effect created to justify the sanctions which have been imposed on mendacious broadcasters. Central to this regulatory development is that it invents a quasi-judicial 'offence' for which legally defined damage need not be proved. This lack of potential or actual damage is crucial.

Regulation focuses on the documentarists' relationship with audiences and it does so at the cost of the documentarists' (3.2) 'Right of Free Expression'. (3.3) 'Documentary and the Common Law' defines the documentarists' legal environment as depending on the contractual relationships between broadcaster, film- or programme-maker and participants (and does not normally include the audience). While documentarists are merely workers *vis-à-vis* the broadcaster, their right of free expression tends to take precedence in conflicts with participants over (3.4) 'Legal Privacy' or in debates about the nature of (3.5) 'Legal Consent'.

Chapter Four, 'Regulation', contrasts the limitations of this legal framework with the expansive detail of regulation. In essence, these (4.1) 'British Codes of Practice' operate to make good perceived lacunae in the law. The majority of broadcasters profess themselves happy with them and there is considerable extra-legal precedent for such overt content regulation as (4.2) 'A Short History of Media Control' reveals. In broadcasting terms, however, this control turns on the concept of (4.3) 'The "Contract" with the Viewer'. This has little legal validity, but this deficiency is largely ignored by the regulators. They tend to have a bias against free expression that is exacerbated by (4.4) 'The Legal Improprieties of the Codes' in general, including looseness of language. In particular, as (4.5) 'The codes and Documentary' argues, the limited vision and uncertain requirements of the regulators cluster around the contentious issue of 'reconstruction'.

The general authoritarianism of the regulators can be contrasted with (4.6) 'Regulation in the US'. It is difficult to avoid the conclusion that in Britain the result of the operation of these codes of practice is a de facto (4.7) 'Failure of Regulation' since the threat posed to the right of free expression outweighs both the limited protection offered to participants and the advantages of the paternalistic coddling of the audience.

The case against the regulators is matched in Part Three by a consideration of the moral inadequacies of the 'Documentarists'.

In Chapter Five the ethical consequences of their right of 'Free Expression' is considered. (5.1) 'Media Practitioners' Ethics' are formally articulated in professional union or guild codes of practice. In contrast to the regulatory guidelines, these are also concerned with the threats to ethical behaviour producers of media messages have to endure. Yet they too acknowledge that their members have moral responsibilities. This discussion focuses on journalists, despite the fact that documentarists are not journalists, because this entire issue of media ethics has been most thoroughly articulated by journalists.

Perhaps surprisingly, because of free expression demands, the extent to which even (5.2) 'Truth-telling and Other Responsibilities' are reasonable journalistic objectives, for all that they are clearly ethically desirable, can be questioned. The result is that, given the restricted position of the journalist as worker and the broader functions of journalism beyond basic reporting, it is not easy to apply any sort of systematic ethical system to public expression in a free society. (5.3) 'Documentarists' Ethics' are even less susceptible to systematic treatment because, although documentaries advance much the same objections to systematic ethics as those raised by journalism, in addition they also complicate matters by claiming artistic licence. Since the nineteenth century, such licence has been deemed to be, at least potentially, amoral.

Chapter Six, 'Ethics', deals with the ethical consequences of this journalistic/artistic duality. Documentary's creative treatment of actuality, while not sanctioning the passing-off of fiction as reality, did embrace a slightly different non-journalistic standard of what constituted truth. Documentarists also argue, in (6.2) 'The "Consent Defence" ', that those who participate in their films know what they are doing and that the limited legal protection given participants in the name of free expression is ethically sufficient. But any consideration of the documentary archive in terms of the effect on participants quickly reveals the limitations of this professional vision of (6.3) 'Informed Consent'.

Similarly documentarists are ready to use (6.4) 'The Audience's "Right to Know" ' (another legally suspect concept but one crucial to journalism) to justify their activities. But they are too ready to abandon journalistic claims to legitimacy and, when faced with ethical concerns, resort to artistic amorality to justify shortcomings.

So, in 'Conclusion', what is to be done? First, 'Documentarists'. Although it is clear that free expression rights undercut the application of ethical systems nevertheless it is possible to argue that documentarists do have, in effect, a duty of care to those who participate in their programmes and this, not an amorphous 'truth-telling' responsibility to the audience, is where their ethics should be grounded.

On the other hand, if there is no legally recognised damage to the audience, the 'Regulators' who control documentary expression in the name of 'public trust' are oppressive in a free society. Indeed, in asking for an end to content regulation, *Lies, Damn Lies and Documentaries* argues that the documentary scandals, far from justifying such content regulation, reveal just how offensive to a culture of free expression it is.

Part One

THE STATE OF DOCUMENTARY

Chapter One
'Fakery'

In the 1990s it became increasingly dangerous to be a documentary film-maker. This was the not the result of a rise in the traditional journalistic perils of covering war, riot and natural disaster. Nor did it stem from a growth in the rarer hazard of provoking the wrath of those filmed – the anger, for example, that fuelled the fatal shooting of Canadian director Hugh O'Connor, murdered when filming picturesque Appalachian poverty in Kentucky in 1967. The new danger threatened not the person but the liberty of the documentarist to work without censorship or, worse, self-censorship.

For the first time legally backed sanctions were being invoked against any who pass off as real scenes those that had been in some way tampered with. In defiance of post-modern sophistications about the slippery nature of the image (and paradoxically at a time when post-modernism itself was under attack in obscure corners of the academy), documentary film-makers found themselves publicly castigated for everything from downright fabrications through less heinous misrepresentations to reconstructions of previously witnessed events and the everyday interventions of film-making. Quite suddenly all these procedures were bundled together as 'fakery'. That the simple act of switching the camera on of itself caused selection and inevitable distortion was ignored. That moral differences could be drawn between total fictionalising on the one hand and reconstructing actual events on the other was disregarded. That everyday filming required repeated actions, requested if necessary, so that moving-image editing norms could be obeyed was largely overlooked. Instead the documentary and documentary-style TV news features were being held to a simplistic vision of observational purity. When this was not maintained, documentarists were left floundering in the midst of a moral panic created and fuelled by those who apparently believed that a camera left to its own devices, as it were, would indeed tell no lies.

The least interesting aspect of this brouhaha is the moral culpability of those who deliberately create events for the camera out of their imaginations and then pass these off as real, or even as authenticated reconstructions of the real.

Such people are simply common liars. They are to media production what paedophiles are to child care.

But how they might be punished raises crucial issues about free speech – especially when no meaningful distinctions are being drawn between their activities and more legitimate manipulations and procedures. And how we think about the ethics of reconstruction and intervention when no mendacity is involved is a crucial concern that speaks directly to the status of the realist image and its claim to be able to represent, in some way, the external world. These are the questions *Lies, Damn Lies and Documentaries* seeks to address.

Let us begin in the UK in the spring of 1998.

1.1 The Great British Documentary Scandal

It was then that the papers found a new story and the headlines were to run for months: 'CAN WE BELIEVE ANYTHING WE SEE ON TV?'; 'CHANNEL 4 IN NEW DOCU-MENTARY FAKE ROW'; 'VANESSA SHOW FAKED'; 'WILL THIS FOOTAGE SINK CHANNEL 4?'; even, 'FAKE SHOTS "ROUTINE" IN TV WILDLIFE PROGRAMMES'. In Britain the media and ethics had previously gone together like a horse and cartography. British media normally only confront morality when forced to by regulators; or, less often, by the court; or, although only in the dim past and even more rarely, by media trade unions. Issues are always reduced to matters of process, procedure and sanction. They are to be forgotten as soon as possible. The public expresses concern about media morality when surveyed but, it would seem, somewhat hypocritically. They apparently lap up as audience and readers the very stuff they professed to think improper when questioned by pollsters.

Of course, their hypocrisy was nothing compared to that of the Press. 'CAN WE BELIEVE ANYTHING WE SEE ON TV?' was the *Daily Mail*'s rhetorical question in the very week in February 1999 when the Foreign Office released documents bringing back memories of that newspaper's inglorious role in publishing the faked Zinoviev Telegram in 1924 – an incident said to help destroy the first Labour government. But the documentary 'fakery' story was in no way under-mined by the ethically dubious status of many of those peddling it.

Central to this 'fakery' scandal was *The Connection*, a film about a new drug-running route from Colombia to the UK. Commissioned for Britain's commercial Channel 3, it was produced by Marc de Beaufort working for Carl-ton Television as a freelance. De Beaufort was of Colombian descent and had an established track record as an expert in this area where his language skills, local knowledge and network gave him a real edge. This expertise had been utilised by Roger James, a senior and much respected programme-maker, who in 1996 was working as Head of Documentaries at Carlton Television, a broad-cast licensee which, in common with its fellow licensees, also acts as a programme supplier to other channels at home and abroad.

The film was originally screened on 15 October 1996 to an audience of some 3.7 million in the *Network First* slot. De Beaufort had previously provided this series with a prize-winning film, *Inside Castro's Cuba*, in 1994. Of the three film's he made between this and *The Connection*, one – *Maradona* – also won prizes. The *Guardian* picked up that all was not as it seemed in *The Connection* some time in the winter of 1997. *Guardian* reporters, one of whom had been freelancing in the department at Carlton, revealed a story of extensive reconstruction (actually downright fabrication) during the shooting of this film which purported to show a 'mule' passing into Britain with heroin fingers concealed in his stomach. A main source was a disaffected Colombian freelance researcher. 'EXPOSED: THE TV DRUGS FAKE' took the paper six months to assemble and splashed across no less than four whole pages on 6 May 1998 with subsequent extensive coverage. It began a major panic, not least within Carlton.

The *Guardian*'s charges could not be officially ignored by the regulator either and so the Independent Television Commission, the grantors of Carlton's broadcasting licence, also readied themselves to deal with the matter. The ITC is the statutory authority for commercial television in Britain, including Channel 3. It has a quite formal contractual relationship with the channels and the terrestrial television companies it regulates to service them. By the Broadcasting Act 1990, Section 6, the ITC is required to ensure that 'every licensed service complies' with the requirements that 'any news (in whatever form)' must be presented 'with due accuracy and impartiality' (6.1.b) and 'that due impartiality is preserved on the part of the person providing the service as respects matters … of current public policy … ' (6.1.c). To secure compliance, the Commission has to produce a 'code giving guidance as to the rules' and has the power to enforce them with sanctions including the imposition of fines and the loss of licence.

The Act is silent, except by implication, on the ITC's responsibilities in ensuring that its licensees maintain the trust of the audience in areas outside of the broadly drawn category of news; but the Code is not. The 'due accuracy and impartiality' of the Act becomes, in Section 3 of the Code, 'Impartiality'. Section 3.7 deals with 'Drama and drama-documentary' and Section 3.7 (i) with 'Dramatised 'reconstructions' within factual programmes':

> The use of dramatised 'reconstructions' in factual programmes is a legitimate means of obtaining greater authenticity or verisimilitude, so long as it does not distort reality.
>
> **Whenever a reconstruction is used in a documentary, current affairs or news programme it should be labelled so that the viewer is not misled.**
> [emphasis in the original]

So from 'Impartiality' we move to 'misled' via 'reconstructions' and this 'Impartiality' section extends the statutory requirement on 'news (in whatever form)' to embrace 'Drama and drama-documentary'.

The language in 3.7 (i) acknowledges the difficulties of defining terms like 'authenticity' and 'verisimilitude', 'distort' and 'reality' only in its use of those tentative quotation marks around 'reconstructions'. In the second paragraph, when it comes to action, though, the Commission boldly bites the bullet and '**reconstruction**' (in bold) loses even these.

It is, of course, disingenuous to expect the Commission to acknowledge in its language the nuances of the old debate about the representation of reality, much less current arguments as to an image's relation to the real and the extent to which distortion is inevitable; or the audience's relation to the image and the flexible nature of its interpretative powers. But as law, or even more as quango-law, this is very sloppy drafting. At a minimum, the doubts that led to the quotation marks around 'reconstructions' should be admitted. Clearly the Commission did not intend that every last shot be constantly labelled – 'as it happened' on the action, 'shot to be cut in' on the noddie, 'filmed before', 'filmed later', 'digital space image', 'trained animal', 'reconstructed on the basis of prior witness' … 'imagined' … 'invented' … 'based on this year's Booker prize-winning novel'. Without some acknowledgment of which everyday practices – if any – are acceptable, the Commission can pounce more or less at will.

Moreover, Clause 6.1 of the Broadcasting Act itself is vague ('any news (in whatever form)') so that, although *The Connection* could be clearly seen as 'any news', the 'due accuracy and impartiality' requirement in general terms is a catch-all. After all, do not advertisers, for example, claim their work as a public service because it gives 'news' of goods and services? Are not the possibilities of 'accuracy and impartiality' drastically limited by constraints of broadcasting time? Is not the requirement for 'accuracy' actually a prohibition against 'inaccuracy' but one that is far more draconian than the law requires because it does not need to demonstrate that damage has occurred? And does not 'impartiality' imply finding a balance between restricted range of positions on any issue but without defining what the range is? These sorts of problems are amplified by the translation of Act to Code. For instance, in the Code, what is to be made of the misled viewer? Is one enough, as it would be in law? Is there any due process to determine who was misled into believing exactly what? Again, the Commission is silent as to what levels and extents of artifice might be acceptable and whether or not any assessment of outcomes is to be factored in. The Code is subject to the elaborate process of judicial review but, given that those most likely to use this are also those beholden to the framers of the Code for their licences to trade as broadcasters, this is less of a safeguard than it might seem.

The result is not guidance but a fairly opaque apparatus of content control. You might know, to take an analogy, that the police will not act if you drive at, say, 75 mph on the motorway but you cannot rely on that knowledge since it is crystal clear that the speed limit is 70. On what knowledge can you rely in making a documentary for an ITC channel? You always shoot reverses for an interview after the interview is concluded. With only one camera, you have to; but you make absolutely sure that the talent repeats the question exactly. You do not then mislead the audience when you cut the reverses into the interview. Nevertheless, you are, in fact, doing 75 in a 70 zone. The Commission *can* declare that the very fact of the cross-cutting misleads the audience into believing in a simultaneity that did not, in reality, occur. 3.7 (i) actually offers less guidance to the ITC's licensees than it appears to do.

The ITC, secure in its quotation marks and ignorances, was already flexing its muscles before *The Connection* story broke, questioning other possible infringements of its Code, especially by Channel 4. Thus in February 1998, following a *Daily Mirror* splash 'CHANNEL FOUR FAKES FILM', a documentary about rogue builders (*Rogue Males*, Dominic Savage) in the prestigious *Cutting Edge* series, was being examined as having a number of faked scenes, including one where two men were supposedly filmed stealing building supplies. The Commission was already operating on the basis of 3.7 (i) and it could easily be used to justify an inquiry into the *Guardian*'s charges against *The Connection*. Not only that, having been created by the 1990 Broadcasting Act as a 'light regulator' replacing the old IBA, it had levied the first ever fine for a code infringement, against Granada, who gave repeated products 'undue prominence' against the rules on commercial goods and services in 1994 (Goodwin 1998: 119). It collected a 'light' £500,000. Faced with this sort of behaviour, Carlton determined to investigate the programme itself and established its own quasi-judicial process, involving an internal investigation of the facts by the company's CEO which furnished evidence to an independent Inquiry Panel chaired by a QC. The panel did not further cross-question the parties concerned. After a further six months it reported:

> *The programme suggested the mule's journey to London was one continuous trip.* This was false. The programme makers and their immediate supervisors readily acknowledge that the journey was filmed in two parts ...

> *The programme led viewers to believe the mule was allowed through customs and immigration at Heathrow and that he entered London.* This was false. Official records leave no doubt that the mule was refused entry ... the refusal did not relate to either drug trafficking or passport irregularity ...

immigration officials at Heathrow were not satisfied he was a genuine short-stay visitor ...

... the mule was claimed to be swallowing fingers of heroin...

No objective or compelling evidence exists for the claim that the fingers contained heroin, rather than (say) sugar, flour or mints ...

... according to the programme, the man interviewed owned the mansion the Colombian police were shown to raid and was the man they were trying to catch. Both assertions were false ...

The programme said the mule filmed on the flight to London was laden with 60 heroin fingers in his stomach and dramatically described him as a 'walking time bomb'. This was almost certainly false. When stopped at Heathrow, the mule was tested for drugs. The test showed none ...

The scene in flight of the mule eating little, putting food in a vomit bag in his pocket, and sprinkling whisky on his clothes to suggest he had been drinking were designed to depict him as a genuine mule. This was almost certainly a pretence for the camera ...

The programme presented the mule, the loader and the Cartel number three as genuine drugs traffickers ... on the balance of the evidence ... the mule, the loader and the Cartel number three were all acting ...

The mule's trip was organised by a drug's cartel. This claim in the programme was almost certainly false ... it is beyond doubt that ... the cost of the mule's flight was charged to de Beaufort's personal American Express account and de Beaufort made no attempt to claim the cost against the production budget ... The mule is now in jail in Spain serving a nine-year sentence for smuggling cocaine ... Notwithstanding [this] ... other more persuasive factors point to a contrary conclusion, namely that the three main characters acted the parts of drug traffickers when filmed for the programme ...

Other payments ... payments over and above reimbursement of expenses or compensation for inconvenience were also made to achieve the trafficker scenes ... about £7000 was not documented or explained ...

The programme said the film crew (meaning the producer and cameraman) were blindfolded by armed escorts and taken to an unknown location for the interview with Cartel number three. Against this the *Guardian* alleged the interview took place in the producer's room at the Meal Hotel in Pereira and that the trellis in the room was an exact match for the trellis shown behind the Cartel number three in the film. The hotel records confirm that de Beaufort stayed there at the time. Investigation ... has identified what indeed appears to be the same trellis in the same room ...

The programme referred to 'a contact within the Colombian network' in a

context that means a network of drug traffickers. This was false. The contact is
in fact a friend and colleague of de Beaufort's in London.

    The programme suggested in one of the UK scenes that several individuals were
being arrested for possessing heroin. This was wrong – albeit the product of a
mistake … *The programme claimed that: 'Two years ago, Colombian drug cartels*
took a momentous decision to target Western Europe with heroin.' The caption at
the end of the programme was 'Colombian drug cartels claim to be exporting at
least a hundred kilograms of heroin to Britain each month' … the statements are
unreliable … (Carlton, 1998: 13–25)

Two weeks after this damning conclusion was reached, the Independent Television Commission levied a fine of £2 million against Carlton for 'grave
breaches of the programme code'. Sir Robin Biggam, ITC chair, commented
that *The Connection* was 'comprehensively in breach of the ITC Programme
Code … and involved a wholesale breach of trust between programme makers
and the viewers' (Anon., 1998b).

A decade earlier, Carlton's chairman Michael Green, during a newspaper
interview, had demanded with that aggressive insouciance that typified the
Thatcher era: 'What is the difference between a television programme and this
lighter?' (Green, 1988). Presumably he now has a better idea. Manufacturing
and selling the lighter would have cost him a hefty fine only if it had actually
or potentially seriously damaged somebody and then only after due process in
a court of law. Manufacturing and selling *The Connection* cost him millions
without any damage being proved or any potential damage being suggested
beyond a general charge that the audience was misled to some undefined end;
and this outside of any court.

The significance of the point about damage cannot be overstressed. Proving
that any speech, any act of communication, either caused damage or potentially
could cause damage of some kind is the only basis on which such speech can
be prohibited (censored) or punished. As 'Cato' (the journalists John Trenchard
and Thomas Gordon) wrote two and a half centuries ago but as seems to have
been forgotten: 'Freedom of speech … is the right of everyman, as far as by it
he does not hurt or control the right of another; and this is the only check which
it ought to suffer, the only bounds it ought to know' (Knowlton and Parsons,
1995: 50). Instead of 'hurt' or 'control' being the measure by which free speech
is to be curtailed, the right was now to be constrained, at least in the case of
these 'speakers', by a prohibition against 'misleading' audiences. 'Misleading'
remains undefined not least since there is no test for measuring its consequences nor even a need to produce any actual misled member of the audience
to attest to such a state of mind. One thing is clear, though: being 'misled' does
not involve the levels of damage the law would acknowledge to be actionable.

This represents a clear and worrying development since damage – direct, indirect or potential – has hitherto been essential. Damage, elaborately and legally defined, is the basis of crime and tort and, for example, actually lies behind such apparently damage-free offences as obscenity (where the damage is potential corruption and depravity), sedition (where the state and the citizens within it are potentially endangered), incitement to racial hatred (where public order and individual safety are potentially undermined), and all the regulations protecting the public from the harm of false trading. (This last, of course, embraces and justifies both the legal and quasi-legal regulation of advertising.) Even blasphemy, the product of a more religious society, can be seen as potentially injuring faith with supposedly real consequences – eternal damnation and so on. This has now fallen into desuetude, perhaps in part exactly because the threatened repercussions are no longer generally seen as valid by many people. Even if it had not done so, then it would still be hard to see how religious faith could be made to compare with faith in the telly.

Damage does not have to be actual but it must be a reasonably expected consequence. Traditionally this is expressed as a prohibition against mendaciously crying 'fire' in a crowded theatre. The liar is liable not only for any injuries that ensue but also for the possibility that people could be injured as they try to flee, whether they were or not. Even this latter test was ignored in *The Connection* case. Quite simply none of this rational applied to that scandal nor, more importantly, does it figure in the ITC Code.

It might be thought that, as the Code is not law, the fundamental legal principle that in a free society 'hurt' or 'control' is the only basis for abridging free speech does not apply; but the Code is mandated by law and therefore has the same force as law. In this instance, however, it is not bound by the same principle as law since its sanction did not involve any proof of damage. To be extremely uneasy about this and the general sloppiness of 3.7(i) is well merited in my view. Concern that a liberty is being taken or, at least, undercut is confirmed by Sir Robin's legalistic 'breach of trust' language.

The trouble is that there was nothing to suggest that ITC sanctions would not apply to simple errors and mistakes, never mind circumstances more legitimate and more routine than deliberate falsehood. There is no question in all this that there was a serious breakdown in the control of the production. The disaffected researcher, in the course of a meeting with James and others prior to transmission to resolve a dispute over fees and expenses which she felt were not commensurate with the dangers she had run, had handed him a memo that, *inter alia*, described the mule as 'fake' while at the same time insisting, in a contradictory fashion, on the hazardous nature of setting the film up. In James's account, he asked for this oral report, which was given with the help of an interpreter, and stressed the risks of the assignment. Danger was much mentioned but 'reconstructions' and 'fakes' were not. In the belief that the money issues had been resolved, neither he nor the other Carlton representatives read the memo as they clearly should have done.[1]

Beginning as a film editor at ATV, James rose to be Controller of Factual Programmes at its successor Central and then Head of Documentaries at its successor Carlton. He had an enviable reputation as a serious, concerned film-maker and was chair of British documentaries' main professional annual meeting, the Sheffield International Documentary Festival. As an editor, he had cut *Death of a Princess* for Anthony Thomas and worked with Ken Loach and Adrian Cowell. As an executive he had supported Juris Podiakis whose *Red Hot* won the Prix Italia. De Beaufort was being nurtured by James in the same tra-dition. That James failed to check the researcher's memo, however opaque, is surprising. That he was widely believed within the industry to be incapable of perpetrating fraud is not.

The ITC and the Press totally failed to take account of the fact that some of these supposed infringements represented fictions which nobody could defend while others arose from such mistakes and routine practices. The UK drug raid, for example, was not shot by de Beaufort and, relying on Manchester police information, it was claimed heroin had been recovered. This was not further checked by Carlton, nor was it questioned by the Manchester Drug Squad offi-cers who vetted the film for accuracy; nor, it can be added, was it, or the film as a whole, questioned by London Metropolitan Police officers or Customs offi-cials who also vetted the programme. The last did not even correct the false statement that the 'mule' got through Customs. In fact, these checking pro-cedures constituted Carlton's Documentary Department's defence: it had itself been misinformed, its vetting procedures had been unexpectedly ineffective and, the bottom line, it had been duped by the film-maker. (The mistake about the raid was also, of course, potentially actionable as a libel.)

I am no more exculpating the catalogue of omissions, errors and fact-check-ing failures than I would excuse the basic mendacity of the film. They clearly should not happen and are, therefore, of little broader interest. What is of far more serious concern, indeed the starting point for this book, is that among the list of omissions, errors and failures are also common, and hitherto legitimate, production practices. These have been rendered unsafe by the fine.

1.2 Documentary as Journalism

Let me take the one sin of commission of which the Carlton Inquiry Panel found James guilty – that the 'mule's' flight to London was in fact two flights taken six months apart. My worry about *The Connection* affair directly arises from the way this was treated.

Cutting the two flights as one was the only 'falsehood' (as the Inquiry called it) of which James was by his own admission aware. There is a specific defence here: since a supposedly illegal act was being filmed, it was useful to the producers to be able to distance themselves from one single instance that might lay them more immediately open to a charge of complicity. That really does not concern me. Rather, it is the general implications of a second strand of the production team's defence – that such practices were commonplace – and the Inquiry's response to this line that has serious implications.

We need to consider the edit at two levels. At the specific level, there is no question that deliberate mendacity was involved and the 'mule' was no such thing since he was not carrying drugs. Therefore the edit raises the issue that the audience was being duped into believing it was witnessing scenes of actual drug running, which they might not have done quite so readily if the commentary had made it clear that there were two journeys involved. The likelihood of the film-makers twice witnessing heroin smuggling was a lot less than a single act of witness, and this would surely have occurred to the audience. It throws into doubt the whole account of the smuggling process including the authenticity of the demonstration of the 'loading'. The Inquiry Panel held that:

> While it was within the legitimate discretion of the programme-makers to film the journey in two parts, they should not have portrayed it as one. Moreover, the two-stage filming led to a serious error in as much as no meaningful steps were taken to establish whether, on the second stage of the journey, the mule was indeed loaded with drugs. (Carlton, 1998: 14)

Given the specifics, this is a not unreasonable conclusion.

The general discussion of the edit by the Inquiry, however, raises a far more complicated problem, one which speaks to the very essence of documentary and its fruitful, but vexed, traditional position between fiction and journalism.

James told the Inquiry that the use of the two journeys was 'acceptable within the grammar of documentary film-making' (Carlton, 1998: 14). I believe that, deliberate fraud aside, in terms of the tradition in which he works, this is true. The Inquiry did not agree. As far as it was concerned, and the ITC and the *Guardian* after it, such an elision of time was not in general acceptable in any serious work even if the two shots concerned reflected a true reality. The edit created a falsity and it was no defence for documentarists to claim that such a practice, part of what in fact distinguished their work from other more journalistic activities, was appropriate. To believe such editing legitimate was, at best, but one view among many:

> This kind of approach to documentary-making is shared by other people in

the industry to varying degrees … The Panel knows that scenes in documentaries are not always what they seem to viewers and that some documentary-makers genuinely believe that they are entitled to edit reality. Notwithstanding this, the Panel is firmly of the view that the scenes depicting the mule's journey should not have been presented in this way. This avowedly serious programme should have opted without hesitation for strict reliability; that it failed to do so attacks trust and causes disillusion in viewers. (Carlton, 1998: 14)

This, in effect, grievously limits 'the legitimate discretion' of documentarists by suggesting anything that works 'to edit reality' is incompatible with 'strict reliability'. For all that this opinion is grounded in a set of widely accepted, albeit historically ignorant and naïve assumptions – many unfortunately shared by practitioners – it is nevertheless extremely fraught.

Documentary-makers claiming *not* 'to edit reality' need to be treated with a great deal more caution than is being envisaged here. Indeed, the more they talk of unedited reality, the greater the need to count the spoons. There are, surely, no 'varying degrees', with suspect film-makers editing at one end and purist purveyors of unedited reality at the other because the latter simply do not and, indeed, cannot exist as the very act of communication inevitably taints any such vision of purity. What the Panel, the ITC and the *Guardian* were suggesting is a simple variant on the nineteenth-century idea that the camera does not lie – or, equally naïve, that it is capable of offering 'strict reliability'. For anybody who has ever switched one on and processed the results in an editing facility, it is hard to know what this 'strict reliability' can possibly mean.

The Carlton Inquiry Panel nevertheless felt that this edit was the start of a 'primrose path of deceit' which led to all the other frauds and dishonesties of the programme. There is, however, no direct connection between the 'legitimate discretion' of this editing technique, a film-making norm, and the illegitimate fakery of other elements in the film. The primrose path leading to fraud starts with the lies of the images not with the edit. To claim, as the Panel does, that the edit is the source of the problem is to direct the path towards the heart of the documentary enterprise as we have understood for the last eighty years. By British documentary standards, such editing techniques were without question (and without prejudice as to whether they are still acceptable) an essential part of 'the creative treatment of actuality', which is how the pioneer documentarist John Grierson defined the documentary in 1933 (Paget, 1998: 117).

Documentary is a quite particular variety of factual film-making. The very first images produced by the *cinématographe* in 1895 documented the world, but the possibility of making compelling narratives out of such footage did not occur until the American Robert Flaherty produced the feature film *Nanook of the North*, conventionally the first documentary, in 1921. This used non-actors performing daily activities (specially arranged for the camera) to paint a dramatic picture of their lifestyle (albeit that of a previous generation). *Nanook's* authenticity is suspect but in the hands of John Grierson and other pioneers around the world this approach, the editing of footage less ambiguously of the real world into stories or, later, arguments, became the basis of a whole new genre of film, documentary. *Nanook* was followed by other full-length films set in exotic locations such as Flaherty's South Sea story *Moana* (1926) or Cooper and Schoedsack's *Chang*, filmed in Thailand in 1927. (They went on to make *King Kong*.) At the same time, the thought occurred that these techniques could be used at home. The documentary canon gained Ruttmann's *Berlin: Symphony of a City* (Walther Ruttmann, 1927) or Grierson's own first film *Drifters* (1929) and a host of films on everyday life, some journalistic and many, especially from continental Europe, personal and poetic.

Grierson himself was very careful to distinguish this new film-type from other sorts of factual cinema, such as the newsreel, the travelogue or the scientific/nature film. He needed to make these distinctions to help him secure funding for his work but, whatever his reasons, the tradition he thereby identified produced quite distinct films. Grierson thought, for instance, that the newsreels – journalism in the cinema – were 'just a speedy snip-snap of some utterly unimportant ceremony', whereas documentaries would go 'beyond' this into a world hoping to achieve the 'ordinary virtues of an art' (Grierson, 1979: 35, 36).

At the outset in his manifesto of 1932, Grierson indicated that he knew full well the price strict observation pays to understanding. Writing of travelogues and nature shorts, he said: 'they describe, and even expose, but in any aesthetic sense, only rarely reveal' (Grierson, 1979: 36). For him, then, documentaries were to be much more; they were to 'pass from the plain (or fancy) descriptions of natural material, to arrangements, rearrangements, and creative shapings of it' (Grierson, 1979: 36). Hence 'the creative treatment of actuality', a mark of documentary difference promising insights into the world, not mechanistic reflections of it.

Thus documentary encompassed the use of images of the real world for the purposes of personal expression. It allowed for poetic image-making, essays, polemics; and, at the level of production, it clearly permitted the reconstruction of prior witnessed events, commentary, non-naturalistic dubbed sound, editing to produce a point of view and all manner of interventions and manipulations. Documentary was not journalism; rather it claimed all the artistic licence of a fiction with the only constraints being that its images were not of actors and its stories were not the products of unfettered imagining. There are obvious logical inconsistencies in Grierson's definition, for what could indeed be left of 'actuality' after it had been 'creatively treated'? But, in the event, the inconsistencies involved opened up a rich seam of creative expression that illuminated much of twentieth-century life. For example, as compared with the newsreels, the Second World War's documentary archive tells us significantly different but equally illuminating things about 'the way we were' (to use a phrase of Lindsay Anderson's about the Griersonian documentarist Humphrey Jennings).

After the war, documentary and newsreel became television staples, although increasingly practitioners of both worried about the limitations imposed upon them by then existing film technology. This technology, especially sound recording systems, compelled the use of reconstruction while the equipment's bulk and weight and film stock's insensitivity to light anchored the documentarist to camera mounts and heavy intrusion. Escaping from these limitations became the main objective of documentary film-makers.

This played into another aspect of the move to television. Although other documentary styles persisted, television encouraged the journalist aspect of the form. *Special Inquiry*, which ran from 1952 to 1957, was the BBC Documentary Department's first major series. Norman Swallow was its producer:

> We were inspired by *Picture Post* and, in television terms, by the Ed Murrow and Fred Friendly series *See It Now*, from CBS New York. They were our two main influences, I think, together with the old British documentary tradition, of course. … actually my favourite pre-war documentary was *Housing Problems*. … It was probably no coincidence that that was the first *Special* we had. (Corner, 1991: 44)

It was quality, pictorial journalism, American news shows and the least 'aesthetic', most journalistic Griersonian documentary that lay behind the programme. In announcing the show, the *Radio Times* said, 'The aim is to forge a new style of television *journalism*' (Corner, 1991: 43 – emphasis added). Moreover, this journalistic approach also allowed for the live studio to be used for cheaply produced introductory stand-uppers, interviews and discussions providing an economic advantage that could not be resisted.

The desire for lightweight synch sound cameras fleshed out television documentary's journalistic 'turn' to ensure that, when the new technology began to come on stream in the late 1950s and early 1960s, the line between documentary and broadcast journalism was ready to be further blurred. The new lightweight 16mm synch film cameras and battery-driven portable tape-recorders allowed film-makers for the first time to shoot documentary footage without elaborate preparations. A whole new style, Direct Cinema, and with it a journalistic ethic of non-intervention and strict observation, was developed. Enter the 'fly on the wall'.

This approach was extended and enhanced by the introduction of light-weight video cameras and portable videotape recorders from the 1970s on. A process of miniaturisation reduced such outfits first into integrated camcorders and then, by the mid-1990s, into the even smaller professional-quality digital devices. All these technical advances, however, simply built upon the original breakthrough to the portability and sensitivity of the first hand-holdable 16mm film cameras of the 1960s. Direct Cinema's journalistic rhetoric of non-intervention and limited mediation allowed documentary to lay a stronger claim on the real than was possible previously. 'Let the event be more important that the filming', argued Direct Cinema pioneer Ricky Leacock. But with each advance, documentary's differences from broadcast journalism were further eroded and Grierson's initial distinction faded. All non-fiction film and video production was becoming 'factual programming' – just as, pre-Grierson, the cinema had only factual film as a category to cover all varieties of non-fiction movies. This change was reflected, as such things always are, by the eventual merging of the old Documentary and Features Departments in the BBC into a new 'Documentary Features Department'.

(There were also those in the 1960s who thought that the new equipment could embrace a quite different type of cinema truth by allowing the film-makers to reveal themselves in the process of making the film. This self-reflexive Cinéma Vérité would then allow audiences to determine the truthfulness or otherwise of what was being shown on the screen. Cinéma Vérité was initially positioned as being in opposition to Direct Cinema's fly-on-the-wall shooting although it too used long, hand-held available-light and sound takes. Primarily the difference was that Cinéma Vérité did not aspire never to intervene in the action. On the contrary, it set up sequences when necessary, revealing that it had done so. This more or less private row between Direct Cinema and Cinéma Vérité in the early 1960s is today as forgotten as Grierson's definition.[2])

Television, now the major site of documentary production in the English-speaking world, bastardised the purities of Direct Cinema by shooting in a style the British industry called 'vérité' which involved merely adding long hand-held, available-light, natural sound takes to the established repertoire of mainstream documentary techniques. Nevertheless, although many of the strictures of Direct Cinema might be routinely ignored (including the prohibitions against commentary and interviews), it seems that, in the popular and print-journalist mind, documentaries were now expected to adhere to a series of observational filming rules about non-intervention, some going beyond anything being done thirty years before. For example, there is, apparently, the idea that documentaries have structures dictated by the order of events filmed, not by the documentarist in the cutting room or editing suite. Direct Cinema, though, never had any such 'rule'. On the contrary, the films in this style were actually marked by extremely sophisticated editing which created effective narratives without reference to the order in which the rushes were taken. Documentary was being limited by the journalism. Its creativity was becoming increasingly suspect as the requirement for strict observation replaced it.

What seeped into public consciousness was the primacy of the un-lit synch hand-held shot as the essence of documentary. The hand-held camera became a central mark of authenticity while older traditions of reconstruction, commentary, music, interviews and the rest were mostly vanquished. In all this 'vérité' material, interviews and much else survived as legitimate proceedings but reconstruction did not. Direct Cinema's untenable, unGriersonian claim to be able to present 'truth' in the form of films consisting only of events as they actually spontaneously occurred before the lens triumphed. In many quarters, documentaries can only be in the Direct Cinema or vérité modes; to all intents and purposes, they could only be extended journalistic reports.

And then, provoked by bare-faced lying in the 'fakery' scandals, even the norms of editing became suspect. To recognise that this or that editing convention was an everyday procedure was now being represented as evidence of the total moral insensitivity and ethical blindness of the documentary world. Ignorance of a century of film-making in general and eight decades of documentary production in particular was essential to the 'fakery' story not just for the journalists pushing it but, even more alarmingly, for investigators and regulators too. No distinctions were being drawn between reconstructing scenes that actually happened, that could have happened and those that never happened and were, thus, entirely fictional. The draconian interpretation of 'reconstruction', for example, was rendering many standard practices deviant – breaches of public trust. Grierson's definition of documentary as 'the creative treatment of actuality' was in effect being tossed aside.

This is why the Carlton Inquiry Panel's *general* rejection of the two-journeys-as-one edit is so important. It seems as if documentary's most simplistic truth claims are now commonly believed to be not only possible but absolutely required. It was as if the unvarnished rhetoric of 1960s American Direct Cinema practitioners – that events must happen before the lens without any intervention, ideally with the film-makers being completely ignored – had indeed become a set of rules for production and breaches of these justified serious sanctions.

1.3 Documentary v. Docudrama

It is possible that this Direct Cinema triumph was aided by the emergence during these same decades of 'drama documentary', or 'docudrama', which combined the use of actors, scripts and sets with the legitimacies of prior witnessed events and, often, documentary-style shooting and editing to reconstruct actual unfilmed or unfilmable incidents. This fictional aping of factual style has a long history.

The use of documentary characteristics dates back at least to Orson Welles's radio version of *War of the Worlds* (1938). It is astonishing that even at the time anybody could have thought it really matched the conventions of actual disaster broadcasting, so artificial was it, but it did. It has become one of the most notorious example of radio's power as thousands of listeners were seemingly convinced that Martians were taking over New Jersey. Derek Paget traces the history of the blurred drama/documentary line on TV back to 1948 although many of the pre-1960 shows he cites were simply attempts at realistic dramatic fiction (Paget, 1998: 142–51). There was, however, a significant line between drama and documentary at this time so that the application of Direct Cinema techniques to 'plays', when that occurred in the 1960s, was still extremely transgressive. Producer Tony Garnett and his directors, such as Ken Loach, were in constant difficulties with the BBC for using 16mm film (instead of 35mm as expected and demanded by the BBC Drama Department 'Plays' and its film operations managers) to seek a confusingly realistic feel. Of course, it could be argued that these techniques plus the heightened tensions of a fiction was exactly what gave films like the 1966 Garnett/Loach classic on homelessness – *Cathy Come Home* – their considerable power. Despite being firmly in 'Plays' slots, they worked exactly because the audience were confused about their authenticity.

Most drama documentaries were less ambiguous, such as the meticulous American reconstruction of eye-witnessed events in the White House during the 1962 Cuban Missile Crisis, *Missiles in October* (Anthony Page, 1974). However 'true' to the events portrayed, obviously William Devane was not John Kennedy, the role he was playing; nor was Martin Sheen, Robert. It was not unusual, in the less star-studded dramadoc films, for the fiction to be disguised as documentary until the final credits revealed that 'real' figures were (less recognisable) actors.

The dramadoc initially required some form of verbatim text that could be transferred to the screen using actors and sets – and that meant legal transcripts. The justification was that the original trial or inquiry could not for whatever reason be filmed. This then becomes the re-enactment of eyewitness accounts of events outside the courtroom but again with actors and sets. Such a procedure, though, rapidly approaches the conventions of our drama in general where the appearance of the 'names and identities of real historical individuals' are a commonplace. After all, there is even an historical Macbeth buried somewhere on Iona. But this is not the same as real people 'acting' themselves in scenes legitimated as following a real-life pattern – the crucial distinction is the presence of the professional actor as against the amateur 're-enactor'.

The widespread popularity of the dramadoc occasioned a tendency to reclassify all pre-Direct Cinema documentaries involving reconstruction as not being documentaries at all. Thus David Meeker, of the British National Film and Television Archive, when including Humphrey Jennings's 1943 classic *Fires Were Started* in a list of the most important films of the cinema's first decades, queried if this reconstruction of fire-fighting in the Blitz (which used real firefighters, but sets for interiors and a blaze started by the film-makers rather than the Luftwaffe) was 'what we would still call a documentary?'

What matters here is that the creation of a form, 'dramadoc', which is all reconstruction, has helped cast the use of reconstruction in the old form, 'documentary', into doubt. In so doing, it served to confirm the triumph of the journalistic 'fly-on-the wall' Direct Cinema style as being the only legitimate documentary form. The result was that documentarists were now lambasted about the 'reconstructions' they had always used, directly denying one of documentary's foundations. It is a paradox that as this was surfacing, the dominance of Direct Cinema itself was ending after nearly forty years. Space was being found in the UK schedules for rediscovery of older techniques, sometimes even embracing the use of 35mm film. One can point to Errol Morris's *The Thin Blue Line* (1988), which used the 35mm and the visual vocabulary of a noir thriller to make a US 'miscarriage of justice' documentary as a significant pioneer of this renaissance. Some mainstream UK television producers, notably Peter Symes at BBC Bristol, brought an understanding of the documentary archive to the commissioning process. Symes's *Picture This* series on BBC 2 was more often than not an *hommage à* Humphrey Jennings and the more poetic strand of pre-television documentary films.

1.4 The UK Scandal Acquires 'Legs'
Despite this increased professional questioning of the viability of Direct Cinema, outsiders, including regulators, were unthinkingly working with the original Direct Cinema claims to be filming unmediated reality. As we have seen, their general ignorance of documentary theory and practice was so all-embracing that this simplistic outmoded approach was arrogantly represented as being superior to that of the past when documentaries were reconstructed and did not meet the 'stringent' standards of contemporary work.

Of course, *The Connection*'s failures to keep to 'vérité' verities was exactly grounded in misuse of this primitive documentary truth claim. Its mendacity engendered a 'moral panic' in the papers, creating an 'inferential frame' – 'documentary fakery' – that brought a flood of supposedly similar misfeasances – the ethically improper performances of otherwise legal activities – to light, sweeping away all the moral complexities of everyday documentary filming techniques, never mind the previously acceptable practices of reconstruction and intervention when legitimated by prior witness. The £2 million fine did not close off the matter although most senior British television executives seem to believe that their best defence lay (and lies) in pretending, ostrich-like, that documentary 'fakery' is an old-hat story which had gone away. On the contrary, there is now an established journalistic inferential frame that allows papers to continue to pounce on television documentary, and other kinds of factual programming, for wrongdoings of all kinds. These include not just downright fraud and misrepresentation, but all aspects of reconstruction and editing as well as ineptitude and naïveté. The inferential reporting frame even manages to blame the broadcasters when they are themselves victims of misrepresentation and fraud.

The BBC docusoap series of 1997 about people endeavouring to pass their driving tests, *Driving School* (Francesca Joseph), was admitted to contain 'invented' scenes. Apparently the much-failed Maureen, the show's most popular central 'character', was not filmed at 4 a.m. practising for her test but at some later hour. The alarm clock had been tampered with; the sequence was therefore 'faked', as was a near collision. Another level of manipulation was queried in an episode of docusoap series *The Clampers* (Kim Duke, 1998). A traffic warden – a real one – was filmed attempting to issue 100 – real – parking tickets in a day when not only did the entire exercise seem more for the cameras than for real but the man himself was apparently no longer on the street, his previous unfilmed success having earned him a supervisory role. He had returned to ticketing, it was alleged, at the behest of the film-makers.

In August 1998, in the sort of incident that would have caused an ethical Griersonian (should such a creature ever have existed) to pause, a film crew was accused of inciting children in the care of a local council to beg on the street and, in the case of one fifteen-year-old girl, solicit as a prostitute. The Nottingham City Council released surveillance footage showing the *Staying Lost* crew making arrangements with the other children. The film-makers claimed they had seen the begging and soliciting earlier and, following an arrangement to return with cameras, were photographing actual behaviour. They also denied the girl was in care (Roberts, 1998: 2–3; Roberts, 1999: 5). The Council threatened Channel 4 with an injunction.

Although not a usual journalistic procedure, for a documentarist to set up the repeat of a previously witnessed event so that it can be captured on film was a well established technique. Nevertheless, it was not surprising that the filmmakers' defence along the lines that the children had been observed in these activities was dismissed. What was startling was that the dubious morality of their actions was seen to lie more in the 'reconstruction' than in the basic exploitation of these children. The far more vexed moral issue (to my mind) of encouraging a child to repeat their own demeaning, unethical and indeed illegal behaviour for the camera – even to expose the failure of a public authority – was less a focus of concern than was the morality of the reconstruction process. Children are protected from media exposure but this was as if to film the children begging without prior arrangements was perfectly reasonable. This, though, is another matter to which we shall return; the point is that reconstructions of prior witnessed events are not lies in the sense that *The Connection*'s fabrications are lies, but that distinction was being lost. The use of prior witnessed events without which the documentary could never have developed as a separate form could not be legitimated in any connection. Reconstruction, however defined, was *verboten*.

'Fakery' continued to expand its reach until it embraced errors and silliness that victimised the broadcasters themselves while nevertheless somehow still remaining the culprits. In September 1998 *Daddy's Girl* (Edmund Coulthard), a programme about fathers and daughters, was pulled at the last moment when it was revealed that one of the 'fathers' was actually the young woman's boyfriend. The couple had been found by the researcher placing an advertisement in the papers. Although budgets now allow little if any time for proper preparation, by journalistic standards advertising as a research practice is lazy and indefensible and it can be argued that broadcasters who use it as a way of finding participants deserved to be duped. In this case they were, most thoroughly.

By the turn of 1999 the British papers were no longer interested only in documentaries. A popular BBC daytime confessional talk programme, *The Vanessa Show*, was revealed to have used 'faked guests' hired through an agency. The programme was quickly cancelled.

In February 1999, the focus returned to the original issues of mendacity and reconstruction. Men in a scene from *Much Too Young: Chickens*, a documentary transmitted in 1997, who were shown picking up rent-boys in Glasgow, were revealed by another disgruntled researcher to have been members of the production team. The Commission fined Channel 4 £150,000 for this unlabelled 'reconstruction' and Channel 4 told Marie Devine, the producer, that she would never work for them again. As with *Staying Lost*, no distinction was made between the reality of prior witnessed events and fabrications while the different, and I would argue more important, ethical question of filming the young when engaged in deviant acts was ignored. That is to say, more at issue here was 3.7 (i)'s prohibition of the unlabelled scene; not, say, Section 6.4 of the Code which is adamant that 'Under no circumstances may children be put at moral or physical risk, for example in factual programmes concerning criminal activity'. Neither the youthfulness of the 'chickens' nor the illegality of the act filmed was as important to the Commission as the failure to indicate that three scenes were reconstructed. That they were shot unnecessarily furtively in low light to enhance the deception infuriated many in the industry. Hence the £150,000 fine: this was the price of having no clear guidance to the everyday business of requesting repetitions or other interventions. Any unmarked reconstruction (even of the most innocuous kind) *could* be subjected to sanction. Any shot taken as a result of any intervention by a documentarist has to be not just suspect but 'unsafe' in a legal sense. In free expression terms the fine on *Much Too Young: Chickens* (in that it does not rely on 6.4) is far more chilling than the fine on *The Connection*.

Two more programmes were in trouble that spring for employing criminals on production teams. In one, *Undercover Britain: Stolen Goods,* transmitted in 1996 and produced by one of the industry's most admired figures, Ray Fitzwalter, a freelance reporter accused an antique dealer of selling stolen goods; but the dealer was working undercover for the police who were actually investigating the reporter, a man with a criminal record for theft. The second 'scandal' involved a researcher on another programme in this series, *Undercover Britain: Guns in the Street*. He too was revealed as having a criminal record and many scenes in the film were alleged to have been set up.

In June the prevalent broadcasters' naïveté in checking sources and participants struck again. The BBC was caught out by a tabloid reporter pretending to be a nymphomaniac who had responded to an advertisement seeking contributors for a programme to be called *Addicted to Love* (Michael Burke). The programme was pulled and the BBC threatened to sue the *Sun* newspaper because the reporter had signed 'an honesty clause' in her release form. This clause had been introduced after the *Vanessa Show* fiasco.

It is hard to know where to begin discussing this. Why was the BBC making documentaries about fucking? How does the *Sun* justify entrapment? Why was an East End barmaid, which is what *Sun*-girl Andrea Busfield pretended to be, responding positively to an ad in the left-wing, middle-class broadsheet *Guardian*? Why didn't the production team smell a rat when the intrepid journalist also refused to reveal her supposed place of work?

In July 1999 Erez Tivoni was brought to trial in Israel for the murder of his four-year-old son and his baby daughter the previous May (Dodd, 1999: 5). Tivoni had faked amnesia and thus persuaded Olivia Lichtenstein, another practised and highly respected serious documentary film-maker, into approving a study of him for the BBC's *Inside Story* series. She was relying, apparently, on the professional opinion of two British psychiatrists and, on their confirmation of his condition, the BBC paid for him to return to Israel. Two weeks after filming concluded he burnt his children to death in a battered women's centre to which his estranged wife had fled. Liora Glatt-Berkovitz, the Deputy District Attorney for Tel Aviv, told the *Guardian* that, in her view, Tivoni was not suffering from amnesia but nevertheless had comprehensively fooled the BBC which was therefore not in anyway responsible for the murders. All the same, the BBC, perhaps conscious of the murky position in which they found themselves, offered full co-operation to the Israeli authorities including the release of all the Tivoni footage. This, of course, speaks to another major ethical media issue – the endless struggle, here abandoned by the BBC, to preserve unseen, especially by police and courts, all materials gathered by a production as legally privileged.

In February 2000 the *News of the World* accused *The Cook Report* of encouraging and abetting a fifteen-year-old to steal a school's computer for an edition transmitted in 1994 and, for two shows in 1998, setting up crimes. Carlton (for it was they again) mounted an inquiry even as the programme's editor, Mike Morley, was on suspension pending yet another internal report about undisclosed difficulties on an untransmitted show about yardies (Gibson, 2000: 8).

An episode of a rather more serious undercover reporter series, BBC's *Macintyre Undercover* (Alex Homes, 1999), on malpractices in a care home, failed to produce evidence upon which the police felt able to mount prosecutions – at least according to the police. This was highlighted as being a waste of taxpayers' money by the *Sunday Telegraph* in June, but it was also firmly placed by the newspapers in the *Connection* context. Subtly it became yet another row about authenticity although there was no suggestion of malpractice on the programme-makers' part. Nevertheless, in the follow-up, it was once again 'BBC IN THE DOCK OVER CARE HOME INQUIRY':

> Questions have been asked about how the BBC is regulated: the ITV company Carlton was fined £2m by the independent television commission when it was found to have faked scenes in a documentary about the drug trade. Although the BBC has not been accused of faking scenes, it is not subject to such strict regulation. (Wells and Wilson, 2000: 5)

All rows about broadcast factual programmes are now being seen in the Press as exemplars of the 'fakery' scandal. That shows no signs of changing any time soon.

In the face of all these accusations and endless attacks, as well as proven misfeasances, sloppy production work and conflicting principles, the industry's leadership has remained pretty silent and certainly has said little in public about the Carlton episode and subsequent embarrassments. There is, after all, the common professional view that the ITC's licensees, such as Carlton, know full well that obedience to the conduct codes is part of the price of doing business and a draconian sanction was easily justified because the rules had been broken so blatantly. Many in the industry felt their integrity was being threatened by the casual mendacity of unscrupulous 'cowboys' (to use a term offered to me by David Elstein).

They felt their own high standards were being tarnished by such activities and were as upset as the papers at these continuous misfeasances and stupidities.

Roger James is of the opinion that the public silence was manifest because Carlton itself was seen as a somewhat tacky operation – cheap lighter manufacturers, if you will, rather than responsible broadcasters. The common understanding within the industry was that Carlton had been awarded the London contract in 1991 because the Conservative government was determined that Thames Television, the long-time London-based service provider, be denied it. One persistent but totally unsupported rumour was that this was because of the 1988 Thames programme *Death on the Rock* that exposed the falsity of the official British account of the shooting by the SAS of three IRA suspects on Gibraltar (Goodwin, 1998: 115). The contrast between a company in difficulties because of tabloidisation and another because of high-minded investigation was obvious.

Be that as it may, Carlton was perceived as lacking a sense of quality from the outset. Carlton acquired Central TV in 1994 in part to counteract this perception since Lew Grade's Central (and its predecessor ATV) had from the 1950s onwards a distinguished record in documentary production. Indeed, James was a part of this fine reputation. Despite this, the acquisition did not in effect transfer the tradition to Carlton and by 1996 the ITC was castigating the company for its failures to comply with the Code, handing out two formal warnings, which precede fines, that year. Major TV events, such as a huge sensationalised studio discussion on the monarchy and the insensitivities of another debate on the Omagh bombing, confirmed Carlton's dubious standing. *The Connection*'s fine was widely seen as not only predictable and justified but also welcome.

James claims, with much justice in my view, that behind this *schadenfreude* it was a case of TV institution after TV institution being picked off before it was realised that the Press was now attacking on all fronts. Initially, some filmmakers attempted what amounted to a footling defence. On the day the internal panel published its report, over forty of them, including many of the major names who had worked with James at Carlton, wrote to the *Guardian* insisting on James's integrity. For all its sincerity and despite his record as a serious documentarist, this read too much like a *faux* spontaneous gesture from those whom James had employed over the years (although when the letter appeared he was no longer commissioning programmes).

The *Guardian*, on the other hand, was on a crusade. For example, de Beaufort's Castro film of 1994 was also declared a fraud because of a claim in the publicity for this film – not in the film itself – that an interview with Castro was an exclusive when, said the *Guardian*, it was rare archive footage. De Beaufort claimed it was shot by Castro's own crew and passed to him; but be that as it may, a splash based on an error in a publicity handout prepared by the Channel 3 Network Centre (ironically, with the assistance of the *Guardian*) does indicate a quite curious news-value was at work in the paper – especially when there was some dispute over whether or not the publicity piece used 'exclusive interview' rather than 'elusive interviewee'.

The broadcasters did not make much of the hypocrisy of the attacking Press although journalism itself was scarcely in ethically good order. (The broadcasters could perhaps have been obeying the old American adage that it is a good idea never to 'pick a fight with folks who buy their ink by the barrel'.) [3] Increasingly, and especially as the vogue for docusoaps began to decline, the broadcasting professional response was to assert that the issue had gone away, the story was over – although palpably, as the *Macintyre Undercover* incident confirms, it has not.

Channel 4 made the industry's only major on-air reaction to *The Connection*, by transmitting a *Hard News Special*, 'Did you fake this film, Marc?', in September 1998 (Per-Eric Hawthorne). The substance of the *Guardian*'s report was confirmed although there were minor rebuttals. The *Guardian* could have been right that the mule did not swallow heroin, but they were certainly wrong in reporting it was Certs mints in the fingers instead. They were almost certainly right that the mule was not carrying drugs in his stomach when he flew to London but they were probably wrong in claiming the mule and the loader had no drug connections. The mule is currently in a Spanish prison for drug running and *Hard News* produced a Colombian anti-drug squad officer who confirmed that on camera both mule and loader had behaved as if experienced in the matter. The programme hit back, too; the connection of one of the *Guardian* reporters to Carlton's documentary department, which had not been revealed by the paper, was reported. The programme also pointed out that the *Guardian*'s interviews – one obtained by door-stepping James at 9 p.m. at his home and one with de Beaufort which he secretly filmed revealing the two *Guardian* men behaving in a most aggressive and confrontational fashion – would never be countenanced by the ITC Code covering the conduct of interviews.

On the other hand, *Hard News* failed to question the *Guardian*'s concern about the two flights being cut as one because it too seemed unaware of the crippling implications of treating such a normal documentary film-making practice as 'fakery'. *Guardian* editor Alan Rusbridger claimed, when interviewed for this programme, that his decision to run many pages on the film was because 'it's about the whole nature of documentary and what the viewer can believe'. But it simply isn't because, barefaced lying aside, documentary uses many such procedures – which was apparently as unknown to Rusbridger as it was to the *Hard News* team. Rusbridger is more than entitled to claim these everyday procedures are unacceptable but it would be better to do so on the basis of a changed view of the morality of film-making and a full understanding of the implications for documentary. The broadcasting industry has been of no assistance in helping Rusbridger and many others, including the regulators, to reach a more sophisticated and better informed understanding of the 'nature of documentary'.

The only other major response to the 'fakery' scandal came from Ray Fitzwalter. When the Commission ruled in March 2000 that his film *Undercover Britain: Guns in the Street* was 'not misleading' after all, Fitzwalter complained to the Press Complaints Commission, the newspaper industry's watch-dog, of the unfairness of the *Guardian*'s initial coverage. But the PCC, noting that the paper had reported the ITC's exoneration of the film, rejected the complaint (Anon., 2000a: 14).

Beyond this, there were several serious private industry meetings following the *Connection* uproar including a well-attended seminar on the subject held by the BBC Governors. These all expressed condemnation of the film but also heard more vigorous defences of documentary's record. They were not reported outside of the trade press. Overall, British broadcasters have been strangely unselfserving when it comes to defending the concept of fundamental freedom, documentary's distinctiveness or the inevitability of mediation. They certainly, *Hard News* aside, have not used their own air to contribute to the debate. There was a sincere professional condemnation of documentary mendacity which inhibited the mounting of a defence of documentary's normal practices for fear that it could be seen as being of a piece with fraudulent programming. Therefore, they have been slow to complain in public about the ignorant, simplistic retailing of 'fakery' as a basis for moral panic by regulators and journalists. Distinguishing obvious unacceptable lying from other justifiable practices ignorantly being tarred by the same public brush proved too difficult.

They have put up with these regulatory attacks perhaps also understanding how much the industry's current structure and production norms threaten or even undermine the ethical documentary and therefore judge it prudent to remain silent. Properly funded research periods, appropriate schedules to allow for care and accuracy, imagination that goes beyond the sensational and the titillating and, above all, acceptance of the possibility of a project failing, are arguably more important to documentary ethics than the class-bound, often ideologically suspect strictures of the authoritarian codes of practice. Given that TV documentaries especially are made by small (and desperate) independent production companies, it is no wonder that so many documentarists are playing fast and loose with reality.

Sixty-three per cent of respondents to one survey of broadcasting employment patterns claimed to have worked for nothing at least once in the previous year. Another survey showed that, already by 1994, 54 per cent of all broadcast workers were employed as freelances or on short-term contracts of less than a year (Dovey, 2000: 37). Securing a documentary commission from a broadcaster can entail promising more than can be delivered. Failing to deliver is then widely seen as a one-way ticket out of the industry. It is easy to see why insecure programme-makers are firstly prepared to offer what they cannot be sure of filming and secondly to fake it when they fail.

Nearly half of industry respondents felt that standards of accuracy had fallen between 1994 and 1999 and more than half felt ethical standards had slipped as well (Dovey, 2000: 38). The production reality was becoming indefensible:

> Channel 4 tendered 60 late-night slots [*The Other Side*] to Ideal World at a total unit cost of about £5000 a pop. After paying each film-maker's flat £1000 fee, the rest went towards production costs. Out of this total Ideal World provided digital camera and basic editing facilities ... [*The Other Side*] are all 50-minute documentaries shown late at night ... The associate producer for *The Other Side*, Maddy Carberry, explained that, 'Initially the idea was to have cheques for £1000 lined up on a notice board, and each film-maker would turn up with their finished, edited film and get their cheque.' (Kerr, 2000)

Of course, none of this excuses *The Connection*. In fact, it was not subject to these budgetary pressures but, as a prestigious international production from a prize-winning film-maker funded by a major TV contractor, it had positively old-fashioned resource levels upon which to draw. This contributed to the professional hostility to de Beaufort and Carlton. They could not even mount a defence based on their straitened circumstances, although the risk of failure was as great for de Beaufort as it was for other documentarists.

We have had only the occasional public statement from programme-makers, normally as part of the publicity for their films, essaying an explanation of a documentarist's fundamental rights of non-mendacious expression; but these have often seemed less than convincing as earnests of good practice. Take a piece by director Joanna Bailey on how she narrowly avoided being duped by another 'false' respondent to the journalistically slovenly but now standard practice of advertising for participants:

> In April of last year [she wrote in 1999] an assistant and I started to research a documentary about open relationships and swinging. It was soon apparent that a big problem would be finding engaging people who had rejected

> monogamy and could express why in an articulate way. We had hundreds of
> replies to various advertisements. (Bailey, 1999: 4)

Such mealy-mouthed justifications for filming yet more fucking, even in the
name of publicising a transmission, can be seen as speaking to a more general
moral insensitivity.

The collective ignorance of the film-makers about their own traditions and
the silence of their paymasters allowed the substantive attack to go answered.
It gave the inferential frame – documentaries equals 'fakes' – real 'legs'. The
Guardian's Mark Lawson, himself a broadcaster, seemed to think that standard
documentary practices constituted 'narrative tricks – revoicing of questions,
ignoring chronology – which had become routine in documentary' (Lawson,
1998: 26). But such things were not only always routine but also integral to the
development of the form. Moreover, a prohibition against them means less than
nothing in terms of a film's or a programme's integrity, given that mediation is
inevitable at one level or another.

Lawson was, however, right to relate the situation to the Thatcherite reforms
of the commercial broadcasting system which began with the 1981 Broadcasting Act. Certainly the imposition of a Thatcherite free-for-all in the
commissioning process had casualised and sensationalised the industry. In this
uncertain world of small independent 'lifestyle' production 'companies' anyone, even criminals, can be a researcher just as anyone can be a producer,
princes of the blood royal included. Television is unwilling to confront the
problem of this marginalised work-force with, increasingly, its lack of training,
understanding and a purpose beyond mere professional survival.

Not much was said about this in the 'fakery' context. One is left, 'Sherlock
Holmes'-like, clutching at one impossible but nevertheless ideologically logical
explanation of industry's private fury and public subdued stance: broadcasting
obtains one real advantage in taking all this flak and paying up uncomplainingly. It can be illustrated by considering, say, the popularity of films about the
occult and paranormal.

While threats to documentary free expression grow because of the feeble-
mindedness of far too many current practitioners and their unwillingness to
articulate a defence of practice based on the traditional pre-Direct Cinema differences between documentary and journalism, at the same time the television
system as a whole is able to claim, by contrast, that the rest of its output can be
trusted, is not 'faked', does not misrepresent. Thus when a documentary pre-
sents me with evidence that there could be, say, UFOs about, I can be secure in
my belief in its truth. The regulators are on guard on my behalf. The more documentaries get into trouble, implicitly the more pristine is all the news, current
affairs and factual programming by contrast. The failure of documentary to

maintain its claim on the real, therefore, has profound ideological power. One can assert that the sacrifice of all documentaries, whether totally mendacious or simply mediated in a normal way, serves to legitimate the remaining output which is not attacked, exposed in the newspapers, fined by regulators. Fining *The Connection*, in effect, suggests that, by implication, there can be no subterfuge or misrepresentation in the vast majority of the programmes on commercial television and elsewhere.

1.5 A Global Scandal

Britain has not been alone in dealing with 'public trust' and the documentary. Credibility has occasionally also surfaced as an issue in the United States, although surprisingly rarely and then in the shape of a concern with general political bias rather than with 'fakery' as such. The major exception that proves this rule is Michael Moore's *Roger and Me* (1989), which attracted widespread criticism about its editing. *Roger and Me* looked at the havoc wreaked by Reaganomics on a mid-Western working-class community, in this case following the closure of General Motors plants in Flint, Michigan, USA, Moore's home town. More unusually, the film, a satiric polemic against the logic of late capital, obtained mainstream distribution, probably because of its unexpected jocular approach. What is important, then, about this theatrical success is less that it achieved a measure of distribution, even a measure of distribution using a Hollywood major (Warners), and more the seriousness of its subject matter – the decline of America's manufacturing base. Moore's bitter sense of humour and monumental *chutzpah* brought his film exceptionally wide exposure, well beyond the specialised release to big city art-houses which was the most it could have expected. It was probably this success in non-specialist mall cinemas all over America that provoked the assault on its authenticity.

The attack concentrated on the impression the film gave that GM forced the death of the town by the closure of one plant in 1986/87, plunging 30,000 workers into unemployment. In fact, GM slowly removed auto-manufacturing from Flint throughout the 1980s with job-losses beginning in 1978. To substantiate this major criticism, it was further noticed that an evangelist's footling visit to bolster spirits actually took place in 1982 not after the big lay-off year as that appears on the screen. Three absurd job creation projects (including an 'Autoworld' theme park) had all collapsed prior to 1986, not as a consequence of the closures of that year as the film suggests. And, finally, Reagan was not yet president when he is seen exhorting workers to find jobs in Texas, but only a presidential candidate (Jacobson, 1989: 16–17).

Two things were at work here. At the time of the release, talking with students at a conservative state university (whose football coach was to second George Bush's 1992 presidential nomination), it was clear to me that they were having profound difficulties squaring the film's obvious, insistent and *alien*, *uncomfortable* political message about the uncaring nature of late capital with their enjoyment of its jokes, its 'little guy takes on the big guys' theme, its *Saturday Night Live* irreverence. It is probable that the positive reception of the film caused such cognitive dissonance to be widespread and the emergence of questions about the authenticity of its chronology and the ethics of its juxta-positionings were a ready remedy for this condition.

To see Moore as a 'gonzo demagogue' (in the words of Pauline Kael's *New Yorker* attack on him) was to fail to see Roger Smith, GM's chief executive, as a corporate barbarian with no civic sensibilities at all. Anyway, the criticisms were actually without foundation since Moore does not say that the film chronicles only the events of 1986/87 and its aftermath or that Reagan was a candidate and so on. In fact he doesn't date anything particularly. The attacks were therefore doubly picayune since not only was *Roger and Me* making no claims to offer a day-by-day account of the events it portrayed, but whether the film was chronologically accurate or not was utterly beside the point. In the overall scheme of things, GM closed Flint and moved production off-shore and whether they did that all at once in one year or piece by piece through the decade could not matter less. The people of Flint were devastated however long it took. The town's attempts to replace work all failed whether before or after 1986. The comforts of priests and politicians were frivolous and fruitless when-ever they occurred. And none of Moore's critics has ever argued that he remotely misrepresented the actual underlying situation in Flint.

Roger and Me has a significance beyond the particular flaccid charges made against it. Although this has rarely been the case in America, the attacks on the film are of a piece with those mounted in other places, including the UK, dur-ing the later 1990s. As with some aspects of British reportage and regulation, an unwarranted supposition about practice was being made by Moore's crit-ics. In this case, it was the assumption that the chronology of the film's narrative had to match the chronology of its shooting schedule if authentic-ity was to be maintained. This particular editing protocol had never been claimed as a necessity even by the most vigorous of Direct Cinema prac-titioners at the height of early 1960s naïveté about the ability of the new portable equipment to capture the real. Now it was deployed to sustain an asi-nine (because irrelevant) attack on Moore's agitprop strategy. That the editing of the film had made some points, even if cheap ones, because of such routine manipulation is neither here nor there as far as the documentary tradition was concerned.

Appeals to unprecedented and largely unattainable standards of non-inter-vention are at the heart of what began to look like a worldwide war against the documentary in the 1990s, with scandals cropping up everywhere. Not all of them were made by liars who wished to conceal their falsehood and simply wanted to materially benefit from their fraud. For example, Pieter Kramer produced a series of films, *30 Minutes*, for VPRO TV in the Netherlands of faked victim documentaries including one, *Born in the Wrong Body*, which had a white man having his nostrils widened and his skin darkened, apparently convinced he should be an African (Mapplebeck, 1999: 11). His purpose was to use the documentary form to illuminate bigotry in an attention-grabbing way.

Given the ideological power of the realist image in claiming to be trustworthy, it is clearly legitimate to use a faked documentary form to force the audience, as it were, to confront its credulity in such images and its prejudices about what they might represent. Such a technique dates back, perhaps, to the obvious biting absurdities of Buñuel's *Land Without Bread* (1932). In that film 'fakery' – such as the commentary claiming a mountain goat has missed its footing when in fact it had been obviously shot off its perch – overlays the desperate reality of the poverty of the people he filmed. It is possible to read the 'faked' elements in *Land Without Bread* as Buñuel's satiric attack on realist film's pretensions, a target as meaningful as his primary objective in exposing the actual horrors of life in Las Hurdas.

As Buñuel demonstrated, public gullibility could be endlessly exploited. Direct Cinema produced so particular an approach that it was immediately aped primarily because of its strong claim on the real. *David Holtzman's Diary* (Kit Carson, 1968) or *This is Spinal Tap* (Rob Reiner, 1983) were total fictions satirical in intent implicitly attacking 'truth films' and 'rockumentaries' respectively. In the same vein, perhaps, was Jean-Teddy Fillipe's '*X-Files*'-style documentary series *Forbidden Documents*, produced for the Franco-German Arte TV channel. This contained faked 'FBI surveillance' and mock old 'home-movie' footage. Worried viewers urged him 'to steer clear of the Devil's work' (Mapplebeck, 1997: 10–11). A New Zealand film, *Forgotten Silver* (Peter Jackson and Costa Botes, 1997), invented a plausible local figure who is credited with a series of astonishing 'firsts' in everything from aviation to colour photography, all backed up with meticulous faked period footage. The public were had and infuriated but the society's simplistic nationalist pretensions (and ignorance of history) were thereby exposed.

What distinguishes these films from the Buñuel is that, however confused the public, there was in fact clear evidence of the fictional provenance of the piece. This is also true of the drama-documentary; so I am here no more concerned with either than with, say, Godard's use of the documentary-style to-camera interviews in his fictions. Misrepresentation, as the British examples show, is the key and none of these film misrepresents.

The French scandals involved outright fakery in two of TF1's *Reportages* series, one of which, like *The Connection*, covered the drugs trade. More enterprisingly, France 3 staged a complete Alpine rescue as real (Dovey, 2000: 34); but the real uproar was caused in 1996 in Germany. It centred on Michael Born, a broadcast newsman who created many sensationalist tabloid packages for television in the early 1990s (Mapplebeck, 1997: 10–11). He turned out to be a veritable Baron Munchhausen although he did not start that way. His coverage as a journalist of Beirut in the 1980s was deemed to be exemplary but he allowed himself to become 'tabloidised'. Accused of setting up a sequence in Bombay where exhausted children were seen making rugs for IKEA, he successfully resisted the company's lawsuit even though he had paid the children to be filmed. (Paying participants to appear in a documentary film is not unknown, as we shall see, although payment transgresses normal news-gathering practices.) He had delivered a report on a farmer who shot cats for sport to Stern TV but without a shot of a dead cat. At this point, Born crossed the line of even normal documentary practice. He claimed, in a real-life version of the sort of stunt *Drop the Dead Donkey* would have used for a gag, to have dug up a deceased feline to get the required image. The cat-shoot would have been on the wilder shores of sensationalist broadcasting even if true, but Born subsequently claimed that the farmer's hobby was a fiction. The next step was but a small one.

He sold Stern TV a scoop, exclusive film of Ku Klux Klan activity in the Federal Republic. This attracted a level of attention beyond Stern TV's expectations although, given German law prohibiting all neo-Nazi activities, it could perhaps have been anticipated. Police rapidly discovered that, far from revealing a new cell, the clansmen were Born's acquaintances wearing white robes run up by his mother. Since neo-Nazi activity of any kind is illegal and it is also an offence to profit from a fraud, Born, who was of course paid by Stern TV, was prosecuted for the hoax and received a four-year prison sentence, despite the fundamental Federal freedom of expression law that: 'There shall be no censorship' (Barendt, 1985: 33).

As with *The Connection*, the issue is not the perfectly reasonable exposure of a liar but rather the nature of the punishment. There is a general assumption in German law that neo-Nazi activity is as anti-social as, say, false advertising. It is a strict liability offence – no proof of intention is required and there is no mitigating defence once it is proved to have happened. In this it is quite unlike *The Connection* where the possibility of emulation or audience action of any kind was never put to the question. Born's footage was presumed to have a potential influence over behaviour and it was of no concern that it was 'faked' since it would have this damaging effect whether fact, reconstructed fact or outright fiction. But, given its history of draconian censorship, the German state's response was still questionable from the free expression standpoint, a view not lost (for example) on the organisers of the Frankfurt Book Festival who

awarded the Festival prize to Born for revealing the 'truth in media reconstructions'.

German-speaking documentarists seem anyway quicker than their contem-
poraries in the anglophone world still to insist on a measure of artistic rights
which can justify much now considered in the UK as 'fakery'. The rhetoric of
the artist had been widely used to warrant, for instance, Robert Flaherty's pioneering interventionist and reconstructional filming procedures in making
Nanook of the North. In the anglophone world, though, this trope has largely
disappeared following the triumph of Direct Cinema. Flies on the wall could
not at the same time claim the prerogatives of great artists. Outside the Griersonian heartland, however, this has been very much less the case. So, to take a
recent example, Austrian Michael Glawogger's *Megacities* was the documentary
hit of the film festival circuit in 1998 but its authenticity was much queried. For
instance, Glawogger filmed Russians reading books but had no hesitancy in
providing them with apposite texts. 'In some cases', he explained, 'that's what
people were reading at the time. But in other cases, I used it to make my own
comments' (Goldberg, 1999: 18). Anglophone documentarists are now not supposed to make personal comments and even less to intervene with the action
in order to obtain the footage that would allow them to do so.

This is but one source of moral perplexity facing today's documentarist. I
want to make a case that the issue of documentary freedom and documentary
fakery is of central importance to the whole question of media control and
media ethics. Although it can be easily argued that, even including unexpected
blips in popularity such as the British docusoap enjoyed in the late 1990s, documentary is a quite minor audio-visual form, yet in its unique claim both to
represent and to interpret reality it offers the hardest of ethical cases. Moreover,
the development of an audio-visual culture of abundance at the end of the
twentieth century ever more clearly revealed how central the documentary
form was to any concept of socially responsible media services – what we can
term 'public service broadcasting'.

Chapter Two
Public Service

Broadcasting has always been more highly regulated than other media. Unlike a publisher or film producer, the broadcaster needs a licence from the state to even begin. Unlike the publisher, but in common with the producer, the broadcaster's product is subject to further state control in the form of content regulation. Free expression is not a uniform right and broadcasting is the most constrained of all media. There are many reasons why this is so (and why it continues to be deemed acceptable), the concept of a state-sanctioned public service being prominent among them.

Public service broadcasting (PSB) traditionally assumed that a responsibility to the audience was of more importance than, say, a commercial duty to shareholders. In this context, documentary, as a quality 'duty-genre', flourished even though (or perhaps exactly because) it did not achieve mass appeal anywhere until the later 1990s. The relaxation and reformulation of PSB allowed broadcasters, however funded, to become more like other businesses. It became clear, as the ratings became ever more paramount, that documentary presence in the schedules was a real mark of public service commitment.

2.1 Documentary as Public Service

John Grierson's initial ambition for the documentary from the late 1920s on was to influence people through film. Getting them to watch was essential. That he failed to find a mass audience, whatever excuses were offered, means that in effect he did not to get to first base. But failed he did. 'Why do we spend our pocket money and our leisure hours at the cinema?' demanded a letter to a film-fans' magazine in 1933. 'To see our ordinary everyday lives portrayed on the screen over and over again? Emphatically not' (Jones, 1987: 23).

The classic documentary was never popular enough to overcome the hostility of the exhibitors and regularly command space in the commercial cinemas. The Griersonian documentary in the 1930s had not sustained for itself the limited theatrical presence achieved by feature-length films in the previous decade and even the revival of the documentary feature in the Second World War did not establish it as a popular form. The vast majority of Grierson's Documentary Movement films were screened in alternative venues and the largest total annual audience claimed for these school, factory and village hall-style events, 18.5 million in 1943/44, was almost certainly grossly inflated. Even if true, 18.5 million only equalled the number of tickets sold by commercial cinema in any four days at that time. Postwar documentarists did not escape from its ghetto. The cinema remained off-limits to them and the form only survived in the mainstream of moving-image culture because it transferred itself to television. In the UK, BBC TV easily absorbed much of the ethos of the Griersonian documentary movement. Grierson's 'public education' developed along the same lines as the concept of 'public service broadcasting'.

The term 'public service' was hijacked by John Reith, the British Broadcasting Company's first managing director, to mean not simply a service used by the public however owned or funded, whether for profit or not. Reith made it clear that public service broadcasting was a publicly funded, not-for-profit enterprise. Initially struggling to steer a third way between the Scylla of private ownership by the radio industry (his actual situation) and the Charybdis of becoming a department of state, he put this particular spin on 'public service' from which it was not to escape until the Thatcher era. For Reith, 'public service' meant that primarily that the 'BBC was not out to make money for the sake of making money' (Briggs, 1961: 235). The idea was abroad, even in the United States, that perhaps the programmes were simply a way of facilitating the sale of radio sets and should therefore be given away free. Such a thought helped Reith resist 'commercialisation' just as the example of officially created but independent supervisory boards of control or corporations established for various industries during the First World War afforded him a model to avoid becoming a directly state-run enterprise (Briggs, 1961: 332; Murdock, 1992: 26). Of course, in addition he was always prepared to use an argument about quality to bolster his case for independence:'It is occasionally indicated to us that we are apparently setting out to give the public what we think they need – and not what they want – but few know what they want and very few what they need' (Reith, 1924: 34). This paternalism with its 'coercive edge' (in Graham Murdock's phrase) linked Reith back to his fellow Scot, Grierson, who then had the BBC's example to follow as he articulated his vision of public education a few years later (Murdock, 1992: 29).[1]

It is no wonder that, in the 1950s, the new BBC TV Documentary Department could be seen as a direct inheritor of Reith's public service programming remit as well as Griersonian film-making values. It was even run between 1953–55 by Paul Rotha, a major figure from the Documentary Movement (Swallow, 1982: 86–9). Rotha, for all the unhappiness of his stint as a television executive, meshed well with a BBC radio documentary tradition that Paddy Scannell suggests was strongly left wing in the 1930s. Indeed, the radio documentary of that era under Hilda Matheson and Charles Siepmann, successive heads of 'London Talks', dealt with many of the same topics of social concern as did the Griersonians – housing, unemployment and so on – but in a far more coherently radical way. With the Charter up for renewal and facing right-wing attacks, the BBC killed off 'London Talks' in 1935 and dispersed its members: 'The dismantling of Talks marked the arrival of corporate control within the BBC' (Scannell, 1986: 14). What was left of the department then opted for safe subjects and ignored the worsening social and international situations.

Nevertheless, by contrast with the pre-1935 phase, Grierson's reformist approach throughout the 1930s looked like nothing so much as propaganda for the somewhat embattled established order. Moreover, the potentially crowd-pleasing pictorialism of many of the films, and occasional populist gestures – such as scantily-clad chorines tap dancing before the radio mike in *BBC: The Voice of Britain* (Stuart Legg, 1935) – were not enough to balance the overall sober tone of the output. In fact, the spectre of audience antipathy to Grierson's public education documentaries was really the only hindrance to the process whereby the Griersonian tradition was transferred to the small screen. Audience hostility haunted the Documentary Department, counterbalancing the appeal of the Documentary Movement's impeccable public service credentials.

Television, against Rotha's judgement, prayed journalism, albeit serious journalism, into the mix to overcome this problem. Public service might be conformable with public education, but documentarists wishing to reach the new mass television audience needed to disguise documentary as journalism. The persistent poetic characteristic of the classic documentaries also remained as the BBC documentary continued to emulate this tradition as well. In 1959, for example, Denis Mitchell won the prestigious Prix Italia for the poetic *Morning in the Streets*, arguably British television's first critically acclaimed addition to the Griersonian canon (Corner, 1991: 52–4). Overall, however, news values replaced the more overt educational worthiness of the original Griersonian project.

These traditions, public service concepts and audiences skewed demographically upwards across the socio-economic bands (as the industry now described 'class'), masked the limited general popularity of the documentary as compared to other television forms. Journalism and poetry did not entirely ensure that the documentary escaped from the ghetto. Nevertheless public service and elite audiences, even if small by TV standards, ensured that the documentary found a more secure place in the new schedules than it ever had on the big screen. As a result, over the past four decades the BBC has regularly reported remarkably consistent percentages of programming described as 'documentary'. For example, in 1955/6 the Corporation pigeon-holed the 'real' into 'Sport', 'News', 'Newsreel and documentation films [*sic*]/outside broadcasts' and 'Talks, demonstrations [*sic*] and documentary programmes'. These last, at 634 hours, amounted to 25 per cent of output (Seymour-Ure, 1992: 338).

In 1958/59 the figures were much the same – 24.3 per cent (Anon., 1960: 226). The arrival of BBC2 in 1964/65 caused something of a blip as 'Talks etc.', with hours increased to 748 across both channels, nevertheless accounted for only 13 per cent of the output (Anon., 1966: 42); but a decade later the original range of 20 to 25 per cent had been re-established with 988 hours on BBC1 (now described as 'Current Affairs, Features and Documentaries') yielding just under 20 per cent of output and 712 hours on BBC2 just over that level (Anon., 1976: 118). A decade after that, in 1984/85, BBC1 had no less than 26 per cent and BBC2 19 per cent in this category (Anon., 1986: 148). A similar consistency, albeit at a lesser level, can be noted in ITV's commitment where the 'Documentary and Arts' category remains fairly steadily around 10 per cent of output across these decades. Channel 4 devoted a positively non-commercial 22 per cent of its time to such programming (Seymour-Ure, 1992: 138).

In 1996, on behalf of the Italian public broadcaster RAI, a new worldwide survey of scheduling practices was undertaken (Preta *et al.*, 1996). This confirmed that the British levels were being sustained into the mid-1990s. It also revealed that the documentary output of all public service broadcasters fell into two bands. One lay between 5 and 10 per cent; for example – Austria's ORF, the Canadian CBC, Croatian HTV, the Czech Republic's CTV, Denmark's DR, Italy's RAI, the Netherlands' NOS, Slovenian TVSLO and Switzerland's SSR. The second, higher band included the BBC as well as France 2, reporting nearly 20 per cent of time devoted to documentaries with a second French channel, TF1, on 14 per cent; and the American public service system, CPB/PBS, 55 per cent.

Only six of the thirty-five organisations responding were private. Their replies supported the perception that however badly documentary does on public television, it fares even worse under commerce. Italy's Mediaset, for example, managed 0.1 per cent of output. Finland's MTV3 did double its output between 1994 and 1995 but only from 0.5 per cent to 1.1 per cent. But in the anglophone documentary heartland, the British commercial channels bucked this trend. ITV reached a level comparable to the lower band of documentary-minded state-funded systems while Channel 4 matched the higher.

These figures were the result of a fairly random collection of broadcasters self-reporting via a questionnaire that failed to define documentary closely; yet the RAI study did make the category 'documentary output' distinct from 'classical music', 'education', ' "minority" programmes', and a large category called 'Information' that included 'news', 'reportage', 'current affairs', 'magazine' and 'parliamentary reports'. Furthermore, although 'documentary' is almost certainly defined differently in these various countries, nevertheless the RAI study is not seriously at odds with previous analysis. Richard Kilborn has cited two other surveys from 1991 and 1994 which also found that European TV stations, commercial and public, between them produced around 4 per cent or 20,000 hours of documentary programming a year (Kilborn, 1996: 142). It therefore seems reasonable to suggest that an antipathy to the documentary tends to be more or less universal among broadcasters, especially on the new commercial channels and outside the anglophone world.

The RAI study further confirmed Kilborn's observation that 'documentaries still fare best in those countries with a long-standing public service tradition' in the Reithian sense (Kilborn, 1996: 143). For instance, the public broadcaster TVE, being in a country, Spain, without such a tradition, claimed no documentaries at all (Preta *et al.*, 1996: 9); whereas (as I have pointed out) in Britain even commercial broadcasters did better than the European average (Kilborn, 1996: 143). This meant that throughout the first decades of the attack on public service principles that British television began to endure in the 1970s, the documentary, an essential mark of such service, more or less weathered the storm.

Kilborn, in suggesting the Reithian public service concept as a primary determinant of documentary activity, rather than a documentary film-making tradition *per se*, points up an essential link. As the global neo-liberal attack on the principles of public service broadcasting developed, it became clear that documentaries and the retransmission of high culture in performance were what crucially characterised such a service. The market place provided, in a generic sense at least, everything else including news and drama, at least in its most popular forms. What were threatened or even totally lost when public service television was commercialised or the Reithian public service ethos diluted were, exactly, documentaries and arts features. Thus documentary's position in the British schedules, as Richard Kilborn has argued, has been buttressed more by the Reithian public service than by its attractiveness to audiences (Kilborn, 1996: 143). It is, therefore, perfectly possible to argue that the health of documentary or its survival are measures of the failure of the Thatcherite attack on British public service broadcasting culture.

This sort of crude counting does not necessarily say anything about the 'health' of the form. About this there is a complex argument because, since documentary can embrace the facile, the sensational and the titillating as well as illuminating, serious work, its continued presence of itself is no guarantee of 'quality'. Although documentary content has not been fully audited, research has demonstrated that in the contiguous area of UK current affairs production there has been a significant move away from foreign coverage and a rise in crime and consumer reporting over the twenty years to 1998 (Barnett and Seymour, 1999: 11–19). In 1993 the British imported from America Reality TV shows that dealt with crime, accidents and disasters of all kinds (and also made extensive use of reconstructions, but labelled them as such). The BBC's version *999* was but one of many European incarnations of Reality or Crime programming (e.g. *Urgences* in France or *SOS – liveller död* in Sweden). The original British version was widely seen as 'TURNING VIEWERS INTO VOYEURS' as one headline put it (Hill, 2000: 19). The charge was that these shows 'tabloidised' TV, a particularly worrying development given the BBC's lead in bringing them to the public (Corner, 1996: 184). The late distinguished documentarist David Munro was not alone among programme-makers when he wrote in 1994: 'I personally don't think the ambulance-chasing, crime reconstruction programmes have any place at all on television; they are voyeuristic and don't achieve anything. ... I believe that every documentary film-maker in this country, every film-maker, every current affairs person, should stand up and say the public deserves better than this' (Munro, 1994: 18–19).

These concerns were at the heart of a widespread 'dumbing down' assertion about British television which, for all that it is grounded in problematic elitist and paternalistic assumptions, is widely supposed also to apply to documentary. Indeed, 'dumbing down' conditioned a general response to the popularity of the docusoaps that followed Reality TV into the schedules. These are undemanding cheaply-produced documentary series on (largely) uncontroversial areas of everyday life that unexpectedly secured for documentary for the first time a regular position among Britain's most popular TV programming types. Despite this success, the shows were not celebrated as a long-delayed triumph of Griersonian principles in a popular form at last but rather castigated as a key example of what 'dumbing down' really meant in practice. In part, this has to be because documentary is central to the idea of public service broadcasting and, too often, to automatic assumptions as to what TV quality is or should be. The popularity of the docusoap obviously renders it 'commercial' in ways that the documentary traditionally has not been and so removes it from this equation. The importance of the traditional serious documentary to the non-commercial values of television is independent of (and, indeed, in defiance of) popularity. This phenomenon of an elite 'duty-genre' persisting for decades in a mass medium is not limited to the UK.

2.2 The American Tradition of Public Documentary Service

The Americans are heirs, as are British broadcasters, to a tradition of state-funded 'public-education' documentary production even though their sense of 'public service' absorbed commercialism, in effect rejecting Reith's anti-commercial spin. The two leading American networks, NBC and CBS, developed significant in-house TV documentary units and, as we have seen, CBS's *See It Now* influenced the nascent BBC documentary department. *See It Now* began in 1951 more or less as an extended news feature series building on radio formats and the single-issue tradition of the cinema newsreel series *March of Time*. By the third season, Fred Friendly, *See It Now*'s producer, and the anchorman

Ed Murrow, whose considerable fame and stature dated back to his coverage of the London Blitz for CBS Radio, became more committed to 'soft' news stories and, therefore, more 'documentary' in their approach. The famous, and extremely brave, attack on Senator Joe McCarthy's Red-baiting in 1954 ensured *See It Now*'s place in the schedules and in American broadcasting history. The series was followed by *CBS Reports* in 1959 and NBC's *White Papers* a year later.

Documentary was also represented in the schedules by the historical compilation series that began with 'Pete' Salomon's *Victory at Sea* (NBC, 1952–3). Jack Le Vien's twenty-six-part series based on Churchill's war memoirs *The Valiant Years* was a prize-winning hit for both ABC and the BBC in 1961. (Notoriously, it used archive film augmented by actors, one of whom had been hired to speak Sir Arthur 'Bomber' Harris's words on camera because the Air Marshal himself was suffering from crippling arthritis when the filming took place (Purser, 1999: 20).) The historical documentary series was joined, amongst others, by CBS's *The 20th Century* ('Bud' Benjamin, 1957–70), narrated by Walter Cronkite early on Sunday evenings, and Salomon's *Project XX*, which appeared intermittently on NBC between 1954 and 1962 (Bluem, 1965: 145–63). It is often forgotten that the compilation film, pioneered in the Soviet Union by Esfir Schub (*The Fall of the Romanov Dynasty*, 1927), has been among the most enduring, non-sport, documentary forms. It has come as close as any other type of documentary to achieving a measure of broad popularity.

In a commercial sense, though, both these and the journalistic/investigative documentary strand were a species of 'cultural loss leader' more designed to maintain public confidence in a system held by some to be 'a vast wasteland' than to maximise audiences, which they singularly failed to do (Hammond, 1981: 250). The history of these series can be read as a chronicle of a species of long-term network public relations exercise, shored up by a sense of civic duty and little else.

This failure to improve on the marginality of the Griersonian documentary for the mass audience does not denigrate those films, particularly in the 1960s, that have been written into the record as controversial and influential TV masterworks – for example, the *CBS Reports: Harvest of Shame* on the plight of migrant workers (David Lowe, 1960) or *Hunger in America* (Martin Carr, 1968), which is credited with facilitating the introduction of the federal food-stamps programme. *The Selling of the Pentagon* (Peter Davis, 1971), on the military's domestic public relations activities, caused such a storm that congressional hearings were held on the matter. Such occasional triumphs of public enlightenment illuminated 'the vast wasteland' and thereby justified the whole commercialised television system. They were well worth the odd hour of less than maximal audience figures (Winston, 1995: 134–5; 153; 213). The irony is that the year of *The Selling of the Pentagon* was also the last year of *CBS Reports* as a regular series, if only as schedule-fodder against whatever was unstoppable, ratings-wise, on the rival networks: *The Untouchables, Wagon Train, The Fugitive, Marcus Welby M.D.*

As Charles Hammond Jr. pointed out: 'Television news documentary regressed only after it was clearly demonstrated that its various subjects had become too heady to be taken steadily. Viewers didn't like to see too much reality' (Hammond, 1981: 251). Documentaries were increasingly to be found in the late-night or high-summer schedule as the programmes, however distinguished, persistently remained unattractive to the mass of the audience. The result was that documentary was utterly unprotected in the neo-liberal era. In 1984 the Federal Communications Commission's guidelines on programming, which had been outlined in 1960, were formally abandoned. The public service element in American commercial broadcasting was significantly diluted. Gone was any requirement for public affairs programming and, within a few years, the networks' documentary departments were consigned to history. A formal public service mandate and nothing else had been responsible for the documentary's presence in the commercial TV schedules for three decades: and, it should be noted, nothing else – despite the broadcasters' oft-made claim that this demise was the inevitable result of the rise of cable and the exponential growth of competition.[2]

In the mid-1990s, although no longer as monopolistic as they had been in the post-Second World War decades, the networks still reached 37 million American homes in prime time and were taking over $30,000 million a year in advertising revenue. The commercial pressure of competition was less significant in documentary's decline than was the neo-liberal change in regulatory environment. Despite the technicist hyperbole about the death of traditional US television, we are actually witnessing a comparatively 'soft-landing' for the networks in the multi-channel, multi-media era. The Reaganite removal of the public service requirement proved crucial to the destruction of the documentary. This, rather than new technologies or rabid right-wing hysteria, caused the networks finally to give up on them. Even the occasional special *CBS Reports* became a thing of the past.

The only regular 'Reithian' (as it were) public service element that remained was the news. It must be admitted that this grew to include the news magazine which, in some sense, echoes the logic of *See It Now*. Don Hewitt's *Sixty Minutes*, 'the Time magazine of the air', was first broadcast on CBS in 1968 (Brook and Marsh, 1981: 688). It held so secure a position in American Sunday night television that it became something of a broadcasting institution. Over the decades the other networks have tried to emulate it with a variety of series but only with limited success. The ratings effectiveness of *Sixty Minutes*, with its three short provocative films a week, was in contrast to the struggles *CBS*

Reports constantly had to find a similar audience. The news magazine format therefore hammered a further nail into the coffin of one-off network documentary. It also helped solidify the idea that documentary was merely news in a longer format.

The networks also found success with cheap Reality TV. These multiplied 'exponentially' (according to *Variety*) across mainstream network, independent and cable channels in the early 1990s. But the same paradox was to work to the detriment of documentary. Although, as one producer said, Reality TV could be 'more compelling than fiction', its very success confirmed that the older, less sensational documentary tradition was a thing of the past (Hill, 2000: 194).

As a corollary of technicist hype, it is also sometimes argued that the 'New Cabled World', augmented by satellite, has more than compensated for the disappearance of the documentary from the US broadcast networks with whole channels now devoted to such output. The truth is that these outlets command very small audiences, just as documentary and other serious programming did on the old nets. The Discovery Channel, for example, had a cumulative rating of 1.1, that is around a mere million homes, at the point when the networks were killing off their documentaries (Russell *et al.*, 1996: 138). Discovery is dedicated to documentary programming but its comparative lack of attractiveness to TV audiences (most of its employees work in its up-market shopping-mall outlets) demonstrates that cable had no more pressing an economic or audience-appeal reason to sustain documentary than did the networks to kill it off. The Discovery Channel, no thanks to its audience appeal, is, because of new technology market-hype, more valuable than the CBS network. However, as with all upscale programming on other equally comparatively unwatched cable channels such as Arts and Entertainment – which grew from CBS Cable when its ownership of this was forbidden by the FCC – or the History Channel, Discovery works for cable just as documentary had originally worked for the networks – a 'duty-channel' as opposed to a 'duty-genre'. They supply programming of a perceived 'quality' which could be used to legitimate the entire multi-channel output. It provided, in effect, the 'public service' legitimisation cable needed.

On the other hand, cable also made one decidedly un-'public service' contribution to the documentary form itself. Freed from the puritanical constraints of mainstream American television, cable's premium movie channels exhibited a willingness to 'investigate' human sexuality and nudity, cheaply producing a form of non-fiction far from the 'sobriety' (as Bill Nichols terms it) of traditional anglophone, Griersonian public education film or the serious journalistic concerns of the networks' tradition. This 'docuglitz', which has some precedents in the cinema, joined even more cheaply-shot videos of X-rated cabaret mainliners and some sport (notably boxing) as the movie channels' major leavening of the Hollywood films that are their *raison d'être*. Although latterly some recognisably serious work has been produced by the premium channels, cable's overall contribution does seem to be that it somehow stumbled on a solution to the previously futile search for a truly popular documentary form. Docuglitz's acceptability to the subscription-paying audience was widely noticed and eventually this extension of subject matter, the most significant since Direct Cinema invaded the privacy of everyday life a decade earlier, also began to influence all documentary production including what was left on mainstream TV.

The final American proof of the centrality of documentary to a public service ethos lies with the history of the politically-battered public television system during this same period. According to Patricia Zimmermann's convincing analysis, *ad hoc* complaints about 'bias' in the Public Broadcasting System (PBS) metamorphosed after 1989 into a sustained right-wing attack not against individual documentaries for supposed left-leaning proclivities as had been the case previously, but against the entire public-funding structure (Zimmermann, 2000). Despite the arrival of specialised cable services such as Discovery, A and E, and the History Channel, which were largely documentary in their content, it was still the case that the biggest audiences for the form were achieved by PBS. This, though, was far from being a good thing.

As far as the Right was concerned, 'PBS has become a purveyor of leftist propaganda' and almost every documentary work of note produced by the system in recent decades was attacked on these grounds, especially any series on the Civil Rights Movement such as Henry Hampton's measured history of the struggle, *Eyes on the Prize* (1987) or John Valdez's exposure of a miscarriage of justice that imprisoned a Black Panther leader for nineteen years (*Passin' It On*, 1993). Major series on Africa, Vietnam, Korea and the Palestinians created storms far greater than their audience appeal would have suggested as reasonable. In the Right's fervid imaginings these and any other works on diversity, gender or sexual orientation became "The unchallenged proliferation of propaganda over taxpayer-supported airwaves ... and a violation of the laws that make public radio and television possible' (Horowitz and Jarvik, 1995: 60).

Reagan had already begun cutting the appropriations of the National Endowments for the Arts and Humanities in the 1980s and packed them with his appointees. Federal support fell by 40 per cent. Now, at the high tide of Republican control of Congress in 1995, Newt Gingrich went so far as to float a plan to phase out PBS (and the Endowments) altogether. Although this was resisted, the principle of public funding without concern for content has been compromised and these bodies, despite their own sometimes less than passionate defence of freedom of expression, have themselves needed a constant defence.

Zimmermann points out that as far as PBS was concerned the attack disproportionately targeted documentaries:

> Congressional debates, political targeting by conservatives, geopolitical restructuring in the telecommunications sector, and new technologies have turned documentary into a political battlefield where casualties are mounting daily in large and small, visible and invisible ways. It is on the discursive and institutional site of the documentary where fantasies of the white, bordered, homogenous and stable nation are being dismantled and renegotiated. (Zimmermann, 2000)

Curiously, though, the American Right did not use 'fakery' despite the fact that arguments about method, of course, have the advantage of appearing to be politically neutral. They take place in the court of truth before the bar of objectivity. On the matter of content itself they are silent, leaving American sensitivities to the principle of free expression enshrined in the First Amendment of the US Constitution intact. Although the Right sometimes came close (as with *Roger and Me*), they never attacked more directly on this front but rather implicitly accepted documentary's claim on the real, complaining only of the film-makers' perceived politics. At the same time, they also rejected any possibility of audience sophistication or scepticism. It was assumed that documentary could unproblematically reflect an external reality and was in consequence powerfully persuasive not least because deeply susceptible audiences easily believed it.

This strategy in the *kulturkampf* was supported by a strand of rhetoric from the academy that took the form of a strident reactionary attack on post-modernism, primarily by tarring all those who queried the evidentiary potential of the photographic image as 'post-modern sceptics' – a novel term of abuse. The effort was fronted by Noel Carroll, a philosopher.

In his second article on the documentary in as many decades, Carroll emerged to defend the truth claims of documentaries in general and, in particular, quotidian TV films about killer whales and Nazi aviation. Films of this sort, Carroll insisted, display 'standards of scientific accuracy and attendant protocols of objectivity' (Carroll, 1996: 287). Carroll's failure to cite their makers is not insignificant since the 'protocols of objectivity' are much aided by such anonymity. His apparently depoliticised analysis disguised the ideological implications of such texts and, indeed, of Carroll's whole position. The *Wings of the Luftwaffe* (1994?)[3] Carroll cites explained the value of German glider research during Second World War to contemporary aviation; yet the difficulty of claiming life-enhancing outcomes for Nazi research of any kind is scarcely, on its face, neutral whatever truth-value is assigned to the argument deployed in the film. That Carroll has nothing to say about this socio-historic context exactly speaks to the ineffable quality of documentary's traditional claim on the real that he is attempting to embrace and which the ideologues of the Right were accusing public television of abusing because of their left-wing bias.

In contrast to the ever-increasing flow of academic writings on the documentary, the contemporary political battlefield has been largely undocumented where, indeed, 'casualties' mount in 'small ... invisible ways'. The American atmosphere is such that, for example, in the late 1980s I can recall being asked, as a dean at a state university who had published on the documentary, to support Barbara Kopple's *American Dream* project against a supposedly simple request from the 'Reaganised' National Endowment of the Arts, a major funder, that she write a script – not an outline or scenario – but a detailed script of her proposed film on paper in advance of shooting. Even at the height of the classic synch documentary period from the mid-1930s to the late 1950s such a thing was never done. There was always space for improvisation, ad-libbing or 'off-the-cuff' shooting (Winston, 1999: 20–33).

Kopple, an observational film-maker who began her career with two Direct Cinema pioneers, the Maysles brothers, simply could not start to meet this request. She was documenting a long-running strike against a meat packaging company, thereby illustrating the destruction of mid-Western working-class communities in the course of the global manufacturing restructuring of the 1980s. The NEH, though, was not crudely questioning this content. They were not concerned that Kopple's previous strike film, *Harlan County, USA* (1976), in which she had almost been murdered by company goons, was sympathetic to the coal-miner strikers it portrayed. Nor, on the other hand, were they inclined to trust her ability to deliver on the basis of the Oscar that she had won with that film. No – all they wanted was an exact account of what they were buying. Perfectly reasonable – to anybody who knew nothing of documentary film. To those who did, this was also very cleverly a perfect censoring method that left First Amendment sensitivities intact. Kopple was able to use her considerable standing (if only in liberal circles) to fight this off on the grounds that no documentary could meet such a demand. She finished the film and won a second Oscar with it in 1991. Such arguments, affecting even the most distinguished film-makers, were becoming nothing more than the everyday reality of the American documentarist's struggle to work.

There is a further irony here in that Kopple is an exceptionally engagé figure to attract NEA/NEH or PBS support. Many more consistently radical documentarists were marginalised by PBS and the Endowments. Film-makers tended to regard PBS, and especially public TV stations within the system serving conservative local communities, with scorn since challenging material tended to have such folk always running scared. This division of liberal-left opinion was, like arguments about the production process, too sophisticated for the neo-McCarthyite ideologues to use effectively either. The *kulturkampf*, with rare exceptions, was focused on the supposedly monolithic political position, glossed as 'bias', of those spending public funds.

Despite all such problems and the hostages to fortune that documentaries often turned out to be, the Corporation for Public Broadcasting and PBS reported to RAI that around 55 per cent of American public television output was documentary (Preta *et al.*, 1996: 52). Although apparently including all its news and information programming, this is still a significant – if politically fool-hardy – commitment which better served to infuriate right-wing critics than to create a mass audience. Traditional documentary did little to correct the marginality of the publicly funded system to the mass audience, although from time to time, as with Ken Burns's series on the American Civil War (1990), it achieved ratings seven to eight times greater than Discovery's average.

US television's history overall certainly supports Richard Kilborn's thesis that audience support is less important to the documentary presence in the TV schedule than is the concept of public service. It is wrong nevertheless to suggest that documentary can have no popular public appeal outside television and cannot attract an audience broader than the traditional minority, well-educated upper-class viewer. In the cinema, the feature-length documentary might not have lived up to the promise of *Nanook* and the city documentaries of 1920s as an attraction but it does have an intermittent commercial presence on the big screen. War-time documentary features gave way to the occasional Disney nature film (starting with *The Living Desert* (James Algar, 1953), the even rarer, voyeuristic release (e.g. *On the Bowery* – Lionel Rogosin, 1954 – a largely secretly-shot feature about Manhattan's Skid Row), or the odd successor to Flaherty's exoticising of tribal peoples such as the equally voyeuristic *Mondo Carne* (Gualitero Jacopetti, 1961) – a 'so-called documentary … showing humanity at its most ignorant and depraved' (Halliwell, 1975: 532).[4] (This last is one of 'docuglitz's' most important precursors.) And there was always the quadrennial Olympic or World Cup movie, initially pioneered by Riefenstahl's *Olympischespielen* in 1936.

Then, in the 1960s, American documentarists discovered the rock concert film. The hand-held casual aesthetic of Direct Cinema meshed perfectly with the anarchic oppositional world of rock. The capacity to work in poorly-lit conditions and to capture available sound allowed for unprecedented access to the backstage realities of the performing lives of rock icons. One of the most important early Direct Cinema films was *Lonely Boy* on Paul Anka, made by Wolf Koenig and Roman Kroiter for the National Film Board of Canada in 1960. The synch sound scenes shot in Anka's dressing room were as fresh a sight on the screen as was an 'unplugged' Kennedy in his hotel suite on the night of the Wisconsin primary election in the Drew/Leacock *Primary* of the same year. It was Leacock's colleague Donn Pennebaker, with his abiding concern for music, who expanded on *Lonely Boy*. His pioneering feature-length study of Bob Dylan's 1965 English tour (*Don't Look Back*) was the first film to mesh rock with documentary to produce a truly popular hybrid. From *Don't Look Back* to Alek Keshishian's *Madonna: Truth or Dare* (aka *In Bed With Madonna*, 1991), the 'rockumentary' has became a regular (if still intermittent) big-screen documentary form.

This strand has been augmented recently by a couple of other sports titles. *Hoop Dreams* chronicled the careers of two young basketball players trying to parlay their skill into professional player contracts and so escape from their straitened circumstances. It was funded by KCTA, the PBS station in Minneapolis/St Paul, and shot over a number of years by Steve James, Frederick Marx and Peter Gilbert. A spectacular reception at the 1994 Sundance Film Festival facilitated a theatrical release prior to TV transmission. At the same festival two years later, Leon Gast's *When We Were Kings*, a documentary about the 1974 Ali/Foreman world heavyweight title contest in Zaire ('The Rumble in the Jungle'), was also so rapturously received that it too achieved a theatrical release. The fact that a succession of documentaries obtained successful commercial theatrical releases speaks to a sense that non-fiction did, after all, have an audience appeal, albeit elusive, that television was not exploiting.

2.3 The British Documentary Achieves Popularity

There was no similar sudden spurt of big-screen documentary in Britain, nor was a documentary channel a jewel in the UK's multi-channel universe. Although BSkyB, for example, took Discovery Europe, this was not a major selling point. There was a shift in the UK nevertheless in the 1980s to a greater level of public acceptance for the documentary but it occurred, in contrast to the US, on the main terrestrial TV channels.

The consistency in the percentage of programming labelled 'documentary' in the 1970s and 1980s masks a significant change in their overall popularity in Britain. From 1946 to 1974, the television documentary never quite made it to the TV Top Ten. Then in that year Paul Watson's twelve-part series *The Family*, a British version of the previous year's PBS hit *An American Family* (Craig Gilbert), was watched by an average 5.5 million. This was at the cusp of the ultimate prime-time accolade of the channel's Top Ten list. Its comparative success was repeated by the military documentary series *Sailor: Sailor*, made by John Purdie in 1976 and his sensationalist *Hong Kong Beat* on the then-colony's police the following season. Finally, Roger Graef's 1982 *Police*, on the UK Thames Valley force, broke through into a channel's Top Ten prime time. Channel 4, with an edition of its news/documentary series *Cutting Edge*: *Shops and Robbers* (Michael Ryan and David Hart), did the same thing in February 1984.

These occasional appearances in the Top Ten nevertheless remained the exception rather than the rule. For example, despite the high percentage of documentaries in Channel 4's output, in its first decade that single *Cutting Edge* was the only one, at 7.8 million, to figure among its thirty top-rated shows (Phillips, 1994c: 27). No documentary of any kind (unless you count Granada's amateur video-bloopers *You've Been Framed*) made it into the top 100 programmes of 1993 (Phillips, 1994b: 28–30). All of which explains the importance of the docusoap phenomenon; for the first time the TV documentary featured regularly among top-rated UK shows over a number of years. 'Documentaries are at last at the centre of the schedules' (Graef, 1999: 15).

Docusoaps are multi-part series, each episode of which features a number of strong, recurring personalities engaged in everyday activities (more or less) whose 'stories' are interleaved, soap-opera style. In the 1990s the format produced a rating bonanza. Although animals are something of a sure-fire thing in Britain and there is a long tradition of nature documentaries, nevertheless the achievement of a 41 per cent audience share in the autumn of 1996 by *Vets School* (Grant Mansfield) was unexpectedly high, exceptional by historical standards. It was the shape of things to come. One episode of BBC1's *Driving School* was transmitted to an audience of 12.45 million on Tuesday 15 July 1997. That was no less than a 53 per cent audience share. Although the 1999 autumn schedules showed signs that the fad for such programmes was ebbing a little, nevertheless at around a mere £65,000 an episode, it is easy to see why the ratings-driven, bean-counting contemporary culture of British television went for the docusoap in such a big way. Docusoaps cost about a fifth of the price per hour of a popular drama – and they hold the audience nearly as well.

As with soap-operas proper, the docusoap makes full use of the melodramatic moment and the cliff-hanger. Topics tend to the banal – holiday settings such as a cruise ship or a sea-side town, doctors and vets at work, hotels and health farms, neighbourhoods with 'interesting' denizens, estate agents. The major participants tend to the hyperbolic. They included the traffic warden trying to write 100 tickets in a day or the woman trying to pass her driving test for the umpteenth time, about both of whom questions of authenticity have been raised – as well as, for example, the comically domineering hotel manager, the hooker, the unflappable wisecracking English airline station manager speaking perfect Russian. None of these last, or the many others who figured in the proliferating series of the late 1990s, occasioned queries in the Press and this was more the norm.

Although the shows were, for the most part, expertly structured, the shooting style is extremely uneasy with these central participants constantly commenting on their own actions to camera, very often literally over their shoulders in a bizarre variant of the old Direct Cinema 'follow-the-subject' shot. Commentary tends to be as structuring as were Flaherty's intertitles in *Nanook*. Without it, most of the footage would have little or no drama. All in all, with its use of commentary and participant comments to camera, the docu-soap technique represents a bastardisation of television's usual vérité bastardisation. It is easy to see why such a style, such topics and such personalities attract criticism within the business. Here are documentaries, say the detractors, made in exploitative and unethical ways, about nothing in particular which overtly and obviously encourage the people involved to overact in a largely uncharacteristic and sometimes sensational fashion.

But, it is worth repeating, the shows achieved an unexpectedly large audience and such popularity, especially popularity achieved largely without crime or (much) sexual exploitation, ought to give pause. To escape from documentary's traditional small-audience elite-demographic ghetto is no mean feat. Making documentaries that, for the most part, do not treat ordinary people as social victims or problems is also to be celebrated. Expanding the tradition's po-faced sobriety to embrace humour, a given of most of these shows, is also a considerable achievement. While it is true that docusoaps created a precedent for cheap production attracting large audiences which has led to a general squeezing of resources and rising managerial expectations for ratings, it can be argued that had not docusoaps achieved the measure of success they did the documentary itself would have started to disappear from British network schedules as it has from the American ones. The traditional small audience would have certainly occasioned the squeezing of resources anyway, if not the endangering of the documentary presence in the schedules altogether. On this view, the price of survival has been the docusoap.

It is possible to mount a perfectly reasonable defence of such shows along all these lines – attractive, victimless, humorous, cost-effective programming; yet when docusoaps became a prime exhibit in the 'dumbing down' debate, the industry was almost silent, shame-faced about arguing its corner and defending these series. On the contrary, the proliferation of such shows was allowed to contribute in a major way to the perception of increasing moral insensitivity and decreasing levels of serious work in the documentary world, as well as general arguments about the 'dumbing down' of television overall; but these various strands – the fakery scandal, output levels, 'dumbing down' – have to be disentangled. None is straightforward.

Only the '100 parking ticket' warden and the incidents with Maureen being woken at 4 a.m. to study for her driving test or nearly having an accident figured directly in the 1998 'fakery' scandals. It is, therefore, simply wrong to associate the media panic about fakery with docusoaps, although this was often done. There is a serious complication nevertheless: the distance between docu-soaps and the 'fakery' scandals does not mean that docusoaps were immune from attack on slightly lesser issues of authenticity. Hidden manipulations, such as putting a the traffic-warden supervisor back on the street, led to the sense that much docusoap material, while perhaps not 'faked', was tainted. Docu-soaps indeed encouraged the unthinking manipulation of many who came before more serious documentary cameras.

This and the dubious 'docuglitz' sex and/or crime programmes cast a shadow across surviving 'serious' documentary, forcing it into an ever more sensation-alist mould. The unwillingness of programme providers and commissioners to fund research and preparation at appropriate levels did not help either. Docu-mentaries became more slap-dash and more sensational than they ever were in the past in order to survive. The docusoaps, therefore, do make an indirect con-tribution to the 'fakery' scandals without being too directly involved in them. The same sort of complexities affect the argument about the level of docu-mentary output. Determining whether the amount of documentary programming is falling or not is complicated because the genre itself ranges from the sober to the frivolous and differs from channel to channel. Its import-ance to the overall culture of TV depends on time-tabling positioning as much as on crude duration.

One thing, though, is clear: docusoaps do represents a new phenomenon given their popularity and high ratings. For all that millions of British homes watched the first popular series in the 1970s, the popularity of documentary remained stubbornly relative. Even as Paul Watson was drawing 5.5 million for *The Family*, *Some Mothers Do Have 'Em* had 23.5 million. In the year of *Hong Kong Beat* (1997), a rerun of the informal documentary about the Royal Fam-ily was watched by 4.5 million but the year's most popular programme, *Morecambe and Wise Christmas Day Special*, was seen by 29 million (admittedly on Christmas Day!). *Police*'s 10.5 million did astonishingly well against *To the Manor Born*'s 16.5 million. Any documentary audience above 5 million was exceptional. On the other hand, by 1998 the docusoaps were regularly reaching 8 to 12 million plus. It is therefore something of an irony that these, the first documentaries really appreciated by the masses, seemed to many observers to be killing off the Griersonian tradition.

As for the level of output, docusoaps were seen as displacing traditional doc-umentaries of social concern, threatening to remove them from the schedules altogether. This apparent substitution did have the positive effect of removing earlier worries about the very survival of this strand of non-fiction program-ming, at least for the moment. The move into prime time does indicate a significant change in the overall impact of documentary on British terrestrial television culture. The impression now was that there was too much documentary material: 'Once there was only *40 Minutes*, now it's forty hours' (Coward, 1996). Yet this was as much to do with the move into prime-time as it was with increasing numbers of programmes. Docuglitz and docusoaps more than compensated for the undoubted decline of investigative work, to ensure that the crude levels of documentary output remained fairly constant across the system.

The argument about 'dumbing down' is also not straightforward. It antedates the docusoap fad and cannot therefore be laid entirely at docusoaps' door. The arrival of documentaries in prime time in the 1980s had led to an increased documentary salience which fuelled the perception that both BBC1 and ITV were already, early in the next decade, moving documentary 'down market'. This perception was reinforced by a change in commercial contractors, occasioned by the operation of the 1990 Broadcasting Act that took effect on 1 January 1993. Two major ITV series, *First Tuesday* and *Viewpoint*, were replaced with one, *Network First*. The view is that this change was entirely for the worse as far as 'seriousness' was concerned. For example, Meridian, one of the ITV newcomers, in its first ten months posted *Coltrane in a Cadillac* (Paul Sommers) as its biggest hit. This was quite obviously not as demanding as, say, the David Munro/John Pilger exposé of Indonesian atrocities in East Timor, *Death of A Nation* (commissioned by Roger James).

In the interest of a balanced view, it must be also noted that this was not quite the fly-blown disgracefulness of docuglitz either. (Carlton, though, a pariah to many British media observers, managed in these early months to insert three current affairs shows into its top-rated thirteen shows – all *Cook Reports*, a series which would find itself caught up in the 'fakery' scandals.) Arguments like these, that all was not lost or – better – quite lost, went against the general perception of 'dumbing down'. There was a persistent worry about documentaries within the more general concern about the neo-liberal undermining of public service ethos that now embraced (American-style) commercially-funded channels as well as the BBC. This was so pervasive that it could not be countered by citing the continuation of good, or even less-than-meretricious, work.

If appearance in the top-tens was the first indicator of changing status, the arrival of Reality TV was the second. It had rung alarm bells with many. Docuglitz frippery, the sensationalising of the 'serious' output by covering crime and sex, exacerbated the worries caused by docusoaps and Reality TV, all within the context of an increasingly casualised industry.

But some of the bases for concern had been around a long time, long before the 'dumbing down' concept entered the debate. Although the crime (at this level) and sex were new, it should be remembered that sensationalism was not. This was especially true if the changing goal-posts of public taste and acceptability are factored in. Sensationalism was as old (at least) as *Man Alive*

(Desmond Wilcox, Bill Morton, 1965) which had copied the studio/film-insert format pioneered by Norman Swallow in *Special Inquiry* but, by importing a tabloid agenda to television, entered a whole new territory. *Man Alive* was one of the key shows establishing the then new BBC2 as an alternative to 'Auntie' BBC1. It covered, for example, agoraphobia (in an edition called *The Frightened Ones*), paedophilia (then called 'child molesting'), the truth about marriage bureaux – all topics unlikely often to catch the attention of the politically-inclined heavies who ran *Panorama*, *World in Action* and *This Week* or the Griersonians who still dominated the various documentary departments around the networks. *Man Alive* lasted until 1982.

I suppose a cynic would say that the growing popularity of documentary would of itself be enough for the chattering classes to begin to cast doubt on the quality of the shows achieving such unexpectedly wide audiences. As Barnet and Seymour have demonstrated, this variant of the usual 'fing's ain't what they used to be' approach can apply to drama and current affairs. It seems simple to make it also embrace docuglitz: contrast ITV's 1980 *Hollywood*, a meticulous thirteen-part history series made by Kevin Brownlow and David Gill, narrated by James Mason with music by Carl Davis, with Helen Fitzwilliam's and Paul Buller's 1996 seven-parter *Hollywood Pets* (about pets in Hollywood!). And then came the docusoaps. As the 'fakery' media panic revealed, some really astoundingly tacky documentary programming was certainly reaching the screen.

Despite all this, I still want to enter at least a few entries on the credit side. For one thing, the end of the dominance of Direct Cinema that was happening at this time allowed for an increased range of documentary styles. Also, admittedly on the minor channels, space was found for non-anglophone films for the first time. A subtitled documentary would never have made it to the TV screen before the coming of Channel 4. And the BBC's Community Programmes Unit largesse in giving 'ordinary people' camcorders to make contributions to *Video Nation* speaks to a vitality, however threatened. The case for an extension of documentary range in the serious area, however marginalised, can certainly be mounted.

As for fretting about docusoaps, what critics of the popular do not address is the anomaly of documentary's traditional limited audience appeal on what is, after all, a mass medium. When Munro claimed that: 'Serious, committed documentaries are popular with viewers here and abroad' (Munro, 1994: 18), one must ask in what sense this is true. In *British Television*, an admittedly idiosyncratic collection of 'over 1100 favourite programmes' from the first sixty years, the only single documentaries to rate an entry were *Morning in the Streets*, *Deckie Learner* (Michael Grigsby, 1965), *Stones in the Park* (Jo Durden-Smith, 1969), *The Tribe that Hides from Man* (Adrian Cowell, 1970) and

David Munro's own *Death of Cambodia* (1979); and, apart from animals, arts and the series which moved documentary into primetime (*The Family, Sailor, Police*), there was only the persistent strand of compilations from the initial *War in the Air* in 1954 (John Elliot, Philip Dorte) through *World at War* (Jeremy Isaacs, 1973) to Martin Smith's *Vietnam* and *American Caesar* (Ian McLeod, 1984). Not many – and even if the most obvious lacunae are added (e.g. Richard Cawston's film 'humanising' the Royal Family, *Death on the Rock* or the *7-Up* series (Paul Almond, Michael Apted), documentary still accounts for only about 2.5 per cent of the 'favourites' (Vihimagi, 1994: passim). There is an element of Divine Right in the demand that documentarists make programmes even if few watch and that, if they are not allowed to, then the system is 'dumbing down'. Grierson's vision of the documentary pulpit and Reith's idea that folks don't know what is good for them still informs many assumptions.

On the other hand, I most assuredly do not want to argue on this basis that all is well in the UK; but so dominant is Cassandra-like woe among the *bien pensants* contemplating television that I think it is necessary to point up contrary factors as they affect the documentary – that there was a large audience for the first time, that documentaries had not disappeared from the small screen, that rediscovered and fresh approaches were being introduced; and that sensationalism was not new, nor was management fearfulness of controversial work. At the turn of the millennium it was still possible to find here and there in the schedule a Dineen or an Agram. Twenty-five years ago there were perhaps more but still only a few – Graef, say, and Cowell, Grisby, Munro, Willis, Watson and Donnellan; but they were not the audience's first choice, were anyway frequently in trouble with the system and, note, all were men.[5] So, I agree, there was now an exasperating lack of seriousness, of moral sensitivity and of resources – but all was not lost, however much these failings damaged broadcasting and aided the 'fakery' scandal.

What was far more worrying was the way in which the 'fakery' scandal advanced the case for media censorship.

Part Two

REGULATORS

Chapter Three
Law

The law is significant for two reasons.

First, the *Connection* decision turns on a technical breach of contract that the ITC is empowered by statute to punish. However, this disguises the reality which is that a subterfuge is at work here whereby a legally empowered quasi-governmental agency, the ITC, in effect creates a new civil wrong, the tort of 'breach of public trust' which would not be available in the courts. The praying-in of the contract breach is thus a fig-leaf. 'Breach of public trust' is crucially important since it facilitates the potential abridgement of freedom of speech and is, therefore, as grievously improper as is Carlton's publication of a public lie. That it why it does not exist as an established tort. In terms of the actual or potential damage, it is arguably far more serious than were the *Connection*'s fabrications. Media law is important as a basis for understanding the context of such content regulation (which we discuss in Chapter Four).

It is also important because it tilts the playing field in favour of the media since it treats freedom of expression as a fundamental human right. In essence, it takes a strong view of this right and, in terms of documentary activity specifically, privileges free expression against any rights of those who become involved in documentary production. (The law has little to say directly about the audience's right to hear, never mind its putative right to hear truth.) This can be particularly clearly seen in matters of invasion of privacy and the processes of obtaining consent. The legal position also, therefore, impacts on the ethics of documentary to be discussed in Part Three.

3.1 'Breach of Public Trust'

The British common law in no way acknowledges the concept of the falsities in *The Connection* as a 'breach of public trust', except in so far as the sanctions were imposed by the ITC which is a legal body established by statute. The Broadcasting Act 1990 not only mandates the Commission's regulation of the content of its services in various ways including the power to fine but it also enacts (6.1) the requirement of 'due accuracy and impartiality' in the transmission of 'any news (in whatever form)'. But I, as an individual member of the audience, have no direct, common law, contractual hold over any TV service that would establish trustworthiness of itself as necessary to the legal relationship. This contractual abyss exists across all broadcasting and is not bridged if I pay satellite or cable subscriptions, licence fees, other unhypothecated taxes or that percentage of the cost of goods and services recycled to broadcasters through advertising charges. I cannot control a newspaper's contents by virtue of the fact I pay its cover price and the same applies to broadcasting. The law does not recognise the arrival of a signal on my receiver as part of a legally enforceable contractual relationship which could allow me to control content so that it accords with my standards of taste, decency, fairness, impartiality and the rest – or anything else.

I am more of a witness to than a participant in the contractual arrangements between advertiser and programme provider or programme provider and regulator on the commercial channels. My individual powerlessness is confirmed by paternalistic statutory protection given to me by (6. 1) of the Act. What I do not have is an action on the basis that the regulations, say those of the ITC Programme Code, have been breached, although, again, I have the general law to hand should I be in anyway damaged by what is transmitted. And 'damage' must mean something more than my finding material offensive or disturbing or even distressing if free speech is to not be abridged.

With subscription television, I do have a common law right to have services provided but my contract does not allow me to interfere with the services' content. Indeed, it took the intervention of the Office of Fair Trading to stop BSkyB from unilaterally changing the terms in its contract with subscribers including a clause giving it an unlimited right to alter service levels arbitrarily; that is, removing whole channels without redress on the subscribers' part (Anon., 1997). This was in effect quite minor since the contract always allowed a measure of flexibility to BSkyB and certainly gave no content control to the subscriber. And, of course, the longest period I could be held to pay a service provider of whose output I did not approve was less than one month since I could then cancel my subscription.

As far as the financial arrangement with the BBC is concerned, the cost of a licence fee is actually a legally sanctioned hypothecated tax. It is triggered by the ownership of a receiver in the same way as payments of income tax are triggered by receipt of income. One has no more contractual a relationship with the BBC because one has paid a licence fee than one has with, say, the armed forces because one pays income tax. The one does not entitle me to obtain programming of a specific kind and 'quality' just as the other does not allow me to demand a change in the uniforms at the Trooping of the Colour.

None of the existing legal restrictions on free expression (all of which require a demonstration of actual or potential damage) apply to *The Connection* –

except in so far as the coverage of the UK drug raid was misrepresented in commentary, potentially defaming the people involved. (The Colombians were acting and so cannot be defamed.) Defamation does not directly affect me as an audience member and anyway 'smacks of an age when social and political life was lived in gentlemen's clubs, when escutcheons could be blotted and society scandals resolved by writs for slander'. It depends on the proof that a damaging lowering of reputation has occurred bringing the plaintiff into 'hatred, ridicule or contempt', which is difficult to do with drug dealers, unless the parties are innocent (as in this case, curiously, the Colombian 'actors' are) (Robertson and Nicol, 1992: 41; Bainbridge, 1994: 444–58). Other common law concepts are equally irrelevant to the Carlton case and to the position of *The Connection*'s audience.

Malicious falsehood, for example, requires that the defamer act 'spitefully, dishonestly or maliciously' and 'cause financial loss' (Robertson and Nicol, 1992: 46). It is, in fact, a form of trade libel and again cannot apply here since no damage was claimed to have occurred.

False attribution, a subset of the copyright protection provision, is not in point either. This deals with cases where a piece of work is attributed to another to enhance its value which might, if the attributed work were of high enough quality, not be subject to defamation. Again, there has to be a person in law who can prove that the false attribution has damaged them (Bainbridge, 1994: 90–92). Nothing there then that applies to *The Connection*'s audience.

Nor is the law prohibiting misrepresentation any more use since it has quite specific and limited meanings. It involves passing off either where you represent your goods as being those of somebody else or where you pretend that your goods have the same qualities as those of somebody else's. Damage must be proved, if only to the goodwill enjoyed in the public sphere by the other party. There is no question of a common law tort of misrepresentation that would constitute a basis (a 'head of liability') by which Carlton could be sued.

Finally in this list of legal prohibitions of fraud, but equally useless to the TV watcher, there is a principle outlined in *Hedley Byrne* v. *Heller*, a 1963 case that created a head of liability if someone gives false information to a second party upon which the second party relies to their detriment (*Hedley Byrne* v. *Heller* 1963). This has been extended to third party reliance (*Smith* v. *Bush*; *Harris* v. *Wye Forest District Council* 1989). Again there has to be damage and, moreover, a special relationship between the parties. Although the concept of the 'proximity' of parties has been extended by the courts, there is no suggestion that it could ever embrace three and a half million viewers at a go (*Capro Industries* v. *Dickman* 1990).

And what damage could any of *The Connection*'s audience prove – that they acted to their disadvantage in seeking to buy the heroin which the film mendaciously alleged was now being passed into Britain by a new route? That the balance of their mind had been disturbed because two air journeys taken several months apart had been represented as one? That they had lost their jobs because they had not left the house for fear of being approached by drug dealers emboldened by this new source of supply? That, as young people, they were moved to seek a job as a drug mule? No – they could show only that they had been 'misled'. On that basis, the *Guardian* thundered that it was 'A betrayal of viewers' (1998: 24). Its commentator, Mark Lawson, said that although the fine will not go to the viewers, yet they would benefit (Lawson, 1999: 26) – presumably by being less likely to be 'misled' by the television.

The film occasioned much such moral outrage as well as the quasi-judicial investigations into the mendacious procedures that produced it and the £2 million fine, but all this is well beyond any legal contract or tort. What we are left with is the concept of a 'breach of public trust', in effect a fraud which does not encompass a contract with the viewer, defamation, malicious falsehood, false attribution, misrepresentation or the tort in *Hedley Byrne* v. *Heller*. Public fraud involves a wholesale breach of trust between programme-makers and viewers but it seems to me that this fraud is a slippery notion since it involves no identifiable member of the public and certainly requires no proof of actual or potential damage if things go wrong.

The statutory requirement for the 'due accuracy and impartiality of any news (in whatever form)' is clearly questionable as being too vague to achieve legal precision (despite being British law) and such a demand has never been made of the Press. It rests on a series of assumptions, all of which can be questioned to one degree or another. The victimless fraud of 'a breach of public trust' is grounded in the prior notion of a public right-to-know – 'to receive information and ideas' – but for this to work the right must be turned on its head.

The concept of a 'right to know' is a recent legal construction and, although important, is, like fraud, limited in significant ways. It addresses the difference between a right to speak (which is unambiguously the right of free expression and as such enshrined in many jurisdictions for centuries) and a right to hear which only finds its legal form in recent enactments. It is often glossed as 'public interest' in the legislation on data protection, freedom of information and the so-called 'Sunshine Laws' enacted by various American states to ensure open government. To suggest that public interest is in play as the basis of a general right not to be lied to in public is to reverse its thrust. The 'right to receive information' on a personal basis, an innovation of the post-Second World War human rights declarations, is a full legal reality in common law jurisdictions only where it is specifically enacted by statute, as in data protection or freedom of information acts. Otherwise, the right-to-know and/or the public interest are aspects of the right of free expression, as for instance, in the UK Human Rights

Act (1998, in force 2000) which asks the court to consider 'the public interest ... where the proceedings relate to material which the respondent claims, or which appears to the court to be, journalistic, literary or artistic material' (12.4.a). The public interest can be a defence against libel (at least in the US); or a justification for the invasion of privacy or the use of material without the consent of the parties involved. To make it the right upon which the Carlton fine depends is to utterly distort it. The public interest becomes a constraint on free speech.

Of course, in terms of the citizen and the state, a public right to know is important but, even today, it is limited in significant ways. We do not have, and never have had, a general public right to know what other members of the public know simply because they know it. There is no right arising from listening to undamaging lies. That is to say, we do not have a right to insist that if we are told something in public which does not in any way damage us that it be what it represents itself to be – unless it is broadcast 'news (in whatever form)'on some television channels.

Note, by contrast, we do not countenance our fellows gaining advantage, say, in the public stock market because of privileged insider information that damages the interest of others in the market. Nor will we allow misleading advertising, exactly because in that context any misrepresentation could indeed cause identifiable damage to specific identifiable consumers. (If it does cause damage, then the issue moves from regulation to law.) Legislation prohibiting misleading advertising is widespread (e.g. UK Misleading Advertisement Regulations 1998), and the ITC has prior constraint powers over commercials. Section 9 of the 1990 Act obliges it to produce a separate code governing them. Since potential demonstrable damage as it is legally defined is involved this clause and the code is not offensive to free speech.

This more general putative right not to be lied to is quite different. It is not illegal under British law to tell lies in public (unless it is broadcast 'news (in whatever form)'; you can't sue politicians, for example, on that basis. Their pledges can become aspirations and all their hearers can do is await the next election. (Although, if they lie enough, e.g. Profumo and Archer, their political careers might just collapse.) The Press would also be in trouble if we had a general prohibition against victimless public lying.

The problem with the Carlton case is not that the Commission was wrong to pillory the mendacity of the film-makers. Confusions about acceptable reconstructions are one thing but fabrications are clearly another and much of *The Connection* was fabricated, for which there can be no excuse. What is extremely worrying is that the ITC, a government regulatory agency, can levy substantial penalties *without proving damage, actual or potential, to any party*. This, in effect, transforms the rhetoric of 'breach of public trust' into a virtual new quasi-legal tort – 'Breach of Public Trust'; and it comes into being at the cost of free expression.

3.2 The Right of Free Expression

Article 19 of the Universal Protection of Human Rights (1948) states:

> Everyone has the right to freedom of opinion and expression; this right includes freedom to hold opinions without interference and to seek, receive and impart information and ideas through any media and regardless of frontiers (Anon., 1992: 13).[1]

More significantly for Europeans, since it is the actual basis for much legislation, is the European Convention on Human Rights, the ECHR 1950 (Anon., 1992: 159–82). Article 10 of the ECHR states:

> 10.1 Everyone has the right to freedom of expression. This right shall include freedom to hold opinions and to receive and impart information and ideas without interference by public authority and regardless of frontiers. (Anon., 1992: 164)

The Committee of Ministers of the Council of Europe also adopted a 'Declaration on the freedom of expression and information' in 1982 which:

> (I): Reiterated their firm attachment to the principles of freedom of expression and information as a basic element of democratic and pluralist society. (Anon., 1992: 270)

The language of UN Article 19 and ECHR Article 10 has been echoed in national statutes. For example, Article 5 of the German Basic Law also guarantees that 'Everyone shall have the right freely to express and disseminate his opinion … ' (Barendt, 1985: 33). Belatedly, especially given that it was drafted by British lawyers, the whole of the ECHR was enacted into British law as the Human Rights Act 1998. This means, among many other things, that (after the Act is in force in October 2000) there is for the first time in the UK a statutory, as opposed to a common law, right of free expression. There is no question but that this is a most significant change. Previously it was the case that ' "freedom of expression" was not a legal term of art in England and Wales' (Feldman, 1993: 560); but it is now. It could well be that this will, in the long run, force a reconsideration of such clauses as the one in the British Broadcasting Act requiring 'due accuracy and impartiality' of 'news (in whatever form)' – at least in terms of the looseness of its language.

As Eric Barendt points out, there is a difference between freedom of expression and Press freedom although the two are often combined, the issue being whether or not the Press has greater freedom, or an enhanced protection for its freedom (Barendt, 1985: 67–72). Normally, the specific mention of the Press or media implies an ensured and detailed protection of their right of free expression. In the 1982 Declaration, the European ministers announced that, among other things, their objectives included achieving:

> II. b. the absence of censorship or any arbitrary controls or constraints on participants in the media process, on media content or on the transmission or dissemination of information. (Anon., 1992: 270)

Article 5 of the German Basic Law is equally specific: 'Freedom of the Press and freedom of reporting by means of broadcasts and films are guaranteed. There shall be no censorship' (Barendt, 1985: 33).

It is clear that these fundamental laws and declarations create a general right of unimpeded expression, and sanction a regulated media system to ensure the right is exercised. Powerful insistencies on freedom of expression as a fundamental human right and the specific importance of that freedom to the media nevertheless do not envisage that each last individual has a right of media access (although that has been made on occasion the basis for abridging a licensed media speaker's expression). Usually, it does not mean that freedom for one party ought to be, illogically, guaranteed by interference with another party's speech. None of this in anyway implies that content has to be controlled. Indeed, the right suggests, exactly, that it should not. On the other hand, this does not mean that expression is unfettered, especially as far as the media are concerned. This is in line with the common law legal tradition and its American First Amendment embodiment.

For the last 250 years in Britain, free expression has meant, at a minimum, not freedom to say whatever one likes – you cannot mendaciously cry 'fire' in a crowded theatre – but, rather, the right to say it and take the consequences. The struggle to create a legal definition of freedom of expression is a central and somewhat heroic theme in the development of Western liberal democracies. Arising from the new sense of the rights of individual conscience that is one of the Reformation's most enduring legacies, the idea was soon mooted that such liberty of religious expression had to be part of a broader liberty of expression in general. '[T]he liberty to know, to utter and to argue freely according to conscience, above all' marks the beginning of a powerful dissenting (if you will) tradition in our political life.

What should ye do then, should ye suppress all this flowery crop of knowledge and new light sprung up and yet springing daily in this city, should ye set an oligarchy of twenty engrossers over it, to bring a famine upon our minds again, when we shall know nothing but what is measured to us by their bushel? Believe it, Lord and Commons, they who counsel ye to such suppressing, do as good as bid ye suppress yourselves. (Milton, 1644)

Milton's motives in arguing for a free press were suspect since Cromwell had burnt his pamphlet on divorce, a then illegal proceeding of which the poet nevertheless wanted to avail himself. Not only that, Milton was prepared to make value judgements. He did not seem to mind too much about burning the odd Catholic who dared to argue freely according to conscience and Catholic books, of course, might well not be 'good' either. Nevertheless: 'As good almost kill a man as kill a good book.' By 1673 Milton was writing of 'freedom of speech'.

The soundness of his plea for the liberty of an unlicensed press is no more affected by his self-interested motivations than it is by the daily abuses of British tabloids or pornographic cavortings on the Internet. On the contrary, it is exactly such mixed motives and bad examples that give the principle of free expression its force:

This sacred privilege is so essential to free governments, that the security of property, and the freedom of speech, always go together; and in those wretched countries, where a man cannot call his tongue his own, he can scarce call anything else his own. Whoever would overthrow the liberty of a nation, must begin by subduing the freedom of speech. ('Cato', 1720)

By the time Blackstone came to comment on the laws of England a few decades later, the idea of specific media freedom, at that time of course only of the Press, was being expressed as a prohibition against censorship in the form of prior constraint: 'The liberty of the Press is indeed essential to the nature of a free state; but this consists in laying no *previous* restraints on publications, and not in freedom from censure for criminal matter when published' (Blackstone, 1765: IV, 151). On the other hand, censure was, and remained a well-established possibility. Machiavelli already understood that, while the many might have a right to 'think all things, speak all things, write all things', princes might take another view. The British prince James VI and I indeed did inveigh against 'freedome of speech' in a proclamation of 1620 (Levy, 1985: 4). Even in liberal thought, (as Locke had taught) 'a state of liberty' is not a 'state of licence'; 'hurt', as 'Cato' understood, must not be allowed to flow unstaunched from speech. The law could prohibit, say, seditious, hateful or pornographic talk (if necessary on the basis of their potentially damaging effect alone) at the same time as outlawing prior constraint on all other utterance. There is no contradiction.

The radical extension in law from a censorship prohibition to a statute enshrining the principle of freedom of expression and the Press more generally was left to our revolutionary cousins across the ocean. The First Amendment to the American Constitution was written within twenty-five years of Blackstone's *Commentaries* by lawyers immersed in his thinking but prepared, on the basis of the liberal tradition of Milton, Locke and 'Cato', to go much further: 'Congress shall make no law … abridging the freedom of speech or of the Press'. It should be noted that during this same period of Enlightenment, this was not a unique development; Sweden, for example, enacted a similar statute.

This history properly constructs the Press, for all its faults, as an engine of basic freedom and makes the individual right of free expression central to our concept of the civil society. It is this, exactly, to which the Carlton fine speaks. Freedom of expression necessarily includes the right to utter unpalatable truths and horrid opinions and, in fact, to tell lies. If no actual or potential damage can be proved, then the right is, or ought to be, unfettered. Misleading or upsetting folk is, by this tradition, regrettable, immoral even, but without damage or the possibility of damage, it is inconsequential and therefore unactionable.

It is a measure of how fragile the culture of freedom is in the UK that current debates about 'regulation' ignore all this in favour of jargonised considerations of 'choice' (rather than 'speech'), of 'consumption' (rather than 'liberty'), of 'customers' (rather than 'citizens'); yet it is not the case that such eighteenth-century liberal concepts as free expression and 'no prior constraint' are no longer workable in the age of proliferating mass communications. The prohibition against prior constraint, for instance, remains the common law as is now acknowledged by the ITC Code: the Commission 'will not preview programmes or consider specific script requirement before production' (Foreword (g), 1998).

It is instructive, in general terms, to note that this has not always been the case. The ITC predecessor Independent Broadcasting Authority did indeed have powers to vet programmes in defiance of the prohibition against prior constraint and it was not unknown for it to ban them. On one occasion, the screen was left blank for thirty minutes in a union protest against the IBA's censoring of an edition of the current affairs programme *This Week*.[2] Eventually, a judgment of the Court of Appeal against another Mary Whitehouse intervention that sought to force the IBA into an action of prior constraint declared its powers to do so to be illegal (*R. v. IBA ex parte Whitehouse* 1985). I would want to suggest that this is a good example of how the structure of broadcasting regulation can be foul of the law and how the law can move to correct it. In so far as my whole argument against regulation rests on its failure to conform with the common law in various regards, *ex parte Whitehouse* is both a powerful rebuttal of a common-sense idea that the broadcasting authority must surely be within the law at all times as well as a good example of what can happen when it is declared not to be.

Despite this case, a rare echo of Enlightenment principle, in general a seeming amnesia about the rest of the eighteenth-century liberal thinking on these matters characterises much European debate and the legal and regulatory structure it has produced. Overall there is a world-weariness about discussing 'freedom' and the like which marches with a parallel enthusiasm for a neo-liberal technicist rhetoric of 'choice'. This is less true of the United States.

Contemporary American regulators are inhibited from dealing with issues of taste or content generally, at least on a formal basis, because the First Amendment has been much elaborated in the two centuries since it was enacted and renders such action clearly unconstitutional. What began as a prohibition against constraints imposed by the federal government has now embraced all 'speech'. 'Speech' is deemed to encompass a multitude of expressions including striptease and burning the flag.

Although opinion polls in recent years indicate that a majority of Americans would today not support a law along First Amendment lines, for many the Amendment remains a bulwark against the inevitable secret tendencies of the state and a guarantor of all other personal liberties:

> In 45 words the founding generation and those who followed them set
> themselves a course unequalled in human history ... And as we are inundated
> daily with reminders that our computers and our satellites and our fibre-optic
> networks make our era an information age, it is important to note that in
> 1791, the builders of this bold political experiment declared a new vision for
> humankind. The absolute key to realising this new vision, they said, was a free
> flow of information. (Knowlton and Parsons, 1995: 8–9)

That vision lies behind, for example, all those state 'Sunshine Laws' that ensure that the public's business at whatever level of government is conducted as far as possible in public. A school principal censored a student newspaper for work produced in a journalism class on the grounds that he felt an unnamed divorced parent was given no opportunity to respond and anonymous girls in an article about pregnancy could still be identifiable. His position was upheld by the Supreme Court, but was widely seen in American Press circles as an extremely serious breach of First Amendment protections (*Hazelwood*, 1988).

Freedom of speech, as we have said, does not license potential or actual damage and therefore does not prevent the law from offering specific remedies for a whole range of consequences – defamation, breaches of state secrets, inciting racial hatred, naming rape victims and so on and so on. Article 10 of ECHR goes on:

> 10.2. The exercise of these freedoms, since it carries with it duties and responsibilities, may be subject to such formalities, conditions and restrictions or penalties as are prescribed by law and are necessary in a democratic society, in the interests of national security, territorial integrity or public safety, for the prevention of disorder or crime, for the protection of health or morals, for the protection of the reputation or rights of others, for preventing the disclosure of information received in confidence or for maintaining the authority and impartiality of the judiciary. (Anon., 1992: 164)

Note that this list of permitted abridgements are 'prescribed by law' and are all grounded in the usual common law prohibition against actual or potential damage – whether it is to the health and well-being of the state, its courts and its citizens in general or to an individual.

But note also that European opinion was also ready to add non-statutory requirements. In 1982 the ministers glossed 10.2, noting that:

> in addition to the statutory measures referred to in paragraph 2 of Article 10 of the European Convention on Human Rights, codes of ethics have been voluntarily established and are applied by professional organisations in the field of mass media. (Anon., 1992: 270)

Legal and voluntary professional limitations are understood and accepted, and so is the distinction within Press freedom that allows for the importation of further specific restrictions on broadcasting. The last sentence of Article 10.1 for example states: 'This article shall not prevent the state from requiring the licensing of broadcasting, television or cinema entertainments' (Anon., 1992: 164), although the court has held this does not mean content control (*Groppera*, 1990).

All these constraints on the right of media free expression in general and broadcasting in particular are themselves logically limited to the same test. Is the restriction '*necessary in a democratic society*'? That is to say, even laws duly enacted can offend against the right of free expression and be overturned by the courts, UK courts as well as the European Court of Human Rights in Strasbourg, if they abridge *necessary* communication. Under the ECHR, it might be legal to have an ITC (and it is) and it might be legal for that authority to have a code of practice (and it is) but it could be that neither the terms of the code nor the sanctions allowed under the code are legal because they constrain or prevent expression in ways which are '*necessary in a democratic society*'.

On balance, over the last half of the twentieth century, the Court in Stras-

bourg was very supportive of the principle in 10.1 even to the point of over-
turning a number of less liberal decisions that had gone against the media in
various European states, including the UK. Since the Court heard its first case
on Article 10 in 1960, it has delivered judgments, including its decisions in the
Thalidomide and Spycatcher cases which originated in the UK, tending to be
more supportive of Press freedom and certainly more liberal than those of the
British courts (*Sunday Times*, 1979; *Observer and Guardian Newspapers* 1991;
Sunday Times and Neil (no. 2) 1991).

In the Little Red Schoolbook case, freedom of expression has been glossed as
'one of the basic conditions for the progress of democratic societies and for the
development of each individual' (*Handyside*, 1976:§49). The Thalidomide case,
which in 1979 gave the Court its first opportunity to rule specifically on Press
freedom, held that the UK injunction, based on the common law of contempt
of court, that prevented the *Sunday Times* from publishing material on the Dis-
tillers' Company was in breach of Article 10. The injunction, although legal
under UK law, illegally restricted a freedom *exactly* 'necessary in a democratic
society' in ECHR terms (*Sunday Times*, 1979:§65; *Case-law*, 1997: 21.10).

The limits of even defamation as a constraint 'necessary in a democratic
society ' were re-enforced in the *Lingens* judgment of 1986, confirmed by the
conclusion reached in the *Thorgeir Thorgeirson* case six years after that. In the
Lingens case, where the Court overturned an Austrian criminal defamation
decision involving a politician, it was held that:

> Whilst the Press must not overstep the bounds set, *inter alia*, for the
> 'protection of the reputation of others', it is nevertheless incumbent on it to
> impart information and ideas on political issues just as on those in other areas
> of public interest. Not only does the Press have the task of imparting such
> information and ideas: the public also has a right to receive them. (*Lingens*,
> 1986§41)

In *Thorgeir Thorgeirson*, the Court protected a journalist who had published
allegations of police brutality, repeating the formulation in *Lingens* (*Thorgeir
Thorgeirson, 1992:§§59–70*).

In the *Castells* case the Court overturned a judgment against a Basque member of the Cortes for publishing an article suggesting the Spanish government
supported attacks on Basque militants:

> 'Freedom of the Press affords the public one of the best means of discovering
> and forming an opinion on the ideas and attitudes of their political leaders …
> it thus enables everyone to participate in the free political debate which is at
> the core of the concept of a democratic society. (*Castells*, 1992:§43)

'[T]he importance of these rights has been stressed by the Court many times. The necessity for restricting them must be convincingly demonstrated' (*Autonic AG*, 1990:§61). In line with this, the Court and the European Commission of Human Rights have also been at pains to overturn or criticise cases where legal action has been used to stifle adverse comment on officials and even where publication has been deemed unduly to influence a criminal proceeding (e.g. *Case-law*, 1997: 27.36, 38, 39).

There has been one decision of the Court that goes against the general liberal grain and it turned exactly on taking cognisance of an existing code of professional ethics. This allowed the Court in 1995 to hold that an attack on an Austrian judge was not protected by Article 10 because it 'was not in keeping with the rules of journalistic ethics' (*Case-law*, 1997: 24.24; *Prager and Oberschlick*, 1995). This judgment, though, has already been challenged and the scope of *Lingens* reaffirmed in 1997. The Court reaffirmed that 'journalistic freedom also covers possible recourse to a degree of exaggeration, or even provocation' (*Case-law*, 1997: 25.26) while the Commission, in considering the same matter, also reinforced the previous balance in favour of Article 10: '...the general interest in a public debate which has a serious purpose outweighs the legitimate aim of protecting the reputation of others, even if such a debate involves the use of wounding or offensive language' (*Case-law*, 1997: 25.26 fn. 26).

The same logic used in *Lingens* had previously led the American courts to establish reduced protection of reputation for public officials bringing defamation actions against the media. In *The New York Times* v. *Sullivan* 1964, the court held that simply making an error in a story about a public official, which would normally constitute defamation, was not enough. Actual malice would need to be proved if the plaintiff were to succeed. *Sullivan* in effect creates a public interest right as has never been done in UK courts although recent legislation has potentially corrected this.

The main source of the power that all who speak through the media, including documentarists, have flows from freedom of expression. Freedom of expression unbalances the law in their favour. Documentarists, recent regulatory attacks notwithstanding, work in a generally favourable legal environment. These legal underpinnings render them comparatively powerful as 'speakers' within the society and need to be examined (as do the regulations which seek to constrain them) if the ethical issues raised by documentary are to be addressed.

3.3 Documentary and the Common Law
Documentary film-makers assert their right of free expression within a network of contracts – with their bosses and with those who participate in their films.

(They do not, however, have much of a legal connection with their audiences, as we have seen.) Let us start with the bosses. If the documentarists are 'independents', which has been increasingly the case in recent decades, they contract for the supply of programmes or programming materials to broadcasters. Otherwise, the film-makers work for the broadcaster and are bound by their contracts of employment in the usual way.

In either case, there is a curious process in train whereby reality is observed by the documentarist and is transformed by filming into a species of private property – stored moving images with sound. The stored images of the real world become the documentarists' property which can then either belong to or be sold on to the broadcaster or passed to the film distributor or to any other user. What was once true only of photography now holds for all technologies of seeing:

> It is an amazing paradox that the 'reality' whose image is reproduced by the negative always belongs to someone. And the paradox of the paradox is that if what I reproduce ... is part of the public domain – streets, rivers, territorial waters – it will become my property only on condition that I reappropriate it. (Edelman, 1979: 35)

For example, the Kennedy assassination is a world historical event which first Abraham Zapruder and then Time-Life, in effect, copyrighted to their own benefit. Zapruder sold his 8mm amateur film of the murder to Time-Life who then defended their right to exploit its use even to the point of attempting to prevent drawings based on the film frames being used by a third party (*Time Inc. v. Geis* 1968).

Copyright in the common law was initially a legal mechanism for the implementation of the regulation of printing. By the mid-sixteenth century English books, registered at the Stationers Company, could be printed, and reprinted in perpetuity, only by members of the Company. Although the issue of perpetuity has been disputed – with acts bringing now lesser, now longer periods of protection – the association of copyright with book production rather than writing meshed well with the materialist tendencies of the common law to the advantage of publisher and printer over authors and other artists. The 1956 UK Copyright Act extended protection directly to the moving image and radio and, as revised in the Copyright Designs and Patents Act 1988, to embrace new technologies.

The French tradition was grounded in the quite different intellectual assumptions of the Napoleonic Code which put the author first – *droit d'auteur*. This was internationalised by the Rome Act of the second Berne Copyright Convention (1928) as giving 'moral rights' to authors, irrespective of the ownership of the copyright (Berne Convention 1928: 6bis). These were given 'independently of the author's economic rights' although in France such a right – *droit de suite* – allows, for example, a painter to claim a percentage of any resale price of a work even if the artist has alienated the copyright through a legitimate sale (Couprie and Olsson, Henry, 1987). The British 1988 Act moved the common law tradition towards the concept of intellectual property as a basis for copyright by allowing an author of a work 'moral rights' that were somewhat similar to the *droit d'auteur*. UK authors and artists can now also protect their work from misuse or distortion even if they have alienated the copyright – but not gain money from subsequent sales (Bainbridge, 1994: 27–30).[3] The French tradition holds the words of a book to be more valuable than the paper on which they are printed. This is more reasonable than the reverse which was the position of the common law until the 1988 modification; but some developments, that of photography for example, have presented problems to the French law which the British managed to avoid. If in France copyright related to author, who authored a photograph – a 'mechanically' produced image?

Because the camera's capability as a scientific recording instrument was heavily emphasised by the French from the introduction of the daguerreotype in 1839 onwards, the idea of it also being a creative tool was downgraded (Winston, 1995: 127–9). The earliest legal view of photography was that it was so mechanical that it did not involve any 'auteur' and therefore a photographer could not have the *droit d'auteur*. This is why Edelman claims that the French law could not initially *saisi*, come to grips with, photography (Edelman, 1979: 44–9). It did not take long, however, for the burgeoning business of the daguerreotype and then the photographic industry with its books of views and reproductions, its postcards and professional portraits to obtain some copyright protection. The mechanical photographer became an artist and the 'creative treatment' of photographed 'actuality' a possibility. Edelman makes it clear that the driver behind this legal U-turn was commerce, not aesthetics.

In the common law tradition there was no hiccup with the advent of photography. Courts were content to insist that the person who owned the photographic plate also owned the impression on it. It was on this basis that Zapruder acquired his nest-egg from Time-Life and Time-Life set about making sure it recouped its outlay and made a profit (*Time Inc.* v. *Bernard Geis Associates* 1968). The documentarist is in like case. One cannot reproduce images from documentaries any more than one can purloin a still from a fiction film or the copy of a painting in a public gallery. Just as the National Gallery owns Turner's *Speed, Rain, Steam: The Great Western Railway* and restricts reproductions of it, so film-maker Fred Wiseman 'owns' the Massachusetts Correctional Institution at Bridgewater, the location of his first film *Titticut Follies*

(1967), licensing showings of its images and restricting reproduction of frames from it (Benson and Anderson, 1989: xii, 29, 33–4, 113–17). Indeed, in most jurisdictions, a Wiseman now maintains a measure of control even after selling the copyright because he can assert his 'moral rights'.

The law is also concerned with the parallel but distinct relationship between documentarists and participants in their films. Unlike the relationship between film-maker and viewer, which only has only a very tenuous basis, that of the film-maker and participant is substantive. The common law sees documentary film subjects as contractors with documentary film-makers, nothing more and nothing less. It sees documentary film-makers as producers of a commodity, the film or tape, in which they have all rights. These rights, however, do not make the film or tape commercial speech. The law cares almost nothing for invasion of privacy for such 'non-commercial' products. It takes little cognisance of non-material damage such as distress. It sees the film-maker as a protected speaker who utters for the public good. The bottom line is that the ownership of the image is legally significant; the ownership of the thing (including personhood) imaged is not.

Nevertheless, the image of any person raises the possibility that he or she too might have some interest at stake in its use whoever owns the copyright of the image. Once the concern that tribal persons supposedly had about a photograph 'stealing their soul' was regarded as risible. Now, just as body piercings among the young at least become accepted in the First World, such tribal reactions seem to make much more sense.[4] We have little control over our public image because our wishes are deemed to be less important than freedom of expression. Public exposure can matter to us nevertheless. At the cost of no little confusion, therefore, the documentarist's freedom of expression can be limited by the participant in different circumstances involving different legal remedies and constraints. Our legal traditions do offer a measure of protection to a person being photographed or filmed, especially if they are not in a public place.

There is the remedy of defamation, but this is exceptional not only in being too expensive for most people to contemplate and, in the UK at least, extremely uncertain in its operation, but more importantly it is irrelevant in that the vast majority of people filmed, both in public and private places, are not thereby defamed. Not only that, there is still a presumption that a prohibition against prior constraint is in operation and a potentially defamed party cannot seek the protection of an injunction. They must wait until the defamation is published and then go to law.

This is not true of actions for breach of confidence, which are designed to protect confidential information, originally in business but now more widely applied. British courts are more willing to injunct publication on the basis that confidentiality has been breached. Breach of confidence is, at its simplest, less a matter of an offence against reputation or an issue in free expression than a protection of intellectual property: 'Information has become property' (Robertson and Nicol, 1992: 172). Breach of confidence actions can threaten media exposure, overriding free expression.

David Elstein, having conducted a training course for executives of a chemical company, was prevented from screening a programme he subsequently made about them for Thames Television even though he was meticulous in not using any information he had acquired during the private training process (*Schering Chemicals Ltd* v. *Falkman Ltd* 1981). In 1982 Robert Maxwell injuncted the *Watford Observer* from publishing a story about the trading difficulties of his printing company, an early warning of his imminent financial collapse. Secrets of a council development plan and the dangers of a chemical company's operations contained in reports by, in the former case, a consultant and, in the latter, the local fire brigade were prevented from being published in 1984; even the injunctions themselves could not be reported. As with *This Week*'s blank screen, the *Daily Express*, in one such situation, left blank spaces in an injuncted report as a protest against the exercise of prior constraint (Robertson and Nicol, 173; Welsh and Greenwood, 1991: 160).

The government has used breach of confidence as a basis for seeking to restrain embarrassing publications that are not covered by the 1975 Official Secrets Act or which would not secure a prohibition because juries had become very loath to convict under the Act. These have failed, and moreover a British decision in a major case, *Spycatcher*, has been overturned by the European Court of Human Rights.

Breach of confidence as a protection of business and government information has been extended into the private domain via a 1967 injunction obtained by the Duchess of Argyll preventing the Duke's publication of his story in the *People*, following their notorious divorce. In 1987 Prince Charles relied on the same principle in removing from circulation a tapped telephone conversation supposedly between himself and Lady Diana. In a further extension in that same year, a judge stopped the *Sun*'s presses (literally) from reprinting revelations run in earlier editions by the ex-nanny of a TV presenter's baby (Robertson and Nicol, 1992: 180: Welsh and Greenwood, 1991: 161). Princess Diana was able to settle out of court an action against a private gym owner who sold photographs he had taken of her working out to the *Daily Mirror*. The settlement was on the basis of breach of confidence.

UK cases often turn on the circumstances in which the information was obtained, although theft of information itself, unless specifically criminalised as by the 1985 Interception of Communications Act (which prohibits private telephone tapping) or the anti-hacking Computer Misuse Act of 1990, is not an offence. It is always possible that the media in paying for information from, say, an employee, especially one whose contract of employment contains a 'secrecy' clause, will be caught offending the Corruption Act. Against this, the bare fact that information passed to the media was stolen will not secure an injunction preventing publication.

3.4 Legal Privacy

Breach of confidence is twin to invasion of privacy. The difference is that, before the Human Rights Act, there was by no means agreement within the common law tradition that any such tort as invasion of privacy exists, given these other remedies of defamation, breach of confidence and a number of criminalised prohibitions. In addition to prohibiting wire-tapping and hacking, UK law also barred publishing rape victims' names or, in many circumstances, the names of minors involved in legal proceedings. In many US jurisdictions, statutory constraints include not only prohibitions against wire-tapping and hacking but also against publishing the contents of the mail, radio messages, academic records, records of the sales or rentals of videotapes, e-mails in public systems, library and bank records and the contents of refuse bags (Anon., 2000b).

There was also, of course, the most time-honoured basis for the protection of privacy in trespass and although this has often failed to 'come to grips with' advances in technology – the telephone wire, the telephoto lens, the eaves-dropping microphone – it still had sufficient force to contribute to a traditional English hostility to a separate tort of privacy, especially when the powerful hostile voices of the Press are heard in opposition as well.

The principle of free expression stunted the development of straightforward general protection of privacy in common law jurisdictions. For example, in the 1950s an English textbook on tort could still regard the whole idea of a separate ground of action for invasion of privacy as positively comic:

> A much discussed point is whether the law of torts recognises a 'right to privacy'. There may be circumstances where invasions of privacy will not constitute defamation or any other tort already discussed. For example, the jilted lover who makes his former sweetheart a present of a bathing costume which dissolves in chlorinated water; ... the newspaper reporters who, regrettably, sometimes stop at no invasion of privacy in order to 'get a story'. No English decision has yet recognised that infringement of privacy is a tort unless it comes within one of the existing heads of liability. (Street, 1959: 411)

As far as the English and Welsh were concerned, privacy, as a legally enforceable notion, was dreamed up specifically as a response to the muckraking gossip columnists of the Boston Press in 1890, by two smart young American lawyers, Warren and Brandeis, in an article for the *Harvard Law Review* (Warren and Brandeis, 1890: 193–220). In fact, an academic American lawyer had come up with the phrase 'the right to be left alone' in 1888 (Cooley, 1888: 29); but, despite this, Warren and Brandeis were somewhat hard pressed to mount a case for a privacy tort.

They did so by extending the concept of ancient lights, by making analogies with copyright and they also used *Prince Albert* v. *Strange*, a case where the proposed publication of unauthorised etchings of the Royal Family was deemed to be both a trespass and an invasion of privacy (*Prince Albert* v. *Strange* 1848). All this enabled Warren and Brandeis to elaborate for the first time the idea of a right to an 'inviolate personality' parallel to the common law right to inviolate property. Most American jurisdictions followed this logic by creating a measure of privacy rights exactly by analogy to other property rights, especially – as far as the media were concerned – by allowing celebrities access to the court so that they could prevent commercial exploitation of their images by others.

The law in America failed initially to 'come to grips with' the idea of fame, much as the law had not grasped photography in France and the technologies of wire-tap, prying lens and microphones everywhere. The logic at the outset was that if one had a public persona, then one had less right to privacy than an 'ordinary' person; but, again, the possibilities of economic exploitation caused a rethink. In the face of a valuable trade in baseball cards, the courts began to elaborate a process giving the famous a right over the marketing by others of their image (*Haelan Laboratories, Inc.* v. *Topps Chewing Gum, Inc.* 1953). This 'right of publicity' was eventually to be codified three decades later in 1985 in the so-called 'Celebrity Rights Act' within the Californian Civil Code (Section 990b) (Gaines, 1992: 200–01).

(Such a 'right of publicity' follows on from a matching right, which some American legislators have long acknowledged, for ordinary people to prevent their images being used for advertising purposes. Occasionally the courts have distinguished between advertising and news. They have then accepted that a person still retains a residual property right in her or his image when it is being used for an advertisement; but even this is relinquished if consent is obtained. In this sense, the freedom of expression accorded such 'commercial speech' is less protected by the First Amendment than other forms of speech including non-advertising media messages.)

Despite the elegance of the Warren and Brandeis argument and the fact that, in these various ways, American jurisdictions have accumulated many statutes and a large body of case-law, the US position on privacy had never really been accepted as a serious one by English lawyers. Nevertheless, the fact was that the existing heads of liability did not cover many situations notwithstanding legal thinking that they ought to. In 1977, for instance, the English law did not allow Lord Bernstein to obtain an injunction preventing an aerial photography firm overflying and photographing his property (*Bernstein* v. *Skyviews and General*

Ltd 1977); nor, in 1991, could the family of Gordon Kaye prevent the *Sunday Sport* from publishing photographs of him in hospital recovering from brain surgery (*Gordon Kaye* v. *Andrew Robertson and Sport Newspapers* 1991). It was in the judgment for this case that, finally, 'the Court of Appeal ruled out the development of a tort of privacy in English law, and urged Parliament to consider legislation on the subject' (Hepple and Matthews, 1991: 799).

This has now changed with the incorporation of the ECHR into British law through the Human Rights Act. Parliament avoided passing a distinct privacy bill but, by enacting the ECHR into British law, has brought in the concept anyway because the Convention incorporates a privacy right in Article 8:

> 8.1. Everyone has the right to respect for his private and family life, his home and his correspondence. (Anon., 1992: 163)

This was very worrying for the British Press, despite the strength given to the principle of free expression in general and media freedom in particular in the ECHR. As Jack Straw told the House of Commons during the second reading of the Human Rights Bill:

> It is worth pointing out that, in practice, the [European] Convention has already been extensively used to buttress and uphold the freedom of the Press against efforts by the state to restrict it. There are at least four leading United Kingdom cases in which the Strasbourg Court has done that – and not one on privacy has detracted from such a line. (Hansard, 1998: col. 775)

Indeed, as we have seen, this is the truth but nevertheless Straw acknowledged the worries the Press had expressed over the possible chilling effects of Article 8 and, as had already happened in the Data Protection Act where 'the special importance of freedom of expression publication' was acknowledged, agreed to make specific reference to Press freedom in the ECHR Act (Hansard, 1998: col. 776).[5]

The UK Act therefore specifically glosses the ECHR in favour of the Press:

> 12.4: The court must have particular regard to the importance of the Convention right to freedom of expression and, where the proceedings relate to material which the respondent claims, or which appears to the court to be, journalistic, literary or artistic material [*sic*] to – ...
> (b) any relevant privacy code (Human Rights Act 1998).

This, in effect, creates a de facto statutory public interest right similar to that articulated in the American *Sullivan* case. The reference to 'any relevant privacy code' alludes to such provisions as those provided by the Press Complaints

Commission and the ITC codes. Despite the added protection of 12.4, the ITC was already consulting about revisions to its Code in the light of the Act in the months before it came into force. It was proposing, for example, that the limitations in Section 2.1 of the Programme Code which deals with 'Privacy, Gathering of Information, etc.' ought to be altered to reflect the ECHR and the British Act. Instead of 'considerations of national security, *the requirements of the Broadcasting Act* and from individual citizen's right to privacy on free speech', it simply might read 'that the guidance given in this Code is consistent with Convention principles' (ITC, 2000: 2, emphasis added).

(I emphasised above the ITC's proposal to remove the Broadcasting Act as a particular legal justification for its guidance on privacy to draw attention to the fact that the constitutionality of other parts of the Broadcasting Act could now be questioned because of the Human Rights Act – including, because of Article 10, the ill-defined requirement in (6.1) for the 'due accuracy and impartiality of any news (in whatever form)'.)

Invasion of privacy implies that there is no prior contact between the parties involved in documentary filming but for the most part there is indeed a formal relationship between the documentarist and the participant, and it is one in which the participant forfeits much legal protection on the use of their image. The basic position is that, as with the use of images for advertising purposes, any significant participant must sign a release form, otherwise the screening of the image can be prevented. Participants need formally to consent to appearing.

3.5 Legal Consent

The matter, however, does not end with the release form. It is not quite so simple – and not just because of the legal restrictions on abridgements of free expression. There is, in effect, a somewhat ill-defined continuum here. At one end, in the news, the strength of the journalist's right to speak is such that the participant need not be contracted to appear. At the other end, in advertising, obtaining consent is crucial because participants have an elevated and, in some jurisdictions, statutory control over the use of their image. Despite the need for consent agreements, documentaries fall somewhere in the middle of the continuum. Documentarists have a greater need to obtain formal consent than do broadcast journalists but a lesser need than do advertisers. Sometimes, they can proceed without formal consent. On the one hand, then, participants in most circumstances must consent and have a basis for intervention if they do not; on the other, if they are not contracted or wish to withdraw a contract they have signed, they are likely to be much inhibited because they cannot unilaterally abridge the documentarist's right to speak.

In practice, film-makers must obtain from participants, excluding bystanders in public places of course, a contract consenting to their appearance; however, unless the terms of the contract specify control of use of the image, then no 'moral rights' are created for the participant. In everyday practice this means that documentarists need and do obtain permission from participants in the form of a release form which normally passes all rights over to the documentarist. The need for written (or, at least, recorded) consent in the USA was established in 1961 (*Durgom* v. *CBS* 1961). CBS was successfully sued by a person who was represented in a docudrama – that is, a dramatic reconstruction of a real-life incident – but who had not signed a release despite the fact the programme had been made with his advice and therefore implied consent.

Once participants formally consent to being filmed they then forfeit control. In this way, the film-maker 'appropriates' the images of people and the advantages of the 'paradox' of copyrighting reality come with that appropriation.

The law of contract places some restrictions on the ability of parties to bargain, but most address quite specific situations and almost none of those is strong enough to overcome freedom of expression assumptions in case of disputes with the media. If one party to a bargain, for example, is sufficiently powerful to be able to coerce another into agreement, the law will not support the contract; but the legal concept of coercion has been very strictly defined. A real physical threat is needed if a contract is to be nullified. Without physical violence, one party can still assert undue influence on another; but here again 'undue influence' has been very narrowly construed – forcing a senile relative into making a will to your advantage would be one example (Atiyah, 1989: 292–9). The same holds true of other situations where a weak party has been convinced by a stronger to sell, for example, a painting or an antique for a fraction of its true value. Conservative lawyers see any possibility of contracts being negated because of 'economic duress' as a 'danger' (Atiyah, 1989: 288). Some relationship between buyer and seller, other than that created by the market, needs to be established for the court to nullify the contract (*Fry and Lane* 1888: 312; Cartwright, 1991: 197–8). Even if the documentarist did have a family or other special relationship with a participant, it is unlikely that these specific limits on contract would defeat an assertion of the principle of free speech.

Common law tradition sees the general ability to bargain freely as an essential social lubricant and places as few restrictions on it as possible. The possibility of easily establishing agreements between people that would then be enforceable took the law some centuries to accomplish but it was an essential prerequisite to capitalism. For a contract to exist there has to be an offer, and an acceptance of that offer for some identifiable reason which the law calls 'an earnest of consideration'. This last need have no material value and certainly does not have to be money. As a legal term, 'consent' is part of, and essential to, the making a contract. Understanding of this process is assumed and demonstrations of ignorance will not affect this assumption. For centuries, the law has therefore warned contracting parties to beware. It has done so because once the contract is made, the law is interested only in its fulfilment and washes its hands of these other factors. In the documentary film-making situation, the participant is a 'buyer' whose understanding is taken for granted unless she or he is a minor or lunatic. Documentarists bring to the usual film-making bargain (of which the participant must beware) the further right of free expression. This is enhances their power and further unbalances the relationship between them.

Consent has been deemed to be unobtainable from minors (Pember, 1972: 244). As for mental competence, the *locus classicus* for the documentary remains *Titticut Follies* (1967). This was in effect banned from general exhibition for more than three decades in part because of the issue of consent. Wiseman, working on his first film, obtained only twelve completed forms from the sixty-two inmates he filmed, and there was a question anyway about the extent to which they could sign a consent.[6] The very fact of their incarceration was that the criminal justice system held them to be mentally incompetent. If they were not responsible for the crimes of which they had been found guilty, how could they be competent parties to contract with Wiseman?

If they were not, then the officials administering the system could be said to be responsible for them as wards of the state and capable of giving consent. Wiseman had permission to film from all relevant authorities who were just such *parens patriae* and this permission implied consent, so he did not need individual consent from the inmates, or indeed the guards (Anderson and Benson, 1991: 10–24). The persons in authority who gave Wiseman permission to bring a camera into the prison hospital had, however, to have the general understanding needed to bargain over the terms under which the film would be made. That they became upset with the film's picture of their brutality and incompetence some months after it was released is neither here or there. (Distress is no basis for attacking freedom of speech in law.) English courts have been unwilling to discover debilitating or damaging distress in cases turning, say, even on Post-Traumatic Distress Syndrome. In Wiseman's defence, then, it must be said that his reading of the *Titticut Follies* situation does represent the usual circumstances of documentary film production. If you consent for yourself or on behalf of others in your care who are unable to consent for themselves, *caveat emptor* – all that will be available to you should you change your mind is an action for defamation or breach of confidence. But clearly, however embarrassing politically, *Titticut Follies* would support neither.

Not untypically, Wiseman adds to this persuasive argument around the consent issue, appealing both to his own rights as a First Amendment speaker and to the public's right to know. He claimed that in his initial approach to the authorities – as the Boston University law professor he then was – he made clear that the purpose of this film was to give his students, and others, an understanding of the problems of the state in dealing with the criminally insane. He rebutted any implications that he had misrepresented himself to the authorities in order to obtain their consent fraudulently (Anderson and Benson, 1991: 10–24). But even if he had so behaved, he could still have used the concept of a public 'right to know' to defend himself from attempts by Massachusetts to censor his film. Isn't the job of the Press (including in this context documentarists) to uncover hidden abuses of state power? And isn't this a sufficiently important task to obviate the necessity for consent at all and also to warrantise subterfuge if necessary?

Titticut Follies remains unique, the only film ever to have had its cinema exhibition legally restricted in America on grounds other than obscenity, blasphemy or sedition. It is not an exception in that it allows the common media professional's echo of the law's *caveat emptor* to those who would participate in programmes and films. Nor is *Titticut Follies* exceptional in highlighting the problems raised by consent, even if they were particularly complicated in this instance because of the character of the participants and the public, yet closed, nature of the location. In this film and everywhere else in documentary, the contract between the documentarist and the participant has the latter yield all rights of control and empowers the former to use public right-to-know to prevent any participant changing their mind. The contract therefore does not address distribution of profits, derogatory use, tertiary market exploitation or a myriad of other issues with which it could deal. It turns only on consent. In fact, it is normally nothing but a release form – less than a page – which allows the documentarist to do what he or she will with the image.

The law does not allow the documentarist a free hand but the power of the concept of free speech unbalances, in their favour, many of the relationships arising from the film-making process. Film-makers are more powerful than their audiences and, normally, more powerful than those who participate in their documentaries. To redress the balance requires intervention regulating the content of documentaries, which the law is adverse from making. Enter then the regulators offering through their codes, whether mandated or voluntary, a sort of equity to compensate for the consequences of the legal privileging of free expression.

Chapter Four
Regulation

The regulation of broadcasting content in the UK implicitly assumes that the common law is insufficient. The law is seen as wanting because it has failed to balance the old right of free speech against new mass media and their attendant intrusive technologies. (There is also a powerful, and not entirely baseless, rhetoric suggesting that, anyway, judges are not to be trusted with preserving this old freedom.) Statutory mandates have therefore been put in place requiring third parties to produce codes of practice that neatly side-step the unwillingness of the law proper to engage with such issues as privacy and distress directly. The difference between law and codes is that the law would not recognise the same standards for sexual and violent portrayal; would not assume the same responsibilities for undamaged members of the audience; would not countenance the same concept of unfairness and would not require anything like 'balance'. Content regulation is, enabling clauses apart, extra-legal and, indeed, actually or potentially hostile to the basic legal concept of free expression.

Those responsible for erecting this edifice of control and many of those living under it claim that the regulation of content is good and serves the public well. Whether this is so or not is certainly worthy of debate; but what is without question is that the regulatory structure at many points expands and extends the constraints of the law proper. These bodies, either directly mandated by statute or others originally set up by the creative industries themselves and now acknowledged by statute (e.g. the British Board of Film Classification or the Press Complaints Commission), are created to do what the law will not – intervene in content beyond the norms of contract, tort and crime. Regulation is sanctioned by statute not only to plug the legal gaps but it can also be supported, as is the case with broadcasters, by a willingness on the part of those regulated to embrace control.

It is also the case that there is a common confusion here that erodes the distinction between content regulation and the regulation of the infrastructure of broadcasting or other media systems for either technical or social reasons. In the developed world the former tends to be a greater threat to free speech than the later.

4.1 The British Codes of Practice

There is a lot more to UK television regulation than the operation of 3.7 (i), the clause of the ITC Code used to discipline Carlton TV. Overall, the UK has a most elaborate structure for the regulation of broadcasting. It is concerned with two main areas, the creation of a system for providing broadcasting signals and the technical standards thereof, and control of the content of those signals. To do this, apart from the government's residual powers of legislation for regulation, there are two licensers who combine spectrum allocation and other infrastructural functions with content regulation (the ITC and the Radio Authority), one unified broadcaster (BBC) and one overlapping body with a public remit to monitor the content of all output but with no say over the basics of the system (the Broadcasting Standards Commission). The ITC's authority to intervene over content comes from the Sections 6 and 7 of the 1990 Broadcasting Act. The BBC's parallel rules for intervention are required in Section 5.3 of the Agreement associated with its Charter.

The ITC code, for example, discharges its overall statutory duty by demanding that its licensees make sure that 'the Code's contents and significance' are widely understood among television staffs and have 'in place procedures for ensuring that programmemakers can seek guidance on the code within the company at senior level' (ITC, 1998: Foreword (e)). Carlton's compliance officer, the senior manager in question at the time of *The Connection*, was Don Christopher, a media lawyer with seventeen years' experience, who resigned over the scandal. The existence of this elaborate structure within organisations 'providing the services' is uncomplainingly accepted by programme-makers not just as a cost of doing business but, as many would argue, a positive mechanism. Ian McBride, Christopher's opposite number at the Granada Media Group, is one such.

McBride is Managing Editor of Granada Media, a self-described 'head of flak', but reached this position after years of aggressively contentious current affairs programme-making, often causing trouble to regulators and even, on occasion, to police and courts. McBride is something of a poacher turned gamekeeper. At the 1999 Sheffield International Documentary Festival, he spoke against a proposition that 'the time has come to abandon all regulation of television programme content'. He was not slow to acknowledge 'the absurdity' of much content control and the proliferation of regulators with whom he has to deal; but, at the end of the day, in his view only regulation stood between the pressures of competition and a 'healthy diet' of programming:

> I feel a creepy unease about any channel's ability to keep the diet healthy if it's
> not required to do so when its competitors are selling some of their burgers by

the squillion. Regulation gives us and the viewers the only guarantee that free-to-air channels will maintain what I believe are three essentials to their success and our creative aspirations: *quality, diversity* and *home production*. Why do I want to continue withholding from us the kind of editorial freedoms that every print journalist, every author takes for granted? **BECAUSE IT KEEPS US HONEST**. (emphasis in original)

McBride made a persuasive argument that, in contrast with the Press, broadcasters cannot entrap people without elaborate consultation and record keeping; cannot resort to subterfuge to get a story without almost always needing to come clean and obtain consent; and so on. The lies of *The Connection*, in his view, 'went to the very heart of the contract with the viewer' and he implicitly endorsed the fine as 'a chilling … reminder of that contract with the viewer'. An ITC survey following the scandal revealed that the majority of those questioned thought programme standards were the same as they had ever been and a majority of that minority who disagreed did so because they thought standards had improved. Although other surveys of professionals suggest people in the industry do believe standards have declined (Dovey, 2000: 38), McBride was nevertheless supported when he suggested:

To me, those [ITC] findings show a public confidence which is important to the viewer and absolutely essential that we maintain … None of this is to say that regulation and our regulators don't need a radical overhaul. Nor do I pretend they get it right all the time. Our courts don't get it right all the time, but that's no reason to abandon the rule of law (McBride, 1999)

McBride had no difficulty in carrying a large audience of documentarists with him at Sheffield virtually nem. con. and I am sure this reflected a real feeling in the trade generally in its response to the fakery scandal. One can criticise professionals as victims of a false consciousness that causes them to operate with unproblematised concepts of objectivity and truth; but, even if this is so, they also have high levels of integrity and scrupulously honour their own code of behaviour. There is also, as I have said, the widespread belief that the most important 'people' being kept 'honest' by regulation are the bosses, the media-moguls 'selling… their burgers by the squillion'. Without content regulation they would be even crasser.

All this might well be false consciousness but it leads most broadcasters including documentarists not to feel unduly constrained by regulation. They willingly accept the regulatory vision of the ITC: 'Licensees may make programmes about any issue they choose. This freedom is limited only by the obligations of fairness and a respect for truth, two qualities which are essential to all factually-based programmes, whether on 'controversial' topics or not' (ITC, 1998: 3.1). The BBC's *Producers' Guidelines* also allows the Corporation to be 'free to make programmes about any subject it chooses' (BBC, 2000: 2.1 ¶3).

The gap between such reasonableness and critics' objections is unbridgeable. For the latter, that 'only' in the Code is the thin end of a censorship wedge; 'fairness' and 'truth' are too much in the eye of the beholder to be anything other than a potential licence to censor; 'essential' is but code for the maintenance of broadcasting as an important apparatus of state power by disguising the inevitable construction of media images as the products of a supposedly neutral recording process; and the quotation marks around 'controversial' give the ideological game in play here away totally.

4.2 A Short History of Media Control

In 1737 Prime Minister Robert Walpole, 'goaded beyond endurance by caricatures of himself in the plays of Henry Fielding', empowered the Lord Chamberlain to censor dramatic works (Robertson and Nicol, 1992: 138). Blackstone, unfortunately, mounted no forceful argument against this although the Lord Chamberlain had been in the prior constraint business for less than three decades when the *Commentaries* appeared. It became apparent that, as far as the common law was concerned that not all media were the same. Despite increasingly strong adherence to free speech including Press freedom, the Lord Chamberlain's contrary censorship power persisted and was consolidated in a new Theatre Act in 1843 which allowed him: 'to prohibit the performance of any stage play "whenever he shall be of the opinion that it is fitting for the preservation of good manners, decorum or the public peace that he do so"' (Robertson and Nicol, 1992: 138).

Shaw was of the opinion 'that the dearth of good English plays between the early eighteenth century and his own debut in the late nineteenth was entirely due to the Lord Chamberlain' (Tynan, 1967: 175). In 1965 the Lord Chamberlain of the day, Lord Cobbold, decided that five scenes from John Osborne's *A Patriot for Me*, Edward Bond's *Saved* and scenes from Wedekind's classic *Spring Awakening*, all at the Royal Court Theatre, were unsuitable for public performance. His language on these occasions tended to reveal the basis of his reasoning. He determined, for example, that another play, given by the Royal Shakespeare Company, was 'beastly, anti-American, and left wing'. The theatre, goaded beyond endurance by such rationales, finally counter-attacked.

After 231 years, the resultant Theatres Act of 1968 abolished the Lord Chamberlain as censor and left the stage to the mercy of general legal restrictions only. In the Act there were also the specifics of what to do about stage obscenity, but these were along lines parallel to those previously outlined in the

Obscene Publications Act 1959. In a final twitch of the corpse of specific the-atrical censorship, Mary Whitehouse, a self-appointed would-be censor, pressed for the prosecution of the National Theatre in 1981 for homosexual obscenity in Howard Brenton's *The Romans in Britain*. When the Attorney-General declined to act, she brought a private prosecution under Section 13, the Sexual Offences Act 1956 but this collapsed when, under cross-examin-ation, her witness to this outrage could not be sure, from his seat in the gods, whether he really saw one actor approach another with his erect penis in hand or with thumb (as Robertson and Nicol put it) 'adroitly rising from a fist clenched over his organ'. Whitehouse and the amorphous forces she rep-resented nevertheless had their day a few years later when, under Mrs Thatcher, a new Obscene Publications Act (1987) was passed although, for example, Sam Brittain (whose brother was in the Cabinet) disapproved of it as 'an highly illib-eral measure' (Goodwin, 1998: 80). There was however no revival of specific theatrical censorship.

The UK theatre may have escaped specific control but films have not: 'The 1909 Cinematograph Act gave local authorities the power to impose conditions on film exhibition in order to protect the public against fire hazards, but they soon began to use them to quench the flames of celluloid passion' (Robertson and Nicol, 1992: 566). Fire in theatres is an apparently reasonable basis for con-trol but it is also actually a fig-leaf disguising ideological purpose. The original 1909 Act echoes the theatrical Suitability Act of 1878 which brought the British public the theatrical safety curtain but, by imposing costs that could not be met, closed 200 independent variety halls and helped many more into the owner-ship of the emerging theatrical chains of the late nineteenth century and a measure of more respectable control (Winston, 1996: 27–8). In the same way the fire risks of nitrate film – a hazard unnecessarily left in place given that safety stock was patented in 1904 – morphed rapidly from certification of premises into a crude censorship of the films themselves by local authorities.

The industry sought to buy off this wildly uncertain and often draconian control with its own Board of Film Censors, established in 1912 and now endorsed by a series of judicial decisions and by statutes which, for example, empower it as an 'other body' to license 'works unsuitable for children' or video-cassettes (Cinemas Act 1985, 1 (3); Video Recordings (Labelling) Regulations SI 1985 No 911). The BBFC, though, was as quick as the local Watch and Fire Committees to cut scenes and refuse licences, spotting on the screen anything from 'Bolshevik propaganda' to 'themes likely to wound the sensibilities of friendly nations' or 'abdominal contortions in dancing' (Winston, 1996: 60; Hunnings, 1967: 50). The reasonableness of offering public guidance and even controlling what the young can see, like the reasonableness of fire hazards, is compromised by an impulse to censor as apparently uncontrollable as the thrusts of a priapic stud in a porn film. (This stud has, curiously conjoined to his satyriasis, reactionary political instincts.)

With these precedents to hand, the content regulation of broadcasting, from the arrival of radio as a mass medium, was a strong possibility. Instead of fire, though, measures of specific content control, largely initially self-imposed informally by unified broadcasters (e.g. the BBC), were subsequently sanctioned by a vision of spectrum scarcity, a need for technical standards and, on occasion, various social goals such as diversity of ownership. Nicholas Garnham has argued that the major drive towards this regulation was simply that the broadcast media signalled a failure of the market that required state intervention: 'The state underwrites a monopoly and the producer's right to a monopoly rent ... [The media's] economic survival under market conditions depends upon the exploitation of monopolies, in the sense of the unique defining characteristics of pieces of information' (Garnham, 2000: 57, 58).

But this does not automatically mean regulation of the 'defining characteristics' of content. Take telecommunications: 'While regulation of the network was considered legitimate, any regulation of the messages passing over the network was and is regarded as an illegitimate infringement of individual freedom, autonomy and privacy, as indeed an infringement of free speech' (Graham, 2000: 174).

The mass media do not benefit from this view since they have traditionally been seen as 'media of public communication and thus institutions straddling the private economic sphere and the public political sphere in a way that legitimized public policy to ensure that these media fulfilled their public functions, functions ultimately underpinned by a liberal freedom of speech theory' (Garnham, 2000: 173). And, paradoxically by this account, to ensure free speech the speech of media speakers must be regulated. Yet this is not compelling since in some societies (e.g. the USA) the Press is as free from content regulation as is telecommunications. Only the broadcasters are affected by it.

It is certainly the case that the control of broadcasting content does not arise from the tradition of censorship alone since it is also clear that scarcity of bandwidth and other technical issues justify regulatory interventions that are theoretically underpinned by a social purpose argument. On this basis it becomes reasonable to suggest that regulation can legitimately achieve a range of purposes from determining signalling power and technical standards for licensed users to preventing the 'pirate' use of spectrum which interferes with licensed signals. Social ends could also justify addressing the issue of media ownership; or limiting the penetration of audience and readership any one publisher/broadcaster could achieve; or denying any right of media ownership at all to foreign nationals.

However, all these worthy objectives – technical quality, universality of ser-

vice, diversity of ownership, the correction of a breakdown in the market, even
– *all* could be sought without threatening free speech with content regulation.
There was no reason, apart from political purpose, to mix and meld these goals
with freedom-threatening codes; but once content regulation was in view then
the censorship tradition of stage and screen became pertinent. In the confusion
between infrastructure and content, censorship and certification procedures
showed broadcasting regulators how a tradition of content regulation, established despite the free speech right, could easily be embraced by the controllers
of the fundamentals of the system. The two levels became inextricably mixed
as in, to take one example, a prohibition against subliminal messages, which is
both technical and substantive (Broadcasting Act 1990, Section 6.1).

It is true that initially broadcasters needed government regulation of spectrum allocation to prevent them from impinging on each other. Received
history suggests that the market place could not deal with this problem and calls
in evidence the bandwidth free-for-all in American radio in the 1920s prior to
federal intervention. Even in the Land of the Free, regulation of the infrastructure of the system was needed. This is in contrast to the Press where 300 years
of struggle had made newspapering possible to 'anybody' (in A. J. Liebling's ele-
gant analysis):

> 'Anybody in the ten-million-dollar category is free to buy or found a paper in
> a great city like New York or Chicago, and anybody with around a million
> (plus a lot of sporting blood) is free to try it in a place of mediocre size like
> Worcester, Mass. As to us, we are free to buy a paper or not, as we wish.'
> (Liebling, 1964: 15).

These days, you would need to add some noughts to the dollars and, in the face
of declining readerships, the amount of sporting blood required has increased
exponentially. The point is that received opinion sees the Press as an area for
free market activity while broadcasting is perceived as being, by its very nature,
a limited resource and therefore in need of regulation.

As the very first case challenging the right of the German *Länder* to regulate
content within the terms of broadcasting freedom (*Rundfunkfreiheit*) promised
by the Federal Basic Law made clear in 1961, the paucity of wavebands, and the
cost of establishing television services, both precluded the formation of a market and therefore justified regulation (Barendt, 1985: 103). In 1967, the US
Supreme Court took much the same view in the *Red Lion* case, forcing a broadcaster to make space for an opposing view on its air (*Red Lion Broadcasting Co.
v. FCC* 1969). The fact that there were more people who wanted to broadcast
than there were wavelengths to allow them to do so justified the US Federal
Communications Commission, the licensing agency, in abridging the free

speech of a licensee by insisting on this 'right of reply' (Barendt, 1985: 103). These are the differences between *Pressefreiheit* and *Rundfunkfreiheit* the free world over. Even in the USA the broadcasters are singled out because there is a distinction drawn between both Press rights and the rights of telecommunication common carriers and them, although First Amendment arguments can be mounted for broadcasters, albeit with greater difficulty (Pool, 1983: 2).

Nevertheless, in supposedly free societies, moving from spectrum allocation regulation and the rest to content regulation does still require some tricky footwork. It can be noted that, once the technical quality of radio broadcasting was not so limited that bunching occurred in the middle of the medium wave, spectrum scarcity began to decline as a compelling justification for system regulation, although it revived with VHF television only to decline again in the age of communications' abundance. My point is that it was never the open and shut matter it is usually taken to be since it has always had a socio-political dimension.

This can be demonstrated quite easily. The Americans created first more radio stations and then more television stations than did the European states, although they used the same technology. That is because, despite basic US spectrum regulation, they tried for as market-driven a system as possible, one that maximised stations even at the cost of reception quality. In Europe, on the other hand, maximising the quality of the signal was prioritised, even at the cost of choice ostensibly to ensure the technical quality of universal service. This was only 'ostensibly' a quality-of-signal issue because it is clear that, for an organisation such as the BBC, the centralised voice which could be thereby created was *also* essential to its national politico-cultural mission.[1] In short, the scarcity justification was as useful ideologically as it was technologically and this has enabled it to persist into the age of cable, satellite and (potentially) Internet abundance in the form of complex licensing that also involves content control. Scarcity of the spectrum, never mind abundance of channels, no more requires the regulation of content than did the danger of fire in cinemas require the censorship of films.

A further proof can be seen here. The multi-channel environment clearly does not need the spectrum allocation its broadcasting and satellite elements require, although it does, as a whole, still present other challenges to the efficacy of the market. At a minimum, a case for governmental infrastructural involvement now rests on the social need to agree standardised platforms for new technologies (including digital broadcasting and despite a rhetoric of 'open standards') in order to protect the public from the uncertainties of competing systems in the market place. Were we not in the grip of a neo-liberal *laissez-faire* orthodoxy (and a collective amnesia about broadcasting history), standardisation processes could be modelled on the testing of systems, such as that undertaken in London in 1936/37 to establish the London Television Standard, or the long-drawn-out industry-wide debate in America that produced the NTSC TV standard of 1941. But we are doing no such thing. Instead, we are now throwing out the bath water of technical regulation while keeping the content regulation baby.[2]

It is a curious fact that in the UK, for example, regulation is seen as a seamless web while freedom of expression can be parsed on the basis of misunderstood technical requirements or social purposes unacceptable to the free Press. These purposes, however worthy, are grounded in a paternalistic concern to the well-being of readers or audiences. What the media do not need is government intervention in content – but then, it never did. The point is that to move from spectrum allocation, ownership rules, technical standards and so on to regulation of content requires the praying in of the Reithian concept of Public Service Broadcasting or a variant thereof. 'Scarcity' is central to the Reithian PSB and PSB is central to the idea of 'a contract with the viewer'.

4.3 The 'Contract' with the Viewer

The Reithian PSB assumption of 'a contract with the viewer' is deemed potent because broadcasting enters the home if not as an 'uninvited guest' then certainly as an 'unpredictable' one. In essence, this posits that, as children watch with parents, the guest could embarrass or distress the one in front of the other. This has always struck me as glib since the same seems to me to be true of other, non-content regulated, media as well. Were I not British, for example, I might be quite surprised to pick my newspaper off the welcome mat and discover a naked young woman posing on page three. (Were I not British, of course, I would be unlikely to care much if I did.) The unpredictability of the daily newspaper – the striking horrific front-page image, for example, as much as the page-three girl – is no more and no less than the unpredictability of programming. To argue that papers are seen by one pair of eyes only while the television screen can be watched by many starts to thin the argument to the point of flimsiness, for all that it is endlessly retailed. To assume that the audience is unprepared for the next shot is to assume they have never seen a television programme.

Reithian PSB supposedly transforms the relationship between broadcaster and public because it promises levels of programming quality and integrity that can be ensured by content regulation only and could not be delivered by market-led or directly controlled government channels. It is a weak chain that leads from scarcity and diversity of ownership to technical standards and PSB to 'a contract with the viewer' and *The Connection*'s 'breach of public trust', but it is a chain nonetheless. The 'contract with the viewer' is a regulatory concept that, however widely accepted in the industry, has no more direct legal reality than does 'breach of public trust'; it is no more sustainable as a secure basis for content regulation than is legitimisation based on supposed scarcity.

A measure of significant neo-liberal verbal confusion has emerged because 'regulation' conflates system regulation with content regulation and, when it comes to content, further melds statute and precedents with legally sanctioned or legally acknowledged codes. In the resultant salmagundi, the fundamental human right of free expression becomes glossed as, for example, a 'basic citizenship entitlement' the more easily to confuse it with the legally spurious concepts of a 'right to choose' or a 'contract' between broadcaster and audience. A great theme in the Western concept of liberty becomes, linguistically, a matter of consumption like any other.

Although each regulatory agency is required to draw up its own code of practice or guidelines, the shape of these is now more or less standard. Take those of the Broadcasting Standards Commission. The BSC represents the triumph of the Whitehousean attack on the perceived liberal metropolitan elite controlling broadcasting, and is twin to the 1987 Obscene Publications Act as an achievement of the repressive tendency in British life.

Statute requires that the BSC draw up a code on *avoiding* 'unjust or unfair treatment' or 'unwarranted infringement of privacy' and offering *guidance* on the 'portrayal of violence', 'the portrayal of sexual conduct' and 'standards of decency' (Broadcasting Act 1996, Section 107 (1), Section 108 (1)). Unlike the ITC Code and the BBC Guidelines, there is no mention of freedom in the BSC's preamble to its Fairness and Privacy Code, only 'responsibilities' (BSC, 1998: 1 ¶2). The parallel code it has on standards also deals with 'freedom' in the context of 'responsibility': 'It is part of the broadcaster's duty to find ways of striking a balance between their creative freedom and their responsibility to their diverse audiences' (BSC, 1998: 1, ¶1).

The BSC's rules and regulations on these 'Standards' (which encompass 'Taste and Decency', the 'Portrayal of Violence' and the 'Portrayal of Sexual Conduct') are prolix: 'Broadcasters should bear in mind that children tend to stay up later than usual on Friday and Saturday nights' (BSC, 1998: 7). 'Matters of decency are based on deeper, more fundamental values and emotions' (16). 'Violence takes many forms' (48). 'People of all faiths are distressed by affronts to their sacred words. This should not be underestimated' (31). And, as is common, no distinction is drawn between responsibilities to the audience as opposed to duties to programme participants. So some injunctions are directed at programme-makers' responsibility to both the audience and participants as mere dual manifestations of the same 'public'. For example, participants are not to be 'exploited needlessly or caused unnecessary distress, nor should the audience be made to feel mere voyeurs of others' distress' (17). The net result is that programmes must not treat badly those of the public who appear on them or offend against taste and decency, encourage crime, lead to disorder, or be offensive to public feeling.

Discovering what is offensive and therefore causes distress, basically unactionable at common law, and to whom it is caused has been the object of much BSC 'research'. This involves the usual social science attempts at establishing 'objective' measures of public opinion; but in this area the exercise is particularly spurious, at least as a basis for policy making. The BSC Codes' foundations are not limited by such popularity polls. They are conditioned by a set of ethical, ideological assumptions that 'research' can boost; or the results can simply be ignored if they fail to do this. Since we are here concerned with freedom of speech, it is possible to argue that the matter is *ultra vires* to 'research' anyway. By this view, say research discovers that the audience does believe broadcasting to be invasive; that should no more justify undermining free speech than public approval for hanging justifies the death penalty.

The BSC seems unconcerned that a fundamental human freedom is at stake. 'Freedom' is rather merely a factor to be 'balanced' against a slew of constraints. Having at the outset of its existence sounded opinion, including conducting a series of 'roadshows', it is never by doubt diverted on this, even when it has evidence that support for its very *raison d'être* is limited: 'Research shows that audiences in Britain have generally become more liberal and relaxed about the portrayal of sex ... *but* broadcasters cannot assume a universal climate of tolerance towards explicit sexual material' (BSC, 1998: 79, emphasis added). The public's increasing tolerance in matters sexual has been reflected in the courts: 'Explicit sexual material' is not necessarily obscene and therefore falls outside the scope even of the 1987 Act (*David John Darbo* v. *DPP* 1991). Despite this, one offended or distressed person, like one of the righteous in Sodom or Gomorra, is sufficient to save the Commission and all its works. And one single objector is, largely, what the BSC deals with – in 1998/09 a mere 4,892 complaints of which 3,133 were taken forward, from an audience of hundreds of millions across the year. The BSC upheld the cases of 817.87 complainants whose sensitivities were, it judged, unjustifiably upset or who were unfairly treated by broadcasters, at a cost of just over £2 million – a public charge of £2,457.47 per successful complainant for a total budget that would buy a dozen major documentaries a year (BSC, 1999: 10, 24).[3]

Confusing audience with participant confuses the 'contract with the viewer' and issues of privacy and consent. The BSC's other code on 'Fairness and Privacy' boldly uses language no British common lawyer would (either before or after the ECHR became British law) in prohibiting invasions of privacy without reference to a basic right of free speech. 'The line to be drawn between the public's right to information and the citizen's right to privacy can sometimes be a fine one' (BSC, 1998: 14). Broadcasters must remember, especially in the context of public figures that 'not all matters which interest the public are in the public interest' (17). The BSC does allow for justified infringement of privacy only if there is an 'overriding public interest'. This is glossed as:

> 'revealing or detecting crime or disreputable behaviour, protecting public health or safety, exposing misleading claims made by individuals or organisations, or disclosing significant incompetence in public office. Moreover, the means of obtaining the information must be proportionate to the matter under investigation' (BSC, 1998: 14).

Otherwise, in contradistinction to the English common law prior to the Human Rights Act and the provisions of Article 10 of the ECHR after its incorporation, the Code does not allow for intrusions.

In line with its general procedures and in the aftermath of the *Connection* affair, the BSC commissioned the highly respected Stirling Media Research Unit to study the participation of the public in broadcast programming (Stirling Media Research Unit, 2000). Its report, *Consenting Adults*, used focus groups and so on to prove public support ('evidence') for the notion that broadcasters should 'introduce a highly explicit code of rights for participants' in a way that is even more restrictive than are the scattered provisions in the current codes (2000: 78). The researchers worry, in true neo-liberal fashion, that this extra code might entail costs but seem to be blithely unconcerned about any other aspect of their recommendation. They follow their paymasters in being almost blind to the vexed conflict between free expression and social responsibility; but they go further in that their report gives no overt cognisance to the idea of an 'overriding public interest', even as outlined by the BSC Code itself – except implicitly in that their proposed new code on participant rights, which 'would unite provisions relating to public participants currently found in producer and programme makers' codes', might have to deal with the public interest exception, although the researchers make only glancing mention of this possibility (2000: 77).[4] Section 12.1 of the Human Rights Act does exactly the opposite of this, rendering the Stirling proposal moot but, nevertheless, as another telling example of how far the erosion of any British culture of media freedom had progressed by the year 2000, *Consenting Adults* can hardly be bettered – not least because of the unimpeachable credentials of its writers as thoughtful media scholars.

Thus Stirling does not even offer a nod in the direction of 'public interest', the right to know, although this is anyway a legally fragile basis upon which to excuse infringements of privacy because, as we have seen, it is distinct from, and less well established than, the right to speak. Yet this right to know is written into the code and it is also in the Press Complaints Commission Code of

Practice which 'upholds the public's right to know' (PCC: 4). In both cases, the stronger right to speak has been thus far ignored, although this cannot continue in the light of ECHR Article 10. The ITC and BBC rules will also have to be revised if they are to conform with the ECHR since free expression was always couched in terms of permission rather than right: 'Licensees may make programmes', 'the BBC is free to make programmes'. These are to be found in sections crossheaded not 'Free Expression', but 'Impartiality'.

The concept of 'impartiality' is expressed through the long-standing British conventions that broadcasters maintain 'balance'; that there be 'fairness'; that children be protected as both audience and participants; and that none, neither audience nor participants, be 'misled'. All news or any other programming dealing with political and industrial controversy or public policy must be accurate and impartial. The requirement that broadcasters maintain this 'balance' is in the 1990 Broadcasting Act which calls for 'due impartiality'. This is glossed in the ITC Code as the representation of different views 'adequate or appropriate to the nature of the subject and the type of programme' (ITC, 1998: 3.2.i). The definition of 'due' is repeated in the BBC *Producers' Guidelines* because 'due impartiality' is required by the BBC Agreement (5.5): 'Due impartiality lies at the heart of the BBC' (BBC, 2000: 2.1 ¶5). The difficulties of maintaining impartiality are acknowledged, at least at a crude level: 'it cannot be achieved by a mathematical balance ... There are generally more than two sides to any issue ... "due" is to be interpreted as meaning adequate or appropriate to the nature of the subject and the type of programme.'

Due impartiality impacts on the 'fairness' with which interviews are conducted (ITC, 1998: 3.8). BSC requires that 'when a programme alleges wrongdoing or incompetence ... those criticised should normally be given an appropriate and timely opportunity to respond' (BSC, 1998: 11). This is echoed in BBC *Producers' Guidelines* Chapter Two, Part 1: 2.7. ('Right of reply' is also guaranteed by Article 8 of the European Convention on Transnational Television (1989) but can take the form of an adjudication published in a viewers' magazine (Robertson and Nicol, 1992: 552). It is the equivalent of the American 'Fairness Doctrine' to which we shall return.)

There is a sensitivity in these codes to using archival material: 'Beware of causing pain or offence' (BBC, 2000: 2, 8). This applies to all participants, not just those appearing in archived images. The ITC Code creates obligations to be fair to innocent parties, that is, ordinary members of the public, filmed with permission of the owners or controlling authorities of premises or public places; or in a 'sensitive situation (for example as psychiatric or intensive care patients)'(ITC, 1998: 2.2.i); or in covering police operations (2.2.ii); or in programmes or items within programmes dealing with 'serious crime, a tragic event or disaster' (2.2.iii). The inclusion of 'scenes of extreme suffering and distress' in any programme is to be set against a sensitivity to 'the risk of sen-sationalism and the possibility of an unwarranted invasion of privacy' (2.5). The ITC Code also draws attention to the representation of children and has fairly draconian regulations governing the use of hidden cameras, secret micro-phones and telephone conversations (2.6, 2.4, 2.3). The BBC *Producers' Guidelines* parallels this and calls for 'sensitivity to offence and outrage' but, again, acknowledges a possibility that 'a material public interest ... outweighs the offence' (BBC, 2000: 2.2.10).

The specific right of the audience not to be 'misled' is mixed up with these responsibilities to programme participants and also comes within the Impar-tiality sections, 3.7 (1) of the Code and Chapter 2, Part 1.6 of the *Guidelines*. Chapter 2, Part 1.3.5 further states that the public are not to be 'confused' by the 'mixture' of 'established fact and what is fiction'. The BSC requires that 'Broadcasters should avoid creating doubts on the audience's part as to what they are being shown if it could mislead the audience in a way which would be unfair to those featured in the programme' (BSC, 1988: 2).

4.4 The Legal Improprieties of the Codes

This would be reasonable enough were not all content regulation that goes beyond the requirements of the law (as this does) potentially unacceptable in a free society. One does not have to take a libertarian view to hold to this pos-ition. It is possible to control speech legally and constrain harmful or hateful expression without offending against the fundamental right of free expression. The key is that constraints must arise through the operation of the law directly. Whatever the faults of the law in practice, and they are certainly manifold in this area, nevertheless legal principles involve a range of basic requirements that these codes, for all that they are mandated by statute, lack.

The first of these is the ancient precept that everybody should be equal before the law. Not everybody – that is, not every broadcaster – stands equal before these rules and is subject to the same sanctions if they break them. While it is true that the Broadcasting Standards Commission does deal with all output, including the BBC, the plain fact is that fines have been applied by the ITC to the channels for which it is responsible alone.

The Radio Authority, which controls UK commercial radio, can fine, but only to the level of £50,000. The BBC *Guidelines* are mute on the nature of sanctions beyond the BBC 'doing all it can to ensure that provisions of the code [i.e. Chap-ter Two of the *Guidelines*] are observed' (*Agreement* 5.3 (b)). It is hard to see the BBC fining itself if infringements occur, although BBC wrongdoings in the first phase of the fakery scandal did involve the cancellation of *The Vanessa Show*. On the other hand, the *Sun*'s attempted entrapment was met with a counter-attacking BBC lawsuit, the altered alarm clock in *Driving School* and dubious near-miss collision with silence (quite rightly, in my view), and the suspect traffic-warden merited a dismissive letter from the responsible executive to the papers, while the Israeli murders were exonerated by local legal officials. The irony of the situation is that regulations designed to ensure 'fairness' towards any who become involved in a television production are themselves unfair, because they differ from channel to channel, to those making that production.

The same objection, that equality before the law is being undercut, applies to broadcasting regulation as a whole – ITC, Radio Authority, BBC and BSC. Here those who are not subject to control include the Press who, as McBride was happy to point out, do not have any quasi-legal sanctions to worry about. Only the general law applies to them. McBride may well be right, of course, that many UK newspapers behave appallingly and probably this is because their controlling body, the Press Complaints Commission, is, unlike the ITC, able only to compel the publication of its adjudications. It is widely seen as a more or less toothless watchdog.

The control of the Press through self-regulation, however widely disdained, nevertheless challenges the claim that regulation is the only way to control content. The UK magazine *FHM*, for instance, with a stupidity in my view well beyond that of Marc de Beaufort's, ran a facetious 'how-to' piece on student suicide (October 1999), citing actual cases and causing real distress to the bereaved families of the deceased. This warranted a well-deserved rebuke from the PCC for what one of the families involved called 'a vile abuse of journalistic licence'. More pertinent than this naming and shaming, the magazine's sponsors and advertisers then withdrew support (Ahmed, 2000: 1–2). The *Sun*'s splash 'THE TRUTH' purported to demonstrate that the 1989 Hillsborough football stadium catastrophe, where ninety-four Liverpool fans were crushed to death, was their fault because they were drunk. Investigations demonstrated that police crowd mishandling caused the disaster. Merseyside responded with a persistent boycott of the paper that is said to have cost its owner Rupert Murdoch some £10 million revenue (Lister, 2000: 5).

The threat to the *Sun* or *FHM* magazine through such market action is far more acceptable in a mature free society than is discipline by a public body. Before the law, a 'Forgers' Gazette' can forge away or a magazine seek cheap outrage with all the wit of a BSE cow as long as they don't damage anybody (distress not counting) while others, broadcasters unfortunate enough to work for channels controlled by the ITC, can be fined or worse for lesser, damage-free activities. Both pro- and anti-regulators can surely agree that such inconsistency is regrettable. I would go further to state that the situation is offensive to the principle of equality before the law.

4.5 The Codes and Documentary

The codes' language is a second major area of problem. With their plethora of undefined terms and rather crude assumptions about production practices, they in no way meet a legal standard of precision despite the rationale that they are guidance documents mandated by Acts of Parliament. For example, the BSC's flow of words, 'public interest' apart, eschews definitions, so 'crudeness', 'cruelty', 'humiliation' and so on lack any sense of legal certainty. The BSC's gestures towards liberal proprieties exacerbate this: 'Challenging or deliberately flouting the boundaries of taste in drama is a time-honoured tradition going back to Shakespeare, Chaucer and beyond.' This truth is then qualified: 'Comedy has a special freedom but this does not give unlimited licence to be crude or cruel, or to humiliate individuals or groups gratuitously' (BSC, 1998: 15). But in law, comedy, exactly, does have a licence limited only by defamation, obscenity and the other legal provisions – and the test for damage is altered to give comedic speech a greater licence than ordinary speech. It is very hard to sue for defamation by cartoon, for example, in the common law – distress and humiliation notwithstanding. So what is the limit of the BSC's 'licence'? We cannot easily know.

There is one aspect of this that is of particular concern to documentarists and it impacts directly on the dangers to free speech inherent in the 'fakery' scandals. The codes construct a general category of 'factual programme' which runs from the news to gardening and talk shows, embracing documentary as it goes. All Grierson's effort in defining a separate form, documentary, and with it differing standards is thus set at naught. It was always assumed (and articulated through the existence of separate production departments, which continue in some places) that, most crucially, documentary procedures were significantly different from news procedures. The forms have distinct histories and different purposes. The use of reconstructions in news (and proper restrictions thereon) was for the Griersonians always a different matter from the use of reconstructions in documentary.

But, as the codes know no documentary difference, so they fail for the most part to distinguish various levels of 'reconstruction' in their language. Their use of this term is particularly fuzzy. For instance, the ITC Code's requirement that 'reconstructions' be labelled for the audience is completely ill defined and apparently based on some quite primitive vision clearly grounded in the rhetoric of Direct Cinema. The implication is that the 'fly-on-the-wall' filmmaker captures reality as it happens and that anything else is suspect. But that is tendentious nonsense. It ignores how the vast majority of documentaries, even those most obedient to Direct Cinema's rules and strictures, are made and it implicitly claims a veracity for observational filming that cannot be sustained.

The Directors Guild knows better than this when it demands that 'The director must arrange and control the action going on in front of the camera ... The director often sets up circumstances in which the required action will happen' (Directors Guild, 1999: 7).

Only the BBC's *Guidelines* begin to speak to this sort of reality. The BBC has been moving on in sophistication from early iterations of rules such as *Principles and Practices in Documentary Programmes* (Cawston *et al.*, 1972). This was very much a rehashing of Grierson's principles in a Canute-like attempt to turn the tide of Direct Cinema observationalism:

> A documentary ... not only shows, it illuminates. It attempts not merely to inform, but to provoke deeper thought and understanding than a cold presentation of facts would do ... even the purest piece of '*ciné vérité*' [*sic*] can never be – and indeed should never be – totally free of the day-to-day business of directing. (Cawston *et al.*, 1972: 5, 11)

In the wake of the 'fakery' scandal of 1998, the BBC attempted to refine the terse references to reconstruction in the *Guidelines*. An addendum, *New Producer Guidelines*, was issued in December 1998 that pointed implicitly to the inadequacy of the current rules on the matter. The section of the revised guideline *Factual Programme Methods: Staging and Re-Staging Events* incorporates this addendum revealing that 'reconstruction' is a far more complex matter than is dreamed of by these other codes, including its predecessor. Although documentary difference is still ignored, general production realities are acknowledged for the first time:

> production methods, especially in television with single location shooting, sometimes mean that it is impossible to record all events exactly as they happen. Many of the techniques that are used to overcome this have long been part of the accepted grammar of programme-making ...

> Such techniques may sometimes involve a departure from the strict chronology of events. Additional bridging shots known as cut-aways may be edited to shorten a sequence ... So long as editing, changes in shot order and, indeed, new juxtapositions of shot do not distort the story and so mislead viewers, this is part of the normal grammar of film production.

> Factual programmemakers may sometimes legitimately ask contributors do things for the camera twice or repeat routine things, which they do regularly ...

As a result:

programme makers must ensure that:

– while it may, on occasions, be legitimate to re-shoot something that is a routine and insignificant action, it is not legitimate to stage or re-stage action which is *significant to the development of the action or narrative, without clearly signalling this to the audience*

– contributors should *not* be asked to re-enact *significant* events, without this being made clear in the film

– if significant events have been arranged for the cameras that would not have taken place *at all* without the intervention of the programme-makers, then this must be made clear to the audience

– shots and sequences should never be inter-cut to suggest that they were happening at the same time if the resulting juxtaposition of material leads to a distorted and misleading impression of events. (BBC, 2000: 2.2.7, emphases in original)

This is a vast improvement on previous attempts at drawing a line between legitimate practices and mendacities and it has now been incorporated into the current iteration of the *Guidelines* proper. Nevertheless, there is still a somewhat inadequate reflection of everyday non-fiction filming in play. These 'sometimes' and 'on occasion's still gesture to received contemporary opinion limiting the 'truth' to fly-on-the-wall filming, thereby transforming the norms of most documentary production into exceptions. There is also a problem yet again with the subjective and undefined nature of much of the language. What constitutes a 'distortion', what is 'significant', are significant routines to be labelled? And to whom is this addressed? Despite being the *Producers' Guidelines*, the definition of 'cut-away' suggests a readership unfamiliar with the craft. Is this guidance or PR?

Above all, the major revision of the *Guidelines* published in February 2000 was still about 'factual programmes'. Documentaries were no longer a separate genre, defined in terms distinct from other fiction forms, especially journalism, and therefore needing distinct 'guidance'. The same vanishing trick can be seen in the Stirling Media Research Institute's BSC study of May 2000 where 'documentary', when it is used in the text, is quite casually either a synonym for, or merely a type of, 'factual programmes'. It seems clear that this continued failure to distinguish various kinds of 'factual programmes', a task to which Grierson devoted considerable effort, threatens the underlying idea of the documentary; but this is now apparently forgotten even at the most sophisticated level of regulatory injunction. There is no reflection of the documentary tradition.

In the real world of documentary film-making, there is a continuum stretching from non-intervention through to the total manipulation and control of the fictional film. At one end is the surveillance camera, at the other *Star Wars* (George Lucas, 1977). Toward the surveillance end is the camcorder observing the police beating Rodney King; toward the fictional end is the drama documentary with actors repeating as accurately as possible what was said and done by others in a real past. Interventions begin with permissions to film and release forms and move through increasing manipulations to the point where documentary validity begins to disappear when 'real' non-actor participants act out not what they did but what they might have done. The wings of imagination thereafter liberate the film-maker totally from the Earth-bound constraints of reality.

The many permutations of reconstruction can be thought of as hanging from a line that runs from non-intervention to total intervention:

- no relationship established between film-maker and participant prior to filming to

- unfilmed interactions between film-maker and participant (the asking of permission to film, for example) to

- specific unfilmed requests made to participants without prior research to repeat or delay action to

- specific requests to participants to re-enact actions witnessed during the research process to

- specific requests to participants to re-enact actions witnessed by the participant or others in the past (what we may call filming the history the camera missed or was prohibited from capturing originally) to

- specific requests to participants to re-enact actions witnessed elsewhere during the research process performed by other people of the same type as the subjects (what we may call filming the typical) to

- specific requests to participants to enact actions which are possible but unwitnessed (what we may call the limits of the creative treatment of actuality) to

- implicit or specific requests to participants to 'act' (that is, to perform before the camera unlikely or impossible actions at the direct behest of the film-maker without the legitimisation of any prior witness in ways unrelated to the subject's actual behaviour and personality, e.g. the vogue for plonking people on desert islands to see what will happen) to

- actors performing according to witnessed accounts (what we may call drama-documentary) to

- actors performing imagined actions (what we may call fiction).

RECONSTRUCTION CONTINUUM

NON-INTERVENTION
    PERMISSIONS
    DELAYS and REPETITIONS
      RE-ENACTMENT OF WITNESSED ACTION
        RE-ENACTMENT OF HISTORY
          RE-ENACTMENT OF THE TYPICAL
            ENACTMENT OF THE POSSIBLE
              ENACTMENT OF THE UNTYPICAL
                ACTING WITNESSED HISTORY
                  ACTING
                  TOTAL INTERVENTION

WITNESS ·IMAGINATION

Note: filming outside of the documentary tradition indicated by italic

'Acting' alone is unambiguously fiction and 'acting witnessed history' is drama-documentary; but all the other points on the continuum can and have been considered legitimate for documentary practice. News is much more constrained being limited to only the first three categories within the continuum. The attempt of the BBC *Guidelines* apart, the other two codes deal with this difficult issue in a crude fashion, apparently simply assuming (as do many in the industry) that the documentary is journalism – feature journalism, say. Although documentary can indeed be journalistic it is not limited to that. Remember, Grierson's 'creative treatment of actuality' produced 'art' and legitimately among the techniques it used so to do was reconstruction. There is, therefore, a symbiotic connection between documentary and 'reconstruction'. The codes' failure to acknowledge this, their resultant unrefined simplicities and even the more sophisticated but still undifferentiated approach of the BBC's *Guidelines* have a limiting and chilling effect on documentaries' ability to illuminate the world.

A 1948 definition of the documentary spoke of it as 'all methods of recording … either by factual shooting or by sincere and justifiable reconstruction' (Barsam, 1973: 1). There is a tendency to see this reference to reconstruction as a necessary consequence of the limitation of film equipment prior to 1960. Such a technicist view, however, ignores both the necessity of reconstruction to the general processes of the creative treatment of actuality and, more specifically, the inevitable presence of what could be strictly defined as reconstruction in the everyday world of film-making where requests for repetitions and other interventions are still commonplace. The codes take little cognisance of any of this and privilege the observational, in fact the single-take. Not only does this render much filming 'unsafe' in terms of the code, it also implicitly reinforces fly-on-the-wall authenticity and legitimacy.

I am not claiming that a more measured and sophisticated view of the gradations of intervention will justify misrepresentation in the documentary. Pretending a fiction is real is still clearly a fraud. Reconstructing a previously witnessed scene is not; which is why the fine on *Much Too Young: Chickens* is potentially more worrying than the fine on *The Connection*. Filming reconstructions of illegal activity is not the same as filming reconstructions of legal activity. (Previously witnessing illegal activity is itself potentially illegal and could place the film-maker in the position of aiding and abetting the offence.) But in *The Connection*'s case the illegality of drug smuggling seemed to matter less than cutting two shots of different flights together. Demanding 'labelling' of all shots not made as the event filmed happened before the lens without any arrangement, intervention or mediation, if strictly observed, would seldom leave images untagged.

As it stands, the ITC's catch-all failure to define 'reconstruction' at all closely, and indeed to acknowledge the difficulty of so doing with the code's quotation marks around 'reconstructions', means that any prior arrangement between film-maker and participant, if it results in the audience being 'misled', is unsafe. No wonder that we now have comic but chilling po-faced public discussions on the morality of using trained 'wild' animals in 'reconstructions' of 'natural' behaviour, or that brows in production offices now furrow when confronted with computer-simulated images of celestial bodies provided by NASA.

One could go on about loose language. Despite the UK Court of Appeal ruling (in the course of dismissing another intervention by Mary Whitehouse) that holding statutory duties such as ensuring 'good taste' and 'due impartiality' are 'imprecise' (*R. v. IBA ex parte Whitehouse* 1985), they are nevertheless still in the regulations a decade and more later. Specifically, 'reconstruction', as far as anybody who has ever tried to make a documentary is concerned, is no less 'imprecise'. Given this legal assessment, such lacunae and over-simplifications are not just against the principle of the common law that rules should be transparent and comprehensive but are also deeply unfair to documentary film-makers.

A final legal uncertainty: 'misled'. Is one 'misled' audience member sufficient to trigger a sanction? (It would be in law and is clearly implied in the BSC's talk of 'universal' acceptance of standards and adjudication of single complaints.) Is a gullible person (one who believes in the reality of UFOs, for example) to be protected from being 'misled' as much as 'the man on the top of the Clapham omnibus'? (It would not be so in law.) Is this gullible person (who also believes in the automatic authenticity of fly-on-the-wall shooting as does 'the man on the top of the Clapham omnibus') to be protected from being 'misled' by all unseen arrangements both before and after filming being tagged, flagged and labelled on screen? Is misleading people on the radio less heinous than misleading them on television? (The £50,000 limitation on the Radio Authority's ability to fine would suggest that, *de facto*, it is.) In the *Connection* case much was made of the audience size, 4 million (for journalistic convenience, 3.7 million according to the ratings) – 4 million 'misled' viewers. Would the £2 million fine – 50p a viewer – be pro-rated if only 400,000 were watching, or forty, or four?

The regulatory regime is inimical to the principles of equality before the law and the requirement of certainty in the laws' provisions. Its legitimations – scarcity, diversity of ownership, the concept of 'the unpredictable guest' (as it were), 'a contract with the viewer', PSB – are weak and febrile as justifications for specific regulation beyond the provisions of the law. In short, such regulation is offensive to that other word which appears without gloss: 'freedom'.

4.6 Regulation in the US

The Americans, of course, as citizens rather than subjects, are more willing than the British to call up freedom in these debates; although, like the British, they have long accepted a fundamental difference between Press freedom and broadcasting freedom since the federal authorities have had a role in the regulation of the latter since the late 1920s. It is possible to see the very occasional intervention of the Federal Communications Commission into situations on the basis of content as a failure to regulate. Nevertheless, it is true and has been from the beginning of the Republic that despite the utility of the First Amendment in offering a measure of potential protection to broadcasters, 'In every generation attempts have been made to impose censorship or ban unpopular views' whatever the medium (Pool, 1983: 38). On the other hand, given that *any* regulation along the same lines in the Press would be fundamentally illegal, the simple fact of its occurrence in broadcasting, however rare, is of major significance.

Curiously, though, the resultant more lightly regulated American television, even on the wilder shores of the new channels, at least outside hotel rooms and video stores, remains more puritanical than does British. This is clearly because Americans, 61 per cent of whom claim Church affiliation, are actually puritanical (and, given the success of pornography as a mainstay of new platforms including the Web, more hypocritical as well). The point is that, however the media reflect American reality, the broadcasting regulator has had only one basis for regular intervention in content, apart from the draconian sanction of licence removal and even that has been eliminated.

The FCC's 'Fairness Doctrine' required that on controversial issues both sides be given an equitable amount of time 'affording reasonable opportunity' to a rebuttal of a position taken in a programme but unanswered. It was one of those attempts to make freedom of speech a workable individual right, at least in part, by overriding the free editorial control of the broadcaster. Although it was never codified, as indeed it could not easily be, because of the First Amendment, it was considered on occasion by the courts. It became settled US law that such a doctrine never applied to the Press but even with broadcasters it was always limited (Hammond, 1981: 44). In 1972, the right-wing Accuracy In Media took the FCC to court for failing to compel NBC into affording a 'reasonable opportunity' to the US pension insurance industry to explain its opposition to pension law reform. AIM claimed that an edition of *NBC Reports*, *Pensions*, had editorially supported the reform in a partisan fashion. At the end of the day, the network never allowed the industry's opposing point of view and when the case eventually was returned to the FCC, the Commission did not press for compliance.

From 1973 on the Fairness Doctrine was most likely to require a licensee to give a right of on-air reply in the event of personal (non-defamatory) attacks or following licensee 'editorials' that invited public response (Hammond, 1981: 225–6). The decision in the *Red Lion* case in favour of this has been counteracted by the Commission itself which reported in 1985 that the doctrine was not in the public interest (102 FCC 2nd 145 (1985)). The court held it not to be binding (*Telecommunications Research and Action Centre* v. *FCC* 1987) and demanded that the FCC either enforced or repealed it (*Meridith Corp.* v. *FCC* 1987). The FCC abandoned the doctrine except for ballot and other political issues but even that was rejected in 1991 (*AFL-CIO* v. *FCC*).

Wyke Rowland is of the opinion that the Fairness Doctrine was a reflection of 'regulatory activism in support of citizens interest groups' in the late 1960s and early 1970s which also found expression in cable access, worries about violence and the provisions made for children, as well as expanded support for the public system. But just as this activism began to bear fruit, as in the Fairness Doctrine, 'the reigning political economic assumptions about how commercial broadcasting was to be handled kicked in and began to press back, hard. So the Fairness Doctrine and other non-technical interpretations of the public interest were short-lived in regulatory practice.'[5] Instead of being seen as a tool with which to beat the supposed biases of the broadcasters from either left or right, the Fairness Doctrine became an unacceptable governmental intrusion into the broadcasters' freedom as constitutionally guaranteed 'speakers'. Like all other attempts at interference it foundered on the rock of a liberal concept of free speech.

This is, of course, not to say that the First Amendment has created an open, free society, not least since it can be seen to apply less to common carriers and broadcasters than print; rather it is to suggest that the First Amendment acknowledges that free speech is a terrain of struggle, which needs at the most to be extremely lightly regulated. American lobbyists (including fundamentalists of all sorts) and the market can exert pressure on broadcasting, at least on taste and decency, just as well as regulators. This is the sort of pressure outlined above in the rare instance of the *FHM* case in the UK. In the 1970s American radicals sought to reduce violence, for example, by urging a boycott of firms that advertised on violent programmes – 'America's most violent advertisers'. The 'religious right' have done the same, endlessly, about sex (sometimes finding it in cartoons or other children's programming where others, less on the *qui vive* for such things, see only innocence). In 1999, African Americans threatened a boycott of network viewing in response to a complete lack of minority representation in the prime-time shows. The result is some element of balance between the right of free speech and the pressure of audience disapproval. If anything this has produced a mainstream television culture of blandness and caution – but it has done so largely without interference and offence to the First Amendment.

Europeans profess distress at the rare naked interference over expression achieved by the manipulation of market powers in the US. They are also concerned overall at the failure to regulate for better quality. The Americans feel much the same unease about unelected quangos regulating expression via lengthy codes in Europe. There is simply a gulf between these two mind-sets. By the American view, if speech is to be free, then it cannot be controlled for any reason except the prevention of 'hurt'. That means it cannot be controlled even in order to improve its 'quality', however that be defined, or for any other reason. Conversely, the maintenance or enrichment of civil society might be considered paramount and therefore a sufficiently important basis upon which to modify media system even at the cost of undermining the principle of free expression. Implicitly, that seems to be the European view. While neither approach is remotely perfect, it is clear which one is closer to Milton and the tenets of free speech.

4.7 The Failure of Regulation

One problem about regulating content for the social good is that agreement as to what that is remains vexed and regulation becomes a tool of particular interest groups. In Britain one could argue that the content regulation is most sensitive to the social assumptions of amorphous Whitehousean forces. It is they who need the regulatory codes exactly because the general audience is more tolerant than they are. It is not a Thatcherite prejudice against the liberal metropolitan elite alone that has fuelled regulation; it is a reaction against the widespread British taste for tacky indecencies of all sorts as well. It must be said that, despite the formal constraints, British experience suggests that such public preference does inhibit the regulators, at least as far as the imposition 'standards' are concerned. The British silent majority does not share these with the regulators and therefore the taste for tacky indecency is not defeated since it speaks with the power, if not of the market place, then of inchoate public opinion. As Peter Goodwin has pointed out:

> This censorious strain in Tory television policy was not unimportant but its effects should not be exaggerated. During the Thatcher and Major years, there was no significant rolling back of the liberal 1960s and 70s in the general tone of what appeared on British television ... The bounds of 'taste and decency' permitted on British television screens widened over these years, despite the Tories overt effort. (Goodwin, 1998: 167)

While this is essentially true of 'taste and decency', the issue of the ITC's documentary fines reveals that the latently oppressive structure of the regulation of 'fairness', put in place in total opposition to the dominant *laissez-faire* ideology governing the development of the broadcasting infrastructure, is still very real. Its ineffectiveness as a control over 'taste' masks its potential as a control over 'controversy'. This threat is acceptable if the row is about premeditated, utterly fictional 'fakery' (such as *The Connection*) but is more worrying if it is about, say, 'Bolshevik propaganda', 'themes likely to wound the sensibilities of friendly nations' and so on – or the grey, and now unsafe, areas of normal reconstruction in documentary.

And here lies the central issue: even if quality is not a synonym for middle-class taste; even if taste, decency, impartiality, fairness, integrity and the rest are not an excuse for politically motivated censorship of 'controversy' or any more or less arbitrary interference, then regulation – at least as it is practised in the UK – would still be offensive to that sense of our civil society expressed in the traditional principles of the law. The question raised by *The Connection* in the context of the legal enactment of freedom of expression is the extent to which a mendacious communication, where no damage is proved, can be subject to sanction, even by a broadcasting licensing authority empowered by statute to levy it. Is the practice code of such an authority more powerful than the law guaranteeing freedom of expression? And does damage-free expression have to be truthful?

There is no doubt that the fine was seen more as a punishment for Sir Robin Biggam's 'breach of trust between programme makers and viewers' than for a technical breach of the contract between the ITC and Carlton. The Commission felt that 'breach of trust' with its clear implication that damage-free expression has to be truthful even if the common law does not; clause 3.7.(i) says the viewers must not be misled.

My questioning of the ITC sanction is strictly limited to concerns about the impact of extra-judicial fines and general regulatory interventions on content by quasi-governmental bodies. Let me say again, I do not want to suggest that documentarists are in any way above and beyond reproach. On the contrary, the documentarist faces a range of difficulties and too often fails to deal with them. Some challenges are shared with all programme-makers – the responsible exercise of the power of the pulpit, for example; some only with journalists – the burden of offering representations of the truth; but some are particular to the documentarist alone and arise from the peculiar 'creative treatment of actuality' that uneasily mixes journalistic encumbrances with the rather different duties arising from artistic manipulations.

The failure of documentarists to overcome these conflicting requirements is not, however, because they are weakened by the constraints of the law and regulations. On the contrary, they too often fall short of unimpeachable behaviour in the admittedly difficult circumstances of trying to be artistic reporters or journalistic artists, because they are powerful *vis-à-vis* those who participate in their films and, in the majority of circumstances, largely unconstrained. As Fred Wiseman once said, 'Constraints? What constraints?' (Anderson and Benson, 1991: 3). The documentarists' power flows from the legal exercise of freedom of expression which, as we have seen, still hedges and constrains all the statutes and codes that seek to abridge it. The result is that documentarists, despite the common law and the codes, can be unethical – and are.

And this is the final charge against regulation. Not only does it offend the fundamental right of free speech and not only does it fail to maintain the legal principles of equality before, and clarity of, the law, it is also falls short in ensuring the ethical behaviour of broadcasters in general and documentarists in particular.

Part Three

DOCUMENTARISTS

Chapter Five
Free Expression

Despite the support for regulation expressed by British broadcasters, there is evidence that the UK codes do not address the concerns of programme-makers – the protection of their own interests against their broadcasting bosses or programme participants. An indication that this is the case can be found by comparing the codes of practice occasionally produced by professionals themselves with the broadcasting regulations we have been discussing.

This is not to say that, for all that these guild/union guidelines are grounded in free speech assumptions, they are unconcerned with the effects of broadcasting on audiences and participants, ignoring in a self-interested way the ethical dimensions of media work. On the contrary; but they do implicitly argue that ethical conduct is best obtained through media practitioners' voluntary adoption of their own guidelines governing everyday professional behaviour. This would obviously produce a superior moral environment, one in which ethical demands engendered no threat to free expression; but this is not possible in practice, as (to take the clearest example) the realities of journalists' work illustrates.

Almost without exception, journalists are not free agents but employees of one sort or another. Not only that: historically journalism has always embraced more than straightforward reporting but the exercise of these other functions – the retailing of opinion or the provision of entertainment – complicates the ethical position and, when added to the demands of free speech, makes the imposition of any system of ethics difficult. For good or ill, journalism as it has been defined by the culture is not actually limited to the truth-telling of reporting; nor has the free speech right allowed it to be restricted by the demands of social responsibility.

If documentary is prised from the mud of 'factual programming' as a distinct form, it further complicates the ethical issue because it is no more limited to journalism than journalism is confined to truth-telling. It also claims to be art and art's morality, or lack of it, raises yet other issues. These have more to do with the documentarists' relationship to those who feature in their work than with the responsibilities they owe their audiences.

5.1 Media Practitoners' Ethics

The partialities of the authoritarian top-down codes, either legally sanctioned or legally acknowledged, can be contrasted with the guidelines drawn up by media professionals themselves. In the anglophone world professional codes of this type tend to be unacknowledged by the state and therefore to have no enforceable status. They are often produced by media guild or trade union organisations and are far more tightly focused on actual work practices. Although they share much with top-down content regulations, they also exhibit a care for their members which is unaddressed in the other codes.

For example, the British Directors Guild Code of Practice on documentaries, which I have already cited, echoes the authoritarian codes:

> Directors have a *responsibility* to keep faith with their contributors throughout the production process … In a documentary or factual programme, it is the director's responsibility to ensure fairness and accuracy. It is a responsibility shared with the producer, the production and the broadcaster but it cannot be abrogated … The director must not deliberately mislead the viewers in a programme. (Directors Guild, 1999: 6, 10: emphasis in the original)

But this code also acknowledges that documentarists are not free agents but mere employees or independent contractors in different language – 'directors must not be forced … the director must not allow a contributor to be misrepresented … allow the viewers to be misled … '. Indeed, 'directors and researchers have a right to object to any perceived mistreatment of their contributors or any distortion of the facts *without being penalised*' (10: emphasis in the original).

This attempt to protect the integrity of the film-maker against the pressures of the broadcaster is carried further in the many journalist codes that exist around the globe. Here the entire world, not just media management, is a potential threat to the ethical intentions of the journalist. The 1987 code of American Society of Professional Journalists is typical. As with the UK Directors Guild, its ethical code of practice also begins by accepting a responsibility for accuracy, objectivity and fair play but then moves on to a number of other moral snares unmentioned by the regulatory codes:

III Ethics:

Journalists must be free of obligations to any interest other than the public's right to know the truth.

> 1. Gifts, favors, free travel, special treatment or privileges can compromise the integrity of journalists and their employers. Nothing of value should be accepted.
> 2. Secondary employment, political involvement, holding public office, and

service in community organisations should be avoided if it compromises the integrity of journalists and their employers …

3. So-called news communications from private sources should not be published or broadcast without substantiation of their claims to news values.

4. Journalists will seek news that serves the public interest, despite the obstacles. They will make constant efforts to assure that the public's business is conducted in public …

5. Journalists acknowledge the newsman's ethic of protecting confidential sources of information.

6. Plagiarism is dishonest and unacceptable. (Knowlton and Parsons, 1995: 5–7)[1]

This SPJ code is laudably unambiguous. No free lunches. Find a second source (i.e. a back-up for 'Deep Throat'). Don't join the Parent Teacher Association. Insist the council sub-committee meeting is public. I cite these codes not to suggest they would avoid the conflicts around free expression (for they do not) but only to point out that media practitioners themselves are capable of another focus when it comes to regulation.

Documentary ethics means, in effect, the ethics of journalism. This is because, firstly, journalists, at least outside of the UK, and others such as philosophers have worried a lot about press morality and have produced a large literature on the matter. Secondly, documentary, like journalism, lays claim to representing the real and, essentially, the 'real' involves other non-actor 'real' people (and, in these days of debate about animal rights, other living creatures too), in contrast to the realm of fiction film-making and broadcasting, because the use of actors as contract workers and the lack of such a claim on the real proceeds on principles of 'amoral efficiency' (Christians and Rotzoll, 1985: 229). (The morality of the effects it has on the audience is a different matter.)

Ethics in journalism appears to be widely perceived as a risible topic. One is reminded of the old story about Mahatma Gandhi. When asked what he thought about Western civilisation, he reportedly replied: 'That would be nice!' The public seem to assess the possibility of ethical journalism in much the same way – it would be nice. Despite this cynicism the newsroom is, like the hospital, one of the few places in our society where ethical matters regularly come to the fore, even if only to be quickly swept aside. They are ignored in part because of their potentially chilling effect on free expression (which is already constrained by the law) and also, perhaps more importantly, because news professionals are convinced that an 'ethical' readership/audience is an even more risible concept than is an ethical journalist. Experience of the market place unequivocally shows that, although the public protests a desire for ethical material when asked by pollsters, as news consumers they are avid for offal. In ethical debates this is held by philosophers, for example, to be no defence for journalism since philosophers will lay blame on the public not for demanding such material but, rather, for doing 'journalism no service by putting up with trivia and trash, accepting execrable standards as the norm' (Belsey and Chadwick, 1992: 1).

Whether a template for behaviour or not, ethics is understood to present an ever-present set of issues for journalism. Formal journalism education, part of the despised Media Studies, remains one of the few places within the university where ethics is regularly taught. Journalists are aware that ethics needs to be dealt with, if only with the contemptuous and macho dismissals of time-honoured newsroom injunctions such as, 'If it bleeds, it leads'.

If minded to care more deeply, journalists will unfortunately find that they are not helped much by the products of the millennia-long business of philosophising about ethics. Ethics in general, and ethical systems in particular, tend to be restrictive in free expression terms. They also tend to be individualistic and posit a free person facing choices as the norm. Like other workers, journalists for the most part are not free. They are responsible to their employers as well as to their readership/audience and to the participants, informants or contributors who interact with them; and these responsibilities can be at odds with each other. The owners need profit and, sometimes, a platform; the consumers information and/or titillation; the participants privacy or, sometimes, a platform.

Journalists obey orders and those orders themselves, while possibly causing ethical difficulties, are normally legal; that is, there would be no legal redress in consequence of publishing material required by editor or proprietor although ethical difficulties might well arise. The reality of the journalists' limited area of ethical manoeuvre does not figure very highly in public debate. Nevertheless, journalists are workers like any others and their managers are allowed to manage them as they see fit. For example, the *New York Times* in August 1985 described a property developer as ' "plotting" real estate deals' and used other emotive (or lively) language. A few days later an editor's note on this piece appeared in the paper: 'Through opinionated phrases and unattributed characterizations, the article established a tone that cast its subject in an unfavourable light ... The pejorative phrases and anonymous criticism created an unbalanced portrait. They should not have appeared' (Klaidman and Beauchamp, 1987: 48). The journalists responsible received this public castigation from their boss, executive editor A. M. Rosenthal, a friend of the developer. I cite this instance neither to question the ethics of the original language nor the soundness of Rosenthal's criticisms (much less his right to make them); but rather to draw attention to this rare public insight into the realities of the news-workers' position.[2]

Most of the time, news-workers and their bosses agree on what they are doing, including the ethics (or lack of them) involved. At the same time, journalists understand that while it is as foolhardy (as it would be anywhere) to argue with their managers, it is a particularly fraught journalistic business to do so on ethical grounds. Ordinarily the journalists' *auto-censure* mechanism *vis-à-vis* management is fully engaged and is particularly effective in suppressing ethical uncertainties. The mortgage demands no less.

In philosophy, though, being an unfree agent does not excuse morally dubious activity. According to the dean of American journalism ethicists John Merrill, Kant, for example, would see a newsroom variant of the 'I was only obeying orders' defence as simply:

> an excuse or rationalization … the journalist could, in Kant's view, act responsibly out of a sense of duty to principle, not out of consideration of consequences …
> Notwithstanding political and institutional control and pressures, the journalist
> … can, and will, find ways to give vent to personal desires and to push back the confining limits of social control. (Merrill, 1989: 65, 118–19)

But the 'I was only obeying orders' line is not entirely without substance, as Merrill well understands, since the consequences of venting desire and pushing boundaries include the possibility of dismissal for breach of contract because of insubordination.

The reality of limited individual action does mean, however, that all ethical systems which assume a free agent are potentially inapplicable to journalism. From the Aristotelian principle of the 'golden mean' through the religious concept of brotherly love – a 'duty of care' (as it were) for one's neighbour – to Kantian 'categorical imperatives', Utilitarianism's 'greatest good', or some contemporary idea such as Rawls's 'veil of ignorance', a free agent is more or less central; and since the journalist is not quite such a being, the system can offer only, at best, clues for behaviour (Christians, Rotzoll and Fackler, 1983: 9–11). Merrill: 'Seldom does any one of these [ethical] paths run discretely through the thickets of daily journalistic experience' (Merrill, 1989: 164), although parts of these systems will come into play on a case by case basis.

When the difficulties raised by the restricted autonomy of the individual journalist are added to the fundamental amorality of the concept of free speech, the limited applicability of systematic ethics becomes clear. Even the most manifest requirements, that journalism be truthful and accurate, say, raise questions because of one or other of these.

5.2 Truth-telling and Other Responsibilities

Obviously truth-telling is a necessary and essential limitation on journalism, and is accepted as such by the profession: 'facts are sacred'. Nevertheless while clearly an ethical imperative, it is at the same time a limitation of free expression.

The very possibility of a conflict between truth-telling and free speech does not appear to have occurred to the pioneering apostles of freedom in the seventeenth and eighteenth centuries. Perhaps this was in part because, if truth-telling had been acknowledged as an important journalistic activity, then the practice of journalism certainly would not have been limited to it; but it was not and we still live with the consequences. Because of this historical reality truth-telling is not the end of the matter. Even the news press had other roles apart from the truth-telling of reporting and it is these that justify the documentary practice of creatively treating actuality (aside from deliberate complete fictionalisation) in ways largely uncomprehended by the 'fakery' debate.

Contemporary ethicists and media critics are prone to forget these other dimensions. Their starting point for these discussions is that 'reporting the truth is at the heart of the journalistic enterprise' (Klaidman and Beauchamp, 1987: 30):

> Just as health is an internal and constitutive end of medicine, so truth-telling about significant contemporary events is an eternal and constitutive end of journalism. As an end it distinguishes journalism from other practices akin to it, but distinct from it – for example those of pure entertainment. (O'Neill, 1992: 18–19)

It is on this basis, in a dismissive footnote, that John O'Neill castigated Rupert Murdoch for claiming that his Presses 'are in the entertainment business'. O'Neill claimed that:

> This distancing of newspaper production from the values of truth-telling and its recharacterisation as entertainment allows the easy relativism exhibited by Murdoch in his Edinburgh lecture of 1989 in which he identified 'quality' with 'satisfaction of market preferences'. (O'Neill, 1992: 30)

It is not that O'Neill is necessarily wrong in this view of the dangers of journalism as entertainment; it is rather than the implicit idea that there is as clear a divide as he infers between the two is ahistorical and an inadequate description of journalistic practice. 'Recharacterisation' suggests an ignorance of what newspapers have been, certainly since the beginnings of the popular Press 175 years ago. Such ethicists tend to hear journalistic rhetoric (e.g. 'facts are sacred' and so on) and, finding its claims wanting in journalistic practice, attack. In consequence, O'Neill's analysis, for example, has nothing to say, beyond condemnation, to journalism as it actually exists and functions in the culture.

Milton assumed that the Press enabled expressions of opinion which were essential to the creation of a market place of ideas, and that such a market was fundamental to civil society: 'For now the time seems come, wherein Moses the great prophet may sit in Heaven rejoicing to see that memorable and glorious wish of his fulfilled, when not only our seventy elders, but all the Lord's people are become prophets' (Milton, 1644). This vision preceded the establishment of the Press's market stall as a source of truth-telling information. The expectation that all the products on that stall would be stamped 'truthful' only came to be suggested in the eighteenth century and was never guaranteed except to an extent by legal action; and even that required not proof of truth directly but of damage first. Truthfulness was a defence to a charge or claim that damage had, or might have, occurred.

Entertainment, impure perhaps, also set up stall in this market place, right next to the one selling information. By the nineteenth century the goods on both were inextricably jumbled. James Gordon Bennett, founder of the cheap penny paper the *New York Herald*, pioneered many innovations including the modern interview and brought a new attention to non-political coverage in the 1830s. At his death in 1872, a rival paper, the *New York Tribune*, wrote:

> It was as a collector of news that Bennett shone conspicuous. Editorially he was cynical, inconsistent, reckless, and easily influenced by others' opinions, and by his own prejudices. But he had an unerring judgement of the pecuniary value of news. He knew how to pick out of the events of the day the subjects which engrossed the interest of the greatest number of people, and to give them about that subject all they could read. (Knowlton and Parsons, 1995: 177)

James Gordon Bennett, and the many who created the popular Press on both sides of the Atlantic, including those who ran the unlicensed radical Press of early nineteenth-century Britain, sold both entertainment and information, at least to a degree. They did so knowing they were in defiance of some idealistic assumption about the purity of information, but the market endorsed their approach. Again, I do not sanction this but simply point out that to ignore this historical reality or to suggest that mixed functions are in some way aberrant is of limited value to any grounded discussion of what ethical media behaviour might be. I am not hereby downplaying the importance of truth-telling to journalism; I am only suggesting that there always have been other 'impure' factors at play in the journalistic enterprise, and for these functions truth-telling is not so central. This impacts on the simple vision in the 'fakery' scandal of the documentarist as truth teller.

The reality of mixed functions therefore impacts directly on the truth-telling requirement in journalism. Consider, for example, the 1947 Hutchins Commission on the Freedom of the Press, established in the USA by Henry Luce, the founder of *Time* magazine. The Commission acknowledged the Miltonian position when it added to the responsibility of the Press (that it provide 'a truthful, comprehensive, and intelligent account of the day's events in a context which gives them meaning') the additional charge that it also create: 'A forum for the exchange of comment and criticism' (Knowlton and Parsons, 1995: 218–22). This distinguished group of non-journalists, in a commendable but disabling display of independence from their funder, then proceeded to ignore the possible conflict between these roles – truth-teller, entertainer and 'common-carrier' of opinion – and the very different ethical standards which each might require.

Instead the Commission went much further. It not only insisted on one standard for truth, it also did so in the particular context of civic responsibility. Hutchins postulated that the Press 'must be accountable to society for meeting the public need and for maintaining the rights of citizens and the almost forgotten rights of speakers who have no Press' (Merrill, Gade and Blevens, 2000). From this position grew the Cold War articulation of a theory of the Press as a socially responsible civic engine as opposed to other libertarian, authoritarian or communist (Soviet) legitimations (Siebert, Peterson and Schramm, 1956). This concept of social responsibility came in the 1970s, in many parts of the Third World, to underpin a fettered Press in the name of development.

The latest proponents of a responsible Press in the West were arguing in the United States in the late 1990s for what they called 'Public' or 'Civic Journalism'. This was an outcrop of the Hutchins tradition, now reinforced by the commutarian ideals of political thinkers like Amitai Etzoni. It found most vigorous expression in the work of Jay Rosen, a one-time reporter who became director of the Project on Public Life and the Press at New York University. He summarised what had become a veritable crusade for Civic Journalism thus: 'In a word, public journalists want public life to work' (Hoyt, 1995: 28). This means, in effect, journalists must engage with the communities in which they live; abandon objectivity, at least in the sense of disengagement; and no longer privilege truth, at least in the sense of self-censoring stories in the name of social responsibility if publication would prove divisive or have negative effects on the community in other ways.

These reasonable calls for a responsible, community-minded Press, like the sensible assumption that journalism and truth-telling are coterminous, also turn out upon examination to be unexpectedly fraught. For example, the civic journalists' claim on a measure of engagement ignores the vexed nature of their assumption that journalism is disengaged in the first place. That it should be so is certainly the traditional mainstream claim – professionally, objectivity is not considered to be a (pretty unobtainable) goal but an achieved daily reality. Moreover, objectivity is held to be easily separable from opinion. The conventions of editorial, features and letters to the editor pages being distinct from news pages allowed for the divide to be maintained in the professional mind and be easily understood by readers; or in the case of broadcasting (as one senior BBC executive always used to put it), 'facts in the commentary, opinions in the synch'.

For all the wide acceptance of these assumptions, radical critics have long disputed them claiming, at a minimum, that the line between objectivity and opinion is very permeable. The truth and the use of facts are not unknown to the editorial writer or the columnist and, as we have seen, the reporters' vocabulary can slip easily away from unemotional scientific 'objectivity' not least because 'entertainment' demands that it does. Factual commentary colours opinionated synch, and the latter also taints the former. More than this, for such critics the very claim of 'objectivity' is itself ideologically charged. However defined, they would hold it to be essentially unobtainable, an abstract notion serving only to disguise the hegemonic thrust of the news (Glasgow Media Group, 1976).

This radical rebuttal of easy professional claims on objectivity and the like also highlights the ideology of language itself; that, linguistically, one person's 'assassin' is always another person's 'freedom fighter'. As Liebling long ago pointed out, opinion permeates words and clichéd journalistic formulations: 'The employer, in strike stories, always "offers", and the union "demands". A publisher, for example, never "demands" that the union men agree to work for a four-bit raise; the union never "offers" to accept more' (Liebling, 1964: 92).

There is profound ideological force in every aspect of language, not just in vocabulary. Compare the use of active and passive, for example: 'RAID PC SHOT BOY FROM 9 INCHES', with, 'A BOY of five was shot through heart by a police marksman from a range of just NINE INCHES, a court heard yesterday' (Fowler, 1991: 72). And so on. The inescapable and debatable connotations of language could easily reduce the truly serious 'objective' 'truthful' journalist to silence. Civic journalists' call for engagement compounds these inevitabilities.

While sharing received opinion about 'objectivity', civic journalists and their predecessors at the Hutchins Commission were prepared to challenge one fundamental mainstream assumption – the primacy of free expression. They were not concerned that rationing truth might fetter freedom. Hutchins construed Press freedom as 'a positive freedom *for* making its contribution to the maintenance of a free society' rather than 'a negative freedom *from* "external compulsions"' (Merrill, Gade and Blevens, 2000). The idea was that a free Press in the West could only be countenanced in the changed circumstances of an age of mass communications if it adopted social responsibility as its *raison d'être* and would have to be curtailed if it refused to do this: '[The Press] must know that its faults and errors have ceased to be public vagaries and have become public dangers. Freedom of the Press for the coming period can only continue as accountable freedom' (Merrill, Gade and Blevens, 2000). 'Social responsibility' was, in effect, warning journalism that it needed to clean up its act or face increased state control. Hutchins was serving journalism its first drink in the Last Chance Saloon. More is therefore at stake here than just pleas for good journalistic behaviour, a moral lead in eschewing sensation or a greater sensitivity to privacy. Civic journalists now stress the social dangers of putting free expression first and dismiss the right to do so as an eighteenth-century Enlightenment excess, irrelevant to the modern world of mass communication systems.

This is alarming to First Amendment supporters. For Merrill, if social responsibility is to mean anything beyond pious exhortation, then such a freedom would need be reinforced with sanctions and meaningful controls, not arising from the actions of union or professional guild, could only be imposed by government. In the name of regulation it is already the case that:

> Politicians mobilized arguments of the public interest and their elected, representative status to defend their interests against what they see, or at least represent as, the increasingly invasive and irresponsible media – a view famously summed up by Balfour's accusation that the press exercises the prerogative of the harlot down the ages, 'freedom without responsibility'. (Garnham, 2000: 165)

The bottom line is that the free speech right exactly requires that it be without responsibility. The argument here is quite clear: either one believes that this right is paramount, that all other rights depend on it in some way and that therefore it should only be very carefully and concretely limited in the interest of preventing 'harm', or one does not and argues that any right, including this one, ought to be matched with responsibilities which, in this case, could well go beyond the law into regulation.

It is plain that whether one thinks it justified or not, this later view, as Merrill has tirelessly argued over a quarter of a century or more, would seriously compromise the freedom of the Press. In 1974 he warned against the Siebert, Peterson and Schramm articulation of the Hutchins position:

> This 'theory' of social responsibility has a good ring to it and has an undeniable attraction for many ... Nobody would deny that the Press, in one sense, would be more 'responsible' if some type of government supervision came about; indeed, reporters could be kept from nosing about in 'critical areas' during 'critical' times. The amount of sensational material could be controlled in the Press, or eliminated altogether. Government activities could always be supported and public policy pushed on all occasions. The Press could be more 'educational' ... Many persons will object to this line of analysis and will say that 'social responsibility' of the Press of a nation does not necessarily imply government control. I contend that ultimately it does, since if left to be defined by various publishers or journalistic groups the term is quite relative and nebulous. (Knowlton and Parson, 1995: 227–8)

In 2000 (with Peter Gade and Frederick Blevens), Merrill was still issuing the same warning against the 'mom 'n' apple pie' seductions of public journalism, rehearsing a panoply of objections against what he see less as a sensible move from freedom to responsibility and more as the substitution of 'community boosterism' for journalism (Merrill, Gade and Blevens, 2000).

There is another problem revealed by the Hutchins Commission's juxtapositioning 'comprehensive' and 'truthful' in their definition of journalism's first duty. We are in the nature of the case only talking about the truth that 'fits' the available news outlet. Even the civic journalists acknowledge this but make incompleteness a virtue because the flood of information in the modern world is deemed to be so overwhelming that it needs to be stemmed in the name of the public good. Radical critics have argued that incompleteness is inevitable and this was an insurmountable deficiency undercutting any meaningful sense of journalistic 'objectivity' – if not as 'unemotional' reporting, then certainly in the sense of 'scientific thoroughness'. Objectivity could only, at best, be a goal. The Hutchins basic vision of completeness, however laudable, is therefore unobtainable practically unless modified; and modification to, say, 'reasonable' or 'practicable completeness' becomes so partial and subjective of itself as to be of little use as a standard, however worthy as a goal. Nor can the civic journalist defend against the ethical difficulty this partiality creates by claiming some unavoidable technicist necessity requires leaving things out.

Philosophers, blind to Press history and, as we have seen, ready to blame all-comers for 'execrable standards', do no better than Hutchins and the civic journalists. The ethicists among them are often quick to insist on the importation of general ethics to support truth-telling; but, in my view, even the most basic of principles such as 'primum non nocere' ('first do not harm', the heart of the duty to 'love one's neighbour as one's self') also needs a gloss in many journalistic circumstances.

For example, if it were indeed true that during the Mozambique flood of the first winter of the millennium there was a paucity of rescue helicopters, what was the world's Press doing commandeering them to cover the story? Yet the ethical indefensible *can* be justified. As one journalist claimed on that occasion: 'It is true that journalists get in the way; but without us, no one [e.g. aid agencies] would be here' (Duval Smith, 2000: 23). 'Harm' can be committed for the sake of a greater good, without prejudice as to whether or not this was the case in this instance. The principle is certainly true especially if we understand 'harm', outside of life-and-death situations, to encompass less than actionable damage – causing distress or embarrassment, say – and that by distressing or embarrassing one subject the journalist exposes a situation that the public ought to know. Such everyday 'harm' is justified by this even if that public knowledge has no discernible effects or outcomes.

Philosopher Andrew Belsey states baldly that 'media ethics should borrow from medical ethics and insist on consent being informed' (Belsey, 1992: 89); but what are these ethics? Their most extensive codification is in the Nuremberg Protocols on the use of human subjects in scientific experiments, a response to horrific Nazi experimentation in the concentration camps. These outline what fully informed consent entails:

> The voluntary consent of the human subject is absolutely essential. This means that the person involved should have legal capacity to give consent; should be so situated as to be able to exercise the free power of choice, without the intervention of any element of force, fraud, deceit, duress, over-reaching, or other ulterior form of constraint or coercion; and should have sufficient knowledge and comprehension of the elements of the subject matter involved as to enable him to make an understanding and enlightened decision. This latter element requires that before acceptance of an affirmative decision by the experimental subject there should be made known to him the nature, duration and purpose of the experiment; the method and means by which it is to be conducted; all inconveniences and hazards reasonably to be expected; and the effects upon his health or person which may possibly come from his participation in the experiment. (Reynolds, 1982: 143)

Again, this is more than reasonable, but when applied to the actual business of journalism it can have a very chilling effect. Indeed, for much reporting, and for the majority of investigative situations, the importation of such protocols would kill the story and destroy the Press's ability to function effectively. The framers of the Nuremberg Protocols can be forgiven for not addressing this media problem but it does not seem to have occurred to the Stirling Media Research Institute either. The *Consenting Adults* report defines consent as 'Permission based on a participant's knowledge and understanding of (a) a programme's format, aims and objectives and (b) how their contribution will be used and (c) the potential consequences for them and third parties' (Stirling Media Research Institute 2000: 7). It simply 'argues that every contributor should be required to give their informed consent to their participation in a programme' (2000: 7). As we shall see in the next chapter in connection with the documentary, such a demand ignores the reality of participants' understanding, as well as most investigative requirements, never mind the idea of free expression (2000: 57–70).

More than that, the proposal does not question the norm of asking for consent at the time of filming. Some suggest that this produces not so much 'informed' as 'prior' consent in that 'Even when formal consent was obtained immediately or shortly after the filming took place it was granted before the subject had an opportunity to view the complete film and assess its effects on himself' (Anderson and Benson, 1991: 133). Not only does the Stirling proposal apparently ignore situations where those involved forfeit their right to grant consent because of their criminality or misfeasance, it also fails to address the very real problems of treating prior consent as informed consent – unless it is proposing that, at a minimum, '(c)' entails a crash course in the difficulties of celebrity and the dangers of notoriety. A true understanding of these factors is as likely to be alien to the media producers' personal experience as it is to their participants' comprehension. Be all that as it may. The proposal on its face seems to be incompatible with the Human Rights Act (12.4) and it therefore almost certainly moot.

The Stirling proposal and the Nuremberg Protocols would be unacceptable in free speech terms, as Belsey of course understands. So, when contemplating justified deception in order to investigate the corrupt, for example, he is reduced to unhelpful uncertainty: 'Perhaps the answer is that deception is acceptable so long as it does not become dishonesty. But the ethical line is difficult to draw.'

It certainly is, possibly because we are finding that, in a free society, we need more from journalists than just truth-telling and this creates an unbridgeable chasm between ethical systems and journalism as an institution. Merrill has come to believe that journalism is inevitably 'a Machiavellian enterprise'.[3] (Machiavelli, had he experienced developed journalism, would presumably agree.) The obstacles to a straightforward application of ethical principles thrown up by the demands of free expression and the realities of news pro- duction, the dangers (as it were) of 'responsibility' and 'objectivity' (as great as those of irresponsibility and bias) turn even the most reasonable of ethical expectations into contentious issues. This does not mean that unsystematic ethics have nothing to offer individual journalists. On the contrary a relativist, situationist ethic has much to say as guidance for the individual journalist. This was Merrill's view in the 1980s:

> 'What I recommend is an individual and rational ethics, one that will centre moral judgement and responsibility on a personal level, that will help sustain ... authenticity and integrity, and that will combine a respect for tried and tested moral principles with a rational flexibility' (Merrill, 1987: 214).

Despite this tentativeness, Merrill was not in favour of bolstering his advice with a full-scale code of ethical practice of the SPJ type; although, teaching young reporters not to accept free gifts or private tip-offs, maintaining inde- pendence and sources as privileged and not stealing the words of others is the main business of American university journalism ethics courses. Attention is also paid to the issues of taste, invasion of privacy and the rest. Because of this and (more) the First Amendment, American journalism resists the imposition of a Press council, even one owned and operated, as is the British, by the industry itself.[4] Merrill's hostility to professional codes is supported by the fact that the one judgment of the European Court in the late twentieth century that ran counter to the flow of decisions supporting Press freedom turned on the judges accepting a failure to meet the standards of a journalist code (*Prager and Oberschlick*, 1995). In a free society, as Belsey said: 'the ethical line is difficult to draw.'

And it is even harder to do so for documentarists.

5.3 Documentarists' Ethics

Journalism and documentary have much in common because of their shared claim on the real. The imposition of ethical systems is just as hard in both instances because documentary too demands freedom of speech and thereby finds itself facing the same conflict between expression and perhaps contradictory constraining ethical requirements. The documentarist, like the journalist, is also usually not entirely a free agent but rather a cultural worker doing the bidding, at least in some measure, of management, commissioning editor, sponsor or funder. Like journalists, documentarists too are in the entertainment business, if only in their need to gain and hold the attention of their audiences. Documentaries, like journalism, have an elevated need to tell the truth if they are to maintain their integrity; but, far more than journalism, they are also vehicles for personal self-expression. Truth-telling in the restrictive sense the current British regulators demand is informed by journalism and by the journalistic claims of Direct Cinema. It is at odds with the broader, 'creative' practices of other forms of documentary.

Despite this caveat, much of the professional journalism codes are easily applicable to documentary as is the 'social responsibility' theory of the Press. Mainstream documentary's underlying Griersonian objective of public education and his vision of film as a tool to ameliorate social conditions is echoed here. Indeed, it could be suggested that Grierson's use of film as an educative force was in some sense a precursor to civic journalism. (I might add that the tendency of the Griersonian documentary to 'run away from social meaning' could be seen as a warning of the pitfalls civic journalism faces (Winston, 1995: 35–9).) There is a shared rhetoric of a public right to know.

On the other hand, documentarists also differ from journalists in many ways. The richness of documentary as a source of moral pitfalls and dilemmas lies exactly in the ethical gap that lies between journalism and documentary. For example, documentarists bear a greater burden than do journalists because their work is less ephemeral. Newspaper 'morgues' certainly preserve cuttings, as do computer-based data banks with even greater ease and accessibility; and initial errors are notoriously difficult to remove. But the news is a daily business whereas documentaries are archived, in so far as the technology allows, in perpetuity. Documentaries, if only in university lecture theatres, are very long lived and some are canonised to have a life even outside the academy. Robert Flaherty's Irish film *Man of Aran* (1934) is regularly screened on the island during the tourist season although local opinion is divided about the film, some finding in it a source of pride, others humiliation because of the picture it paints of their forebears' grinding poverty. George Stoney, whose note on the original film and his own updating of it (*Man of Aran: How the myth was made* (1978)) is provocatively entitled 'Must a filmmaker leave his mark?', believes that, on balance, the Flaherty film might well have contributed positively to maintaining a population on Aran; the near-by Blaskets are now deserted.

In Wiseman's Direct Cinema classic *Hospital* (1968), a young mid-Westerner is given Ipecac in a New York public hospital to clear his stomach after taking a drug in Central Park and is filmed, quite comically, retching for many minutes. He is now, one trusts, a respectable citizen in his fifties, but this image of him is still in circulation. This is the more typical situation since films seldom affect whole communities, as is the case with *Man of Aran*. It is the persistent image of the individual caught in a moment of weakness or deviancy that raises this ethical difficulty. For example, one of the inmates in Wiseman's *Titticut Follies*, rehabilitated and released, has given evidence in court that his appearance in the film cost him work. He once had to sit through a screening in a class he was taking at the University of Massachusetts (Benson and Anderson, 1989: 112–13). This understanding of film's longevity lies behind the Maori insistence on controlling in perpetuity images of Maori life held in the New Zealand film archive.

There is also a real distinction between documentarists and journalists in their relationship with their subjects. Journalistic detachment, outside of the personalised feature or column, is so ingrained a requirement that when a journalist reveals a relationship arising from a connection made in the course of reporting, it is considered morally vexed for that reason alone. This even colours the ethics of a journalist effecting the rescue of a orphan from a war zone. Documentarists are different not just because they are empowered as mediating artists supposedly more distant from their subjects. The involvement of documentarist and participant post-transmission or release has never figured much in discussions about documentary, whether scholarly or professional. American documentarist Thomas Shachtman was one of the few who has ever come to mention the issue. Of one participant, a young girl, he asks: 'Would I be her friend after it was all over? My answer was and is, yes. Do I see her often? No. I am not in her life to stay and I know it' (Shachtman, 1977: 66). In his autobiography Joris Ivens, arguably one of documentary's major pioneers, only talks in terms of human warmth and individualism of the farm family he met in St Claresville, Ohio and filmed for *Power and the Land* (1940) (Ivens, 1969) – possibly, according to his biographer, because he saw in them a domestic ideal which he could never attain (Schoots, 2000: 153–4). Otherwise, Ivens's account of all the others who had participated in his films lacks similar depth.

Confusingly, though, documentarists can often be closer to those helping them than are journalists because they film members of their personal circle. In journalism, involving relatives is more or less restricted to columnists but from the 1970s on it became an anglophone documentary commonplace. The coming of the 'Me Generation' in the US and the simultaneous arrival of Direct Cinema equipment encouraged a vogue for personal autobiographical films involving more than usually complex relationships between the film-maker and others appearing in the documentary. Films about mother and grandmother, brother, girlfriends appeared (Winston, 1995: 202–203). Relatives with major health difficulties started to look like godsends for the documentarist.

For example, Ira Wohl's *Best Boy* (1979) deals with the specific issue of how his family would cope with Philly, his mentally handicapped cousin, after Philly's elderly parents died. We can note that the usefulness of the film to Philly was probably less (since the intervention in his life could have happened anyway off-camera) than it was to Ira who won that year's documentary Oscar (Katz and Katz, 1988: 123–4; 129–30). Ethically, such a family connection can be fraught with exploitative possibilities making the relative with a camera much more powerful than any stranger with a camera. John Katz and Judith Milstein Katz argue that in such situations family obligations can upset the balance of power between documentarist and participant even more than the confusions and obfuscations that arise between strangers – how can you say no to your son or grand-daughter or cousin? It is also the case that the possibility of exploitation by the film-maker is increased; and, anyway, these personal films tended to be at the very least more beneficial to the film-maker in advancing a career than they are for the rest of the family. Film affects not only the (presumably) continued relationship of film-maker and subject after the film is completed and exhibited; it also exposes the relationship for as long as the film rests in the archive.

For documentaries in general, 'objectivity' in any of its many meanings applies even less certainly than it does in journalism (where, anyway, it causes more difficulties than are generally acknowledged in professional discourse). Nor is the automatic assumption in journalism that the public have a right to know (another somewhat more problematic concept than it first seems) always pertinent since documentaries do not necessarily have to be journalistic and cannot therefore always lay claim to it. Documentaries *can* be the equivalent of journalistic features but, despite contemporary received opinion, they can also approximate to opinion pieces, editorials, columns, *belles-lettres* essays, polemics, agitprop, autobiography, poetry.

Most of all, it is clear that all the problems associated with 'truth', 'objectivity' and 'responsibility' are exacerbated by documentary's demand that it be allowed to treat actuality creatively. For example, the more personalised, opinionated or poetic 'treatment' involved in documentary removes any need for 'completeness' in the sense the Hutchins Commission understood it for journalists.

The twin pressures of representing actuality and doing it creatively means that ethical systems cannot any more easily pertain to the documentary than they do to journalism. Remember that we have inherited an amoral vision of the artist as a being apart from the norms of society (Williams, 1983: 36). As Ruskin wrote in advice to the young painter: 'Does a man die at your feet, your business is not to help him, but to note the colour of his lips' (Williams, 1983: 149). The artist has not only to note the colour but implicitly in doing so also has the right to mediate its representation creatively. This suggests a different, amoral position where the demand for objectivity and truthfulness becomes more secondary than it is in journalism.

Chapter Six
Ethics

Documentary is not fiction, but neither is it journalism exactly, for all that it was widely perceived as being so at the end of the millennium. Although its claim on 'actuality' requires that it behave ethically, its unjournalistic parallel desire to be allowed to be 'creative' permits a measure of artistic 'amorality'. In short, the application of even journalistic ethics (themselves complex) to documentary is not straightforward.

The ethical sensitivities of the documentarist have been much eroded because of this constant implicit claim on artistic licence. However, this does not sanction the passing-off of material as, in some way, a privileged image of reality when it is knowingly a fiction. The issues of such 'actual' or 'pure' (as it were) fakery is morally uninteresting. It cannot be made interesting by erecting a need for truth-telling, strictly construing what that is and protecting the audience when lying has no consequences. It is an open and shut case and it is also, even today, quite rare. What are common and increasingly vexed are the everyday subterfuges inevitably used because in the very nature of the case the camera cannot simply deliver an unmediated reproduction of the truth. Production means mediation.

The central question for documentary ethics is how much mediation is ethical? Our ability to answer this question is currently much hampered. First, in effect losing a distinct idea of how documentary differs from other factual programming in general and news in particular destroys the basis upon which a distinct documentary ethic can be made to rest. Second, we have a heightened sense of audience protection – the very fact of content regulation assumes *caveat emptor* is not enough. At the same time we have confused media responsibilities to the audience with the ethical duties owed participants as if the outcomes of taking part were the same as spectating. Finally, the concept of 'fakery' has been so broadly construed that, in its naïveté, it echoes the old error – 'the camera cannot lie'.

6.1 Sincere and Justified Reconstruction
Not only the law but also photographers themselves had to 'come to grips with'

the ethics of the new technology in the nineteenth century. Little was said at the outset about the dangers of manipulating the camera to distort reality and nothing much about the morality of so doing. The expectation was not only that the camera would not lie but that it *could not,* so the silence was understandable. Scientific enthusiasm fed what was to became a common misconception, one that was endlessly exploited by photographers.

One hundred and fifty-five years after Francis Arago in Chamber of Deputies and Joseph Louis Gay-Lussac in the French House of Peers successfully argued that the French nation should acquire the Daguerre patents for the world, Labour member Andrew Bennett rose in the House of Commons to request 'that leave be given to bring in a bill to require news media to prepare a code of practice to cover the principles by which pictures may be edited, altered and changed using computer techniques' (Hansard, 1994: 951). Bennett's proposal signals how little more sophisticated we are today than we were at the time of photography's birth: 'Most people are aware of the old adage "the camera never lies". It seems to me that many people still believe it. ... Most people believe pictures, particularly those accompanied by a well-respected voice on the television.' Bennett, in effect, claimed that we had not made much progress since Arthur Conan Doyle insisted on the veracity of the Cottingley photos of fairies.

The scientific heritage, now bolstered by new levels of technology, continues to swamp any awareness of the potential for manipulation. Anyway, why would we have moved on? For most people, the actual experience of snapshots, home movies and camcorders is that images do indeed accurately reflect the world. The everyday camera does not lie and this is the source of the expectation that the documentary will not lie either. But the truth of the amateur camera depends on the knowledge of how accurately the image reflects a remembered reality or can be so thoroughly contextualised by the viewer that all partialities and distortions are corrected for. Public images can seldom hope to match this but the experience of amateur image masks this difference. The limitations of the relationship that any photographic image has to the reality it reflects are beyond everyday experience. The possibility that that relationship, its faults already disguised, can be further distorted is understood only on an abstract level. Manipulation, distortion and fakery have thus far required professionals (although the home computer is well on its way to changing that).

The professionals have always been at hand. For example, within forty-eight hours of the end of the Battle of Gettysburg, Timothy O'Sullivan and Andrew Gardner were on the field making images of the aftermath for their *Photographic Sketch Book of the War.* Plate 41, entitled *Home of a Rebel Sharpshooter,* shows a Confederate corpse sprawled in a trench. Plate 40, again of a dead soldier, is called *A Sharpshooter's Last Sleep* (Collins, 1985: fig. 12). This body is not so obviously a member of the Confederate Army. In fact, it is quite hard to tell which side he was on but Gardner's published caption suggests he was a Union man. Both corpses are in a similar attitude lying in the lower third of the frame but the terrain is different. The 'Rebel' is in a trench while the other lies on more open ground. The 'Rebel's' rifle is propped between his legs against the rocky side of the trench whereas in the other image the rifle lies at the man's head. Experts have identified the spots as being about forty yards apart. Others have identified the corpse as being identical in both shots. The only explanation is that Gardner was lugging a body around with him, re-costuming it as he went and even, some suggest, turning the head despite rigor mortis (Fulton, 1988: 23–8).[1]

In a very rare nineteenth-century public row, Doctor Barnardo's Homes were unsuccessfully sued by an outraged Baptist clergyman for a libel that was, in effect, a public fraud. From 1874 Barnardo used 'before' and 'after' shots of street urchins in advertisements soliciting support for his charity. He sold the images in packs of twenty for 5/- or single cards for 6d. The uproar occurred in 1877 when the minister discovered that the shots were taken on the same day. Although it was accepted that this was a misrepresentation, there was clearly no damage to anybody. Any hint of public fraud collapsed in the face of Barnardo's good intentions (Collins, 1985: 24–5). By the time Barnardo died in 1905, the orphanages had made over 55,000 images.

The perfect composition of the image of four marines raising the Stars and Stripes on Mt Suribachi, Iwo Jima in 1945 caused the editors of *Life* pause. The photographer, Joe Rosenthal, always claimed it was an authentic picture of an unmediated event but it is generally agreed that the flag in the shot was a replacement for the one initially raised. The issue is: Who arranged for the replacement? The suggestion is that the larger flag was prepared for hoisting at Rosenthal's instigation and the implication is that this vitiates the authenticity of the image – despite the fact that the photograph, without question, shows four 'real' marines (three of whom were to die in the battle then raging) with a 'real' flag on the actual island of Iwo Jima. These doubts did not prevent the photographer winning a Pulitzer Prize in 1945 or the photograph from being used for a war bond poster, appearing on a 3c stamp and becoming the basis of a statue placed outside the Arlington National Cemetery in Washington. Manipulated or not, the image has been described as a record of 'the soul of a nation' (Fulton, 1988: 160–61).

In 1950, *Life* published a rather different 'soul of a nation' image. The magazine commissioned Robert Doisneau to photograph the romantic French, specifically engaging in such activities as kissing on the street. *The Kiss* is the perfect image of young Parisians in love. A debonair man, tieless, tousled hair, scarf casually tucked into his jacket, has his arm round a lithe young woman.

She leans back into the embrace as he kisses her oblivious of the people around. One of these, a gaunt-faced 'Frenchman' with beret, coat, tie and pullover, appears to be staring past the couple in studied disapproval. In fact, Doisneau treated the assignment as a photo/love-story shot and cast an actor, Jacques Carteaud, and his girlfriend, Françoise Bournet, as the couple. The stereotypical Frenchman in the beret behind them has been identified as the late Jack Costello, a Dublin auctioneer, on a motorbike pilgrimage to Rome, a bit lost in Paris looking for his travelling companion (Lennon, 1993).

There has never been a public scandal about the lead photograph of a famous W. Eugene Smith *Life* photo-essay on Albert Schweitzer but, again, it can be questioned. Smith had complained about the quality of the photo labs prints that *Life* photographers usually put up with. He had demonstrated his prints were superior and the editors therefore allowed him the privilege of avoiding the labs. We can note that he routinely adjusted his images at this stage, always in line with accepted professional practice (Willumson, 1992: 248–50). Manipulations included correcting underexposure in portions of the negative and bleaching to achieve high-contrast prints that would reproduce well on the press. This did not offend against *Life*'s policy at this time, the 1950s, although further manipulations other than cropping were not permitted.

Toilers, captioned 'Schweitzer and a carpenter watch hospital building', shows the doctor, in white shirt and pith helmet, standing before an unfinished structure. Behind him, on the structure, sits a African. Both are looking out of the frame towards something that seems to be causing them concern. They both looked worried. Silhouetted against Schweitzer's shirt is the handle of a saw and a gesturing hand (Anon., 1954: 161). This is actually a composite, a real superimposition. The arm and saw-handle are from another shot. The editors of *Life*, who had forbidden such practices, never knew. The deception (if it can be so called) was discovered, over thirty years later, by Glenn Willumson going through Eugene Smith's negatives (Willumson, 1992: 211–13).

Eugene Smith was working in a tradition of extensive manipulation. For nearly half a century to 1900, newspaper and magazines had used photographs as reference material for engraving because they could not be directly reproduced. Even after half-tone and photogravure first enabled direct reproduction, the low status of photographs as accurate evidence of the news persisted. For example, in 1926, the *New York Daily Graphic* circumvented a judge's ban on courtroom photography by superimposing head shots of the jurors on a specially-taken shot of its own reporters. Circulation jumped 100,000 and the paper composited so often that 'composographs' became a term of art (Anon., 1950: 95).

Despite all this, it would be as foolish now to doubt every image in the archive as it was, previously, naïve to believe them. For instance, it has also been suggested that Robert Capa staged his *Death in Spain* (aka *Death of Loyalist Soldier*), the famous photograph of a Spanish loyalist militiaman at the moment of death as he runs down a slope, his rifle flung wide in his right hand. The lack of uniform and the curiously ornate leather cartridge belt have been questioned. And how come, if this is the moment of death, the rifle is still being gripped? It was finally established in 1996, however, that this is indeed the last moment of loyalist militiaman and member of the anarchist trade union's youth movement, Frederico Borell Garcia from Alcoy at the Battle of Cerro Muriano in defence of Cordoba seven weeks into the war, on 5 September 1936 (*Observer*, 1996).

There was a significant difference between the popular view of photography ('the camera cannot lie') and professional journalistic use of photographs as, initially, merely a guide for engravers and subsequently a basis for dark-room manipulations of all kinds. It is not surprising that this willingness of the professional to intervene in the reality before the lens was transferred from photography to cinematography wholesale. In the first years of the cinema, 'reconstructions' of major events from battles in the Spanish American War and the Boxer Rebellion to whole prize fights were commonplace. They were almost completely without the legitimacy of prior witness. That is to say, they were not reconstructions of what the film-maker had witnessed during the research phase. Instead the attempt to secure their authenticity was grounded only in the journalistic accounts used as the basis for their scenarios. The earliest film-makers were also not above simply relabelling films. The same single-shot film, *The Sea at Brighton*, in a British film catalogue of the day becomes *The Sea at Zeebrugge* in a Belgian one.

Two decades later, Allakariallak ('Nanook') was building Flaherty an open-sided, enlarged half-igloo to facilitate filming the pioneering documentary *Nanook* and Grierson had a trawler cabin constructed on the dock-side to obtain interior shots for *Drifters*. Dogfish filmed at a biological station stood in for the unfilmable shoals of herring. The subterfuge of the dogfish, like the naked fictions of many early newsfilms, was deemed not to be acceptable in the long run; but reconstructions of prior witnessed events were. The use of the shot/counter-shot and continuity norms of the Hollywood fiction film had always been a mark of documentary's 'creative treatment of actuality'. These and the limitations of film sensitivity, lighting instruments and, especially, synch equipment, all designed for studio use, made reconstruction so inevitably a part of documentary that it had to be built into any new working definition. By 1948, as we have seen, this meant 'sincere and justified reconstruction' was as good as 'factual shooting'.

The interior Royal Mail sorting carriage built on the sound stage at Beaconsfield Studios for *Nightmail* (1936) is a typical example of 'sincere and

justifiable reconstruction' in the documentary as is Joris Ivens's use of two miners in *Misère au Borinage* (1934) dressed in hired police costumes acting out an
incident that had occurred during the strike (Winston, 1999b: 160–62).
According to Albert Speer, Riefenstahl necessarily and sincerely got Rudolph
Hess in close-up to repeat without an audience his emotional Nuremberg ora-
tion in Berlin for *Triumph des Willens* (1934) when the original footage turned
out to be unusable (Winston, 1995: 120–21). British film director Humphrey
Jennings, not the Luftwaffe, burned St Katherine's Dock in 1942 for *Fires Were
Started* providing the archive with some of its best 'actual' images of the London
Blitz (Winston 1999a: 32). As Allakariallak told Flaherty: 'The *aggie* [film] will
come first' (Ruby, 1980: 66). It always did – and does.

6.2 The 'Consent Defence'

It is in this soil that the documentary tradition grew. Ethics were never a fer-
tiliser:

> 'Being film people, we'd take advantage. We used to go round to sweet vicars
> living in a twenty-room house and with a congregation of ten, mostly old
> women. And I'd say, "What a beautiful house and beautiful church. May I
> photograph?" Of course, I was showing that he was living in this enormous
> house and having ten parishioners' (Sussex, 1975: 89).

Harry Watt's techniques in the 1930s are by no means unknown today; and
only the foolhardy would claim vicars, and everybody else, are now so media-
savvy as to no longer fall for such casual subterfuge. If nothing else, much of
the 'fakery' scandal suggests – screams – an overall undiminished public ignorance of documentary film's everyday processes. There is still abundant
opportunity for unethical behaviour.

This is not to deny that there is also, without question, a rising media awareness in our societies but, rather, to suggest that it has obvious common-sense
limitations. People do not necessarily know how to behave in unfamiliar situations and making documentaries remains outside common experience. As the
BSC Code, somewhat less clichéd than usual and surely this time right, puts it:
'Many potential contributors will be unfamiliar with broadcasting and therefore may not share assumptions about programme making which broadcasters
regard as obvious' (BSC (Fairness and Privacy), June 1998: 3). Hence the Stirling Media Institute's extreme bias in favour of restricting media power over all
participants. After all, dealing with the media can vex even the most sophisticated; which is why there is a proliferation of business executive media-savvy
courses whose existence speaks to a problem of understanding and presupposes
a need for special skills not widely available elsewhere.

There is no question but that the *aggie* too often comes first with little reck-oning of ethical costs. Fast-talking one's way to winning co-operation or permission from participants is still a factor in professional competence and success. The facility to do this is now exacerbated by the need for programme-makers to deliver what they promised to increasingly sensationalised services, with ever more limited resources. Today's Harry Watt has to con the vicar suc-cessfully or see his future film-making prospects threatened – and he has to do it quickly before his meagre budget runs out. Any measure of dubious or even unethical behaviour is justified after the event by the existence of the contract signed by the participant, the release form. These agreements create, in defiance of those who take the BSC Code's view, what might be called a professional 'consent defence' – that people (except minors or the mentally incapacitated) do know what they are doing. In the 1970s, Direct Cinema film editor Ellen Hovde was already claiming: 'I think people are aware in our society of what a camera is and very aware of what they ought to be doing in front of it' (Rosen-thal, 1980: 352). Joanna Bailey, director of *Swingers, Faithful to You in My Fashion*, surely better represented the situation (even in America) when she mused in 1999: 'It's odd how many people don't appreciate that being in a docu-mentary does actually involve the possibility that Auntie Maud might see it' (Bailey, 1999: 4).

Either way, this 'consent defence' retrospectively justifies the everyday little white lies and omissions that often characterise the 'bargaining' between film-maker and participant – downplaying the levels of disruption involved in having a film-crew about, being wonderfully optimistic about how long the filming will take, not being fully forthcoming about who else is involved, for-getting to mention possible fall-out when the documentary is transmitted or released and so on.

The consent defence applies whether or not participants benefit and never have second thoughts on their role; whether or not they benefit a little but also suffer so that they come to regret co-operation; or whether or not they just suf-fer and rue the day their involvement started them on a disastrous path.

Some of those 'discovered' by documentarists do well out of the experience. In recent years Russian-speaking Jeremy, the 'star' of *Airport*, turned up fronting a live transmission from Moscow on Millennium Eve. Jane McDonald was filmed working as an on-board singer in *The Cruise* (Chris Terrill, 1998) and released her first album as a result. Wannabe singer Emily Boundy was seen working in a shopping mall while taking singing lessons and looking for a show-biz career. Before the series *Lakesiders* (David Hart, 1998) had concluded she had signed with EMI.

Positive experiences have always been possible. We would have to put Mag-gie Dirran, who played the young 'mother' in *Man of Aran*, on the plus side of the ledger. Forty and more years after Flaherty's film crew quit the island, when she was filmed again by George Stoney in 1978, she could vividly recall with obvious pleasure every last move Flaherty had asked her to make. She was not alone in finding *Man Of Aran* had a beneficial effect on her life. Barbara, the daughter of Pat Mullen, Flaherty's local 'fixer' and interpreter, married John Taylor, Grierson's brother-in-law and crew member, and became a famous character actress in Britain. Two others islanders worked in the Irish theatre. The money some earned from the film company was the deposit for a house or the stake for a business. The original *Man of Aran* is the 'historic benchmark by which most older Islanders measure their existence' (Stoney, 1978: 2).

Other participants, even some who featured in less than flattering domestic observational films, have also unambiguously benefited by pubic exposure. Pat Loud, the mother in the pioneering Direct Cinema TV series on family life, *An American Family* (Craig Gilbert, 1973), wrote a book about her experience as a television 'star' and started a New York literary agency on the back of her notoriety.

Oumarou Ganda, one of the main participants in Jean Rouch's ethnographic feature *Moi, un noir* (1957), was a casual labourer in Abidjan, Côte d'Ivoire. After his participation in the film, he became an important West African film director. Market researcher Marceline Loridan became a sound recordist after *Chronique d'un été*, in which she was a central figure and eventually married the great documentarist Joris Ivens.

Often the 'consent defence' would be notionally strengthened because the participants were uncomplaining or even enthusiastic collaborators. On *Nanook*, for example, Allakariallak had supported Flaherty and made many suggestions about the *aggie*; but such agreement between participant and film-maker (as was the case with this first documentary of all) can be nothing but a conspiracy to misrepresent. The ethical shortfall of so doing must then belong more to the film-maker than to the participant, however much they help. Allakariallak connived at his own representation as a technical naïf (which he wasn't), living in an igloo (which he didn't) and re-enacting his father's generation's experience (when he had a contemporary Inuit lifestyle) – but his agreement to all this allowed Flaherty to take advantage of him.

Contemporary sensitivities about reconstruction and misrepresentation are seemingly blind to a form of documentary where no pretence is made that the situation being documented existed separately from the filming. Ricky Leacock used to insist that, for the Direct Cinema documentary, the event always had to be more important than the filming. Rouch, for Cinéma Vérité, made filming the event central and put himself on the screen to reveal that he was doing this. The current gambit for setting up situations involves, for example, getting right-winger and hippie, or homophobe and gay to confront each other; or ex-partners to meet up with each other. These events are arranged and filmed by unseen film-makers, in distinction to Rouch's practice. Such films' value as reflections of the world (classically, documentaries' justification and purpose) is, at best, extremely limited. All moral fall-out firmly falls onto the film-maker, despite the clear consent and collaboration of the participants who, after all, are engaged in situations not remotely of their making.

The strategy has also been deployed to create voyeuristic 'documentary' series where students are given accommodation in return for being filmed constantly. With the development of the Net and minicams, 'voyeur.com' (as it might be termed) has become a new pornographic extension of this documentary technique. (We usefully learn from this advance that nubile young women living together have an unexpected propensity to play strip-poker.)[2] More respectable, if only barely, was the BBC's attempt to start a community, hand-picked by producer Jeremy Mills, in the year 2000 on an uninhabited Hebridean island, billed as a 'landmark observational documentary'. I am reminded of *Hook* (Steven Spielberg, 1991), a feature whose central premise was 'What would happen if Peter Pan grew up?' A US National Public Radio cinema critic at the time dismissed this as being about as interesting as asking 'What would happen if Moby Dick was a trout?'. Judging by the early returns from the Isle of Taransay, transmitted in January 2000, *Castaways 2000* also promised to be as interesting as a trout-quest. (A real documentary could perhaps be devoted to the tabloid Press corps sitting on the mainland waiting for disasters.) Much was made of the involvement of various academics in setting the series up but this ploy was as convincing an earnestness of seriousness as was the presence of ponderous 'experts' in German soft-porn films of the 1970s. The ethical responsibilities will come home to roost if any of the 'castaways' should be seriously damaged by their experience, however much and however obviously they consented.

Although quite rare, such transparent fundamental interventionism was not unknown in the past. *Altar of Fire*, Fritz Staal and Robert Gardner's 1975 ethnographic film of an ancient Verdic ceremony, was created with the willing co-operation of the Brahmins of Panjal, Kerala State but directly at the behest of the film-makers. The *agnicayana* fire ceremony had quite simply fallen into desuetude either in the 1950s or perhaps even in antiquity. The film gives no hint of this nor that, in effect, the Nambudiri Brahmins were working for American anthropologists who are seen on camera merely as interviewees validating the antiquity of the event (Schechner, 1981: 8).

These films all involve relationships between the film-maker and the participants that add a dimension to the normal contractual bargain. The participant does not agree to allow the film-maker to document his or her life but rather joins the film-maker to document situations of the film-maker's creation. In my view, this surely has to be more fictional than the reconstruction by film-makers of prior witnessed events created by the participants, although the former is currently accepted as 'documentary' while the latter, increasingly, is not.

The vogue for documentary autobiography further illuminated the flimsiness of the 'consent defence'. In Ira Wohl's *Best Boy*, for instance, his cousin Philly's parents consented on his behalf, so we can leave aside his own limited capacity to consent (Katz and Katz, 1988: 123–4; 129–30). Maxi Cohen's *Joe and Maxi* (1978) helped her, she claimed, to 'see' her father, Joe, but the difficulty of the 'consent defence' does not go away since Joe, for example, objected on camera to Maxi's public exercise in family therapy, not unreasonably insisting: 'I am not a document, I am a person' (Katz, 1978: 47). Even in the most benign circumstances, say in Ross McElwee's gently ironic personal account of his less than perfect relationships with the Southern women of his native region (*Sherman's March*, 1986), there is a sense that the family would just as soon the film-maker put the camera down but could not quite say so since they had a vested interest in their relative's maintaining his or her curious livelihood. (Joe thought that Maxi was a film-maker instead of having a proper job like being a secretary, but at least he thought it was a job, however improper or improbable.)

Sometimes it is the participants who seek out, and even exploit, the film-maker. Andrew Bethell, whose searingly candid multi-part study of the Royal Opera House, Covent Garden (*The House*, 1996) contributed to the downfall of its management, was approached by Blackpool's PR, a woman described by Bethell as coming 'from the "there's no such thing as bad publicity" school of PR' to make the series that became *Pleasure Beach* (1998).

There are other situations where the participant consents in dangerous circumstances while fully aware of the consequences – as when a dissident speaks out to the camera about a repressive regime in whose power the speaker will remain after the film crew departs. If the participant is fully aware of possible consequences and sees co-operation as a coherent political strategy, then the burden of the ethical dilemma has been lifted from the film-maker by the participant for his or her own ideological reasons.

As an extension of this, it is possible for a participant to be more exploitative of the film-maker than he or she is of them, and not only in political contexts. In this case the consent defence is beside the point, whatever the outcome for the participant. Apart from business and politics there can also be sex, as when a participant has an agenda that is served by sexual exhibitionism, for example. Given the current vogue for prurience, film-makers can be not only voyeurs but also aiders and abettors of all sorts of varieties of documentary 'flashing' (as it were). The phoney as participant, where the participant's agenda is to con the broadcaster into allowing an appearance, is the most extreme example of this reversal of the normal balance of power. Even when there as no presumption of misrepresentation, repeated performances by 'members of the public' can be suspect. The Stirling research noted: 'Surprisingly, 47.5 per cent of our participant interviewees had appeared in two or more television programmes. Some of the forty participants had appeared in as many as seven or eight programmes' – or so they claimed (Stirling Media Research Institute, 2000: 23).[3]

Of all these participatory modes only in those where the film-maker genuinely seeks to redefine the relationship is the ethical in-balance corrected, potentially at least, whatever the outcome for the participants. The National Film Board of Canada pioneered the exploration of this with, first, variants in the production of a number of fairly conventional observational films. One, *Things I Cannot Change* (Tanya Ballentine, 1966), rang warning bells at the Board since the family concerned was unexpectedly ostracised by the community after the film was screened for revealing the poverty of its circumstances. Many at the Board felt that a better way had to be found for giving the disadvantaged a voice.

With this problem in mind, Colin Low attempted to redefine the documentarist's role in a series of films about the island of Fogo, off Newfoundland. The community was being threatened with the loss of its fisheries, its one industry, and enforced depopulation by the provincial government in St John's. The films were exceptional in that they were designed as a means of communication for the islanders specifically to reach their government, which was otherwise deaf to their arguments, rather than as documentaries for a general audience.

The National Film Board then lent its resources to train Native America filmmakers, producing, for instance, *You Are on Indian Land* (1969), in its day a rare documentation of the tribal viewpoint. This found ready emulators among those ethnographic film-makers around the world who were increasingly sensitive to the charge that their discipline is, in Rouch's phrase, 'the eldest daughter of colonialism' (Eaton, 1979: 33). The movement among Aboriginal Australians, for example, to use media to underwrite their land claims has produced films where the ethnographer has acted as enabler rather than artist – combining Low's approach on Fogo with the logic of the Mohawk/Iroquois unit. Caroline Strachan and Alessandro Cavadini worked for and with the Borroloola people to make *Two Laws* (1981) in which the community not only documented their history but were filmed discussing how best to do it.

The next stage in Canada began when the Film Board decided to give the community the then new portapak reel-to-reel video tape-recorders and let them get on with it themselves. George Stoney, then at the Board, created a structured programme of work to explore this issue right across Canada, *Challenge for Change/Pour un société nouvelle. VTR St.-Jacques* (1969), a conventional 16mm film by Dorothy Todd Henaut and Bonnie Klein, documents a pioneering example of community access video. Although the film-makers were responsible for training the videographers/editors they otherwise wrote themselves out of the video work as professional documentarists – just as Strachan and Cavadini were to do as professional ethnographers. With the coming of the camcorder, the model of *VTR St.-Jacques* has been followed most assiduously at the BBC's Community Programmes Unit, initially under the leadership of Michael Fentiman, producing the *Video Nation* output. The BBC lent camcorders and trained participants who were then free to offer insights into the minutiae of their lives, normally by a piece to camera.

6.3 Informed Consent

The second category of participants, those who benefit a little but regret a lot, are mainly to be found among the 'stars' of domestically-based rather than work-based series. They pose a greater challenge to the ethical strength of the consent defence because the more they regret, the thinner the consent defence becomes; on the other hand, the more they benefit, the stronger the defence. Margaret Wilkins, the dominant personality in Paul Watson's early docusoap *The Family*, fully exploited her fifteen minutes of fame following the original transmission with a brief spate of celebrity appearances and a newspaper column. Nevertheless, in a follow-up film (*The Family: The After Years*, 1988), she revealed to Watson that she felt cheated and now understood that the way to deal with documentary film-makers is to 'stick out and get as much as you can get'.

The naïve vision that a television appearance means instant riches is a very good example of the limits of 'consent' but, just as importantly, Margaret's post-transmission behaviour bolsters the film-maker's 'defence'. Watson's on-camera response to Mrs Wilkins complaint was acceptably dismissive to professional ears: 'Margaret, you'd just put the licence fee up by 500 per cent.' Moreover, the aggrieved feelings Mrs Wilkins harboured were balanced, in the professional mind, by her willingness to remain in the public eye for the sake of fame, however ephemeral, and fortune, however small. Any challenge to the consent defence is negated by the participant's own behaviour and those minor sins of omission on the part of the film-maker during the bargaining process that exploit the limited understanding of the public are justified.

This is most clearly seen in another long-form study of a family produced by Watson, *Sylvania Waters* (Kate Woods and Brian Hill, 1992). Noeline Donaher, that series' 'star', was moved, by her own account, to allow her family to be used because: 'I was nearly positive I heard the amount of a quarter of a million dollars mentioned' (Donaher, 1993: 29). Having offered herself and her family,

'then the bomb dropped: Laurie [her partner] asked the burning question of: how much do we get? All hell broke out. [Daughter] Joanne went white with rage and whispered in my ear: Count me out for that sort of money. Just count me out … [Laurie] said they were paying $10,000 so we should just forget it.' (Donaher, 1993: 32–3)

Ms Donaher does not explain why they nevertheless allowed Paul Watson to convince them otherwise except that, in the midst of a serious recession, perhaps even the small(ish?) fee was something of an inducement. They also thought the publicity might help them find a sponsor for the racing car they had recently bought. But one can read into the lack of a full explanation in the book (which, like Pat Loud, she authored and from which I have been quoting) both a refutation of the consent defence and a tacit monument to Watson's interpersonal skills and negotiating ability.

This family's experience offers a perfect example of the limits of prior consent. Although they agreed to filming they clearly had no clue that they were being set up as (in the terms used by the *Sydney Morning Herald*): 'Australia's new ambassadors: a family whose members are variously materialistic, argumentative, uncultured, heavy drinking and acquisitive.' Ms Donaher, even after the event, appeared incapable of understanding the process to which she had consented: 'Oh, Paul Watson, why did you have to take this line; why did you do this to us?' When her casual racism is captured by the film-makers, her response to public backlash is to ask: 'Why did they show this? Okay, we might have been told we'd be filmed warts and all but to deliberately set this up against me is, in my mind, quite evil' (Donaher, 1993: 52, 63, 64). Noeline Donaher 'thought of hiring a male stripper' to spice up a 'girls' party' at which she was selling a diet product (Donaher, 1993: 99). Kate Woods and Brian Hill, Watson's two directors, were presumably less than appalled at this suggestion.

The film-makers (without Watson) faced Donaher at the 1993 Edinburgh TV Festival still insisting that their purpose had been Griersonian public enlightenment. No wonder Ms Donaher remained confused. A more logical explanation – that they were interested in exposing her ugly bigotry and ignorance and her comic crassness, for example – might have better explained the situation to her. But it was not forthcoming; and why should it be? For Watson, Woods and Hill, Donaher's extensive self-publicity, which included not just the book but a pop record and commercials, more than justified their failure to ensure that her consent was informed. The rumour at Edinburgh was that Donaher had privately offered to do a further series, thus implicitly confirming for the film-makers the ethical soundness of their dealings with her.

This is not a question of intelligence. People exposed in another Paul Watson film, *A Wedding in the Family* (2000), admitted to a journalist that

the documentary was not *quite* as they'd expected. Anna's original understanding was that Watson 'wanted to make a social comment on the family at the turn of the millennium, using a wedding as a vehicle'. When she saw the ad in the hospital where she works, her first thought was how nice it would be to have 'a keepsake with all our family in it.' (Freely, 2000: 14)

After transmission, they were interviewed by Maureen Freely. They were smart enough to know that, as she was offered a crumpet with her tea, she might well write that 'they were so Middle England because we have crumpets with our tea'. It is fair to assume they would have had no such acute insight when they gave prior consent to Watson.

A third category of participants is less ambiguous. Some consent without understanding that there will be no benefit for them. There are occasions where innocent parties unambiguously suffer: 'For a long time after [*Man Alive*] went out, sometimes for years afterwards, they had been got at by neighbours, or family, or colleagues who, for one reason or another, were angered, outraged, ashamed, envious or offended by their television broadcast to the nation' (Williamson, 1983: 8). Harold Williamson, who had a well deserved reputation as a most sensitive interviewer in the 1960s, admitted that some of those he had used even had to move home and others lost their jobs.

This was nothing new. The two males who constituted the other two thirds of the central family in *Man of Aran*, Coleman 'Tiger' King, who played the 'father', and Michaleen Dillane, the 'son', 'found they couldn't live on Aran as former film stars' and disappeared after the publicity tour that premiered the film (Stoney, 1978). Angelo, the car-worker in *Chronique d'un été* (Jean Rouch and Edgar Morin, 1960), lost his job, as we see on the screen, because of the filming. Attempts to find him other work, including a job at Billancourt film studios from which he was also sacked, were off screen (Morin, 1985: 21).

Participant regret is not always a certain indicator that they have been dealt with unethically. In *Titicut Follies* situations, where public servants are exposed as inadequate or worse, second thoughts about allowing the film-makers in can reinforce the central message of the documentary: not only were participants at fault in what they do, they were so insensitive to their everyday failings that they co-operated in being filmed. For such participants to complain is provide justifications for the film-maker and to wipe out the ethical difficulties thrown up by any misrepresentations involved in obtaining access.

Titicut Follies is typical in that objections arose when officials realised how negatively the public was seeing them. Participants approve of a film and, subsequent to public exposure, turn on it. Hugh Hefner had no difficulties with *The Most* (Gordon Sheppard and Richard Ballentine, 1962) until 'Critics and audiences saw the film and found him a crass egomaniac. It was only when others saw him as he did not see himself that he objected to the filmic portrait' (Katz and

Katz, 1988: 133, n.3). Kate Woods showed Northwood Golf Club the film she made of them for *Cutting Edge* (Channel 4); but, 'blind perhaps to its own prejudices and bigotry' (and despite *Sylvania Waters*), the club raised no objections. Post-transmission public reaction to these prejudices and bigotry embarrassed them into vigorous protest (Brooks, 1995: 14). In all such cases the moral position of the film-maker is bolstered by the consent defence, for all that those concerned palpably did not fully understand the consequences of their actions.

Except where documentarists actively work to remove themselves from a controlling position, in all these other cases, whether the outcomes for the participants are good, mixed, or bad, the consent defence is far from being perfect. Most of the time it does little more than counterbalance any whiff of coercion that might have been involved in obtaining consent.

As we have seen, the law, limiting coercion to its original meaning, has little to say to film-makers since it insists on a level of threat seldom if ever present.[4] But coercion outside the law has expanded its meaning to embrace the idea of compulsion without physical threat. For the sake of *Man of Aran*, Flaherty persuaded some fishermen to go out in a spectacular rough sea on which they would not ordinarily have ventured (Rotha, 1983: 116). He threatened no force, as legal coercion would require, but he had offered each man the equivalent of a year's earnings to risk their lives for this climatic sequence, having wasted months thinking of how to finish his film. The consent defence is well founded in this instance in one sense since the men did know, better than Flaherty, what risks they were taking; but they also needed the money Flaherty was offering. This is a good example of what Carolyn Anderson and Tom Benson have called 'the *myth* of informed consent' (Anderson and Benson, 1991: 7–25). Flaherty himself well understood this: 'I should have been shot for what I asked these superb people to do for the film, the enormous risks I exposed them to, and all for the sake of a keg of porter and £5 a piece' (Rotha, 1983: 113).

Good Woman of Bangkok (O'Rourke, 1991) highlights the confusions, contradictions and frailties of the 'myth'. Dennis O'Rourke, one of Australia's most distinguished documentarists, received A$100,000 from the Australian Film Commission and, following the break-up of his marriage, went to Thailand deliberately 'to fall in love' and film that process. From the outset the object of his affection was going to be a Bangkok prostitute (Berry, 1997: 37). O'Rourke picked up the Good Woman of the title, lived with her, filmed her life story and then sought to manipulate her fate by buying her a small farm to allow her to quit the Bangkok sex industry. She took the money and returned to the bars. The 1990s equivalent of Flaherty's £5 and a keg was this series of purchases, woman and farm, by O'Rourke. The prostitute was, if you will, a professional consenter because of her oppressed economic circumstances while O'Rourke was something of a classic oppositional serious documentarist much concerned (albeit in this instance in a rather curious fashion) with issues of neo-colonialism.

The film provoked expected outrage since it unambiguously concerned itself with exploitation and was exploitative in the way in which it did so. Amidst the mess of aims and objectives he articulated in the furore that surrounded the film's release, O'Rourke said: 'I wanted to explode myths about the documentary filmmaker as cultural hero, and I thought, "Damn it, I will become the client of the prostitute and I'll make a film about that"' (Hessey, 1997: 133). It is, of course, easy and indeed correct to dismiss this as self-serving twaddle, even if the point about the cultural heroics of radical documentary film-making is taken. Feminist critics, singularly unimpressed with this rhetoric, were damning in their condemnation of the film.

Nevertheless, Linda Williams, after leading an initial charge against the filmmaker at the Berlin Festival, came to value it because at least it had the ethics of honesty (albeit the honesty of the implicitly chauvinist voyeur). For Williams, O'Rourke gave the woman a voice and, in fact, failed to 'save' her in an approved Gladstonian fashion, since this meant that she did manage to assert herself against him:

> Consider, for example, the contrast to Bonnie Klein's 1982 documentary about the sex industry, *Not a Love Story*. Klein's film is made in a spirit of sisterly equality with its main informant – a stripper named Linda Lee Tracy – who becomes a kind of collaborator in the making of the film … She even submits to a pornographic photo session in order to reflect on-camera the degradations caused by the sex industry. This degradation then provides the impetus for Tracy to eschew the life of a sex worker and achieve a 'happy' ending, as if freed by the feminism of the film-maker from the needs to perform sexually for men. Klein's film would thus seem to be a successful intervention in the sex-career of its subject, and for this very reason a more manipulative, less honest, and less ethical film than O'Rourke's. (Williams, 1997: 87)

While I agree that the whiff of exploitation and manipulation hangs very heavy over *Not a Love Story* too, it is hard to share William's somewhat benign view of O'Rourke. O'Rourke's honesty certainly does not disguise the unequal balance of power between film-maker and subject in the way that Klein's does; but such inequality remains the besetting ethical problem of the documentarist/participant relationship even in the most casual, normal and undeviant of circumstances. It does not go away simply because it is honestly paraded. The Good Woman supposedly maintains her integrity by remaining an economically depressed whore; not it would seem an outcome most would think liberating nor an ethically sound foundation for the film. O'Rourke's presence in the film, like Nick Bloomfield's strangely innocent forays into the world of deviant commercial sex, is ethically suspect – not because the subject is sex and all bargains are around it are illicit but because almost all bargains around documentary, whatever the subject matter, are unequal. This is true of traditional documentary film-making procedures although it can be altered, as I suggested above, by a fundamental renegotiation of the relationship reducing the film-maker to an advocacy/enabler role, the sort of function envisaged by film-makers like Bonnie Klein herself when she was involved in the NFBC programme *Challenge for Change.*

The bottom line is that the price of a rice farm, or the other lesser transactions that preceded it in the sex bars of Bangkok, like a £5 note at the height of the Depression in one of the poorest corners of Europe half a century earlier, constitute offers that do not really leave 'the person involved … so situated as to be able to exercise the free power of choice', as the Nuremberg Protocols suggest as appropriate. The very epithet 'consent' needs to be glossed if any hope of ethical film-making is to be attained. Certainly, it cannot be 'an offer you can't refuse'. The ethical problem comes in considering how fully 'informed' it has to be before it becomes a constraint on free expression.

It would be the end of the ethical problems of documentary film-making simply to suggest the adoption of the Nuremberg Protocols (or the Stirling report's crude rewriting of them) as a basis for film-making. Unfortunately, the Protocols no better mesh than do full-scale ethical systems in general with the realities of the media industries or the demands of free speech. As I have said, all, or most, difficulties would never occur if these rules were the norm; but then most of the films would not exist either. This is why I do not for a moment suggest that it would be a good thing to import such an un-nuanced vision of informed consent, much less the Nuremberg Protocol standards, to the documentary, or any other media form including journalism. Any 'absolute' requirement of voluntary consent alone would obviously have a discouraging effect on free expression. As the Stirling research confirms, the audience understands it is not always appropriate for media to insist on consent at all, never mind informed consent, in the coverage of criminality. This also has to be true of documentaries about corruption investigations, or in *Titticut Follies* situations. One can also argue that fully informed consent is not ethically required where a consenting participant is potentially in harm's way but is contributing to a greater good.

Take the series *Police*. One episode, *A Complaint of Rape*, detailed the procedures involved in the UK in the early 1980s when a raped woman complained to the police. There was no question that public understanding of this process was minimal at that time and by remorselessly focusing on the insensitivities of the male detectives conducting an interview with a woman claiming to have been raped the film revealed levels of police insensitivity that were deemed unacceptable. After transmission the procedures were changed. The film was therefore, without question, morally justified, all the more so since Graef and his crew went to considerable lengths to ensure the woman could not be identified. Nevertheless, although the woman was anonymous and filmed from behind and the soundtrack bleeped clean of all references that could have distinguished her, the *News of the World* found and exposed her. Had the protocols been applied, then this possibility would have had to be explained and, probably, her consent would have been withdrawn. The newspaper certainly reported that she had been upset by the cameras (Winston, 1995: 235). On the other hand, there would have been no public outcry and the sexist behaviour of the police towards rape victims would have continued.

The Protocols and the Stirling consent definition are recalled here simply to offer a picture of what full ethically sound informed consent means and thereby to point up the difficulties of obtaining it in a straightforward way when the issue of free expression is involved. Benson and Anderson point up the difficulties in this conflict of principles. Informed consent could well limit the usefulness of medical experiments but nevertheless society demands it. Free speech, on the other hand, ensures similar limitations are not acceptable in the media context (1989: 100–3). As the *Titticut Follies* and *Police* examples make clear, there can be a greater good involved, justifying less than fully informed consent. This greater good is often described as the public's right to know. This right, like the consent defence, furnishes the documentarist with ethical armour. The end justifies the means.

6.4 The Audience's 'Right to Know'

The public right to know is frequently used rhetorically, in parallel to the consent defence, to justify minor misrepresentations such as those that got Watt into the vicarage. Yet, for all that it is ubiquitous, the 'right to know' defence is quite often difficult to argue. In the *Man of Aran* case, for example, what right does the public have to know of a fishing situation, potentially fatal, created by the film-makers, not the participants? It is certainly not true that film-makers commonly put people at risk of their lives, so the Aran fishermen constitute an extreme case; and as with most extreme cases it is easy to find ethical fault. Surely no show must go on at risk to people's lives whether they consent to take part or not? But what of the BBC's castaways?

In cases where no real consent is obtained because the corruption or criminality of those filmed is being exposed, the right to know becomes the sole justification. The right to know justifies fundamental misrepresentations if the participants are themselves so morally culpable as to no longer warrant the protection that informed consent gives to more innocent parties. This is encoded as a legitimate exception for breaching privacy, for example, in the British regulations. Despite the Stirling Media Research Institute's conclusion, as we have seen, the exposure of crime or disreputable behaviour, threats to public health and the like do constitute 'an overriding public interest' that wipes out the need for any consent and justifies misrepresentation and subterfuge on the part of the broadcaster (BSC Code on Fairness and Privacy, June 1998: 14). This now has a statutory basis in the UK (Human Right Act 1998: 12.4).

The basic ethical problem raised by the right to know where innocent participants are exposed to their own detriment is that the right does not envisage any consideration of 'outcomes'. The rape episode of *Police* is a very rare example because an outcome, the reform of procedure, actually occurred; but the right to know did not depend on that. The implication of the right in general is that the audience will be so informed as to be able to act, although there is no requirement that they do act. Invading the privacy of the poor, for example, to document housing problems can be easily justified by the public's right to know and the fact that decades after *Housing Problems* (1935) it is still possible to make the same film, more or less, is no bar to doing so. Housing problems and documentaries about housing problems are, like the poor, always with us. We always have the right to know about poor housing – and the right to do nothing with that knowledge. This in turn gives the film-maker the right to disturb and expose the poor. In general, despite the widespread justification of documentary on a 'right to know' basis, it is surprisingly difficult to cite films, like *A Complaint of Rape*, that have actually had any noticeable effect in the world.

One of the famous 1960s *CBS Reports*, *Hunger in America*, highlighted poverty to make the case for the introduction of the federal food stamp programme. The effectiveness of the show, which began with a premature Native American baby dying in an incubator, is said to have contributed significantly to the campaign for this reform. It can be argued that the reason for the effectiveness of *Hunger in America* or *A Complaint of Rape* is that they did not start a public debate but contributed to one. Food stamps were a major issue for public debate when the film came out. Serendipitously, rape was already in the headlines when *Police* was transmitted because of some quixotic judicial opinions on rapists, so quixotic that even Margaret Thatcher was moved to condemn the bench for its leniency.

There have also occasionally been noticeable outcomes without a background of public debate. Documentaries have been effective in exposing miscarriages of justice, for example, on a fairly regular basis. The most overtly news-like documentaries have a record of amplifying whistle-blowing. Despite this, the vast majority, even those exposing social problems, have no discernible direct effects. Within a decade of *Titticut Follies*, Wiseman had realised this:

I no longer have the view that I had in the beginning that there might be some direct relationship between what I was able to show in the films and the achievement of social change ... I guess I've gone very far away from the clichés and bromides that I started with, especially the simpleminded social work view of help and intervention. (Anderson and Benson, 1991: 156)

Documentaries may, of course, have indirect effects, contributing to slow and unobservable changes in public opinion. In the 1930s Grierson claimed that the purpose of documentary was exactly this: 'to command and cumulatively command, the mind of a generation' (Grierson, 1970). It is hard to avoid the conclusion, though, that this has almost never worked in anything approaching the 'simpleminded social work view' of effective social change. The persistence of the social problems the Griersonians tackled, their constant continuing availability to be filmed, suggests that, whatever the public thinks, the public actually does very little. The right to know is, without question, a powerful part of an environment of free expression; what I am pointing to here is that it is less potent as a basis of ethical documentary production. Documentarists hide behind the public right to know just as they exploit consent.

A children's home visited in the 1970s to expose the utter barrenness and futility of the young lives in care can be revisited in the 1990s to make exactly the same point (*Aycliff*, Michael Whyte (1977): Hugill and Moory, 1992: 4). Nothing has changed. The issue of exacerbating the situation by publicly exposing the children in each generation is ignored. The public right to know is invoked but no one asks: 'To what purpose is this public knowledge put?'

Kate Blewett produced an amazingly disturbing exposé of official mainland Chinese 'dying rooms' where children in state care were being simply left to die: '*The Dying Rooms* was broadcast on Channel 4 in 1995 and has been seen by over 100 million people in over forty countries. Wherever it was shown it created a whirlwind of outrage. Four years later China's orphanages are beginning to deliver proper humanitarian care' (Blewett, 1999: 4). Although the more cynical might perhaps pause over the notion that China is seriously susceptible to external opprobrium concerning its internal conduct, Blewett was convinced enough by this experience to believe she could use documentary to alleviate the lot of poverty-stricken British children. *Eyes of a Child* (1999) was not made for entertainment but pure Griersonian enlightenment: 'Our ultimate aim is to bring pressure on the government ... I hope this film will draw attention to the 5 million or so kids in the country desperate for the voice they need to emerge from the shadowlands of Britain' (1994: 4).

I cast no aspersions on Blewett's sincerity, much less her skill, tenacity and indeed, bravery. It is just that the history of documentary suggests that she will be able to repeat this sincerity, tenacity and bravery in film after film for all her working life giving voice to generation after generation of kids in the shadows (should she chose to do that). All one can hope for is that she and the rest of her generation come to Wiseman's understanding of 'liberal clichés and bromides' and (unlike him, it must be said) act on that knowledge. There is, of course, not much hope of this and not just because the industrial system is, more or less, insisting on cheap sensationalism. In Blewett's case, documentary clichés are implicit even in the title of the work. *Eyes of a Child* was a glib misnomer for a film that maintained its director's traditional controlling role. There was no sense, as there was with the Fogo films, of a specific targeted audience (i.e. 'the government'). Poverty was represented, as usual, as a sort of inevitable condition. This was a documentary of the begging bowl not of the barricade.

Tom Roberts, whose *Staying Lost* caused Nottingham City Council such concern in 1999, ploughed the same well-worn furrow. He too had produced searing accounts of marginalised foreign children, this time on the streets of St Petersburg. Of the British children he sought out on the streets of Nottingham, he wrote:

> I do not believe that giving someone the odd cigarette or the occasional burger convinced them to give us their consent. We are offering them something more important – recognition and a voice … As documentary film-makers, giving them a voice is the best gift we can give … There is legitimate public interest in the widespread failure of our national system of care. (Roberts, 1999: 5)

With the best will and strong desire to believe in Roberts' integrity, it is hard not to hear this as self-serving. Who benefits more? *Cui bono?* as the law would ask: Roberts, his reputation as a serious film-maker enhanced (as indeed it was by this series), or some juvenile virtual spokesperson for the underclass? In fact, is not the latter exposing herself to perhaps more harassment for having spoken out, given that what is not remotely in question here (at least as far as I am concerned) is that the child care system in the UK is a disgrace? The issue is whether or not involving its victims, with all the moral questions and exploitative dangers that this raises, is the best way to use the supposed power of the media to correct this. Roberts, and most professional opinion, obviously believes that it is. They certainly have not thought of another approach in four decades of such observational filming.

The late Dennis Potter, responding to the original *Aycliff*, was unimpressed with the altruistic rhetoric of those documenting the underclass: 'the violence and disaffection of delinquent, working-class youth provides exactly the kind of pungent offal which attracts the flyblown eyes of those who work in television' (Winston, 1995: 234). Potter's bitter denunciation is much bolstered by

the persistence of the problems that documentary exposure is supposed to mil-
itate and the parallel persistent rhetoric of participant empowerment and
public guidance where little or no evidence exists to show these actually occur.
This rhetoric antedates the TV documentary. Photographer Dorothea Lange,
for instance, told Florence Neil, the subject of her famous *Migrant Mother*
(1936), that 'it would never be published and that it was to help people in the
Depression'. That was the last Mrs Neil knew of 'the lady'. 'Lange ... knew as
well as anybody that the conditions she photographed were the consequences
of capitalist crisis and neither acts of God nor arbitrary misfortune. Nonetheless, as a photographer her instinct was ... to present her subjects as objects of
compassion and concern' (Solomon-Godeau, 1991: 179). The photograph, one
of the most enduring twentieth-century images, certainly did not help Mrs Neil
or her children, not one of whom even graduated from high school. One of
them who was in the photograph, Mrs Neil's daughter Katherine McIntosh, was
interviewed by Peter Lennon after the image had appeared on a stamp and a
signed print of it was sold at Sotheby's for $244,500. Mrs McIntosh commented:
'What upsets us is that people are making money out of our mother's pain. But
we are proud that she has become part of history' (Lennon, 1998: 2).

    Man Alive's Williamson revisited many of the programme's original partici-
pants to persuade them to do follow-ups: 'They all needed coaxing [he wrote
in 1983] to tell their stories but, in the end [participants] decided to trust television again because, all of them said, someone might benefit from their
experiences' (Williamson, 1983: 8). Sixteen years later one of the adults Blewett
encounters 'hoped that by showing the imprisonment of the cycle of poverty,
someone would rescue' his young abused charge (Blewett, 1999: 4). There is as
little evidence of such beneficent outcomes in general as there is of these voices
being heard to some ameliorating effect in particular. These are all little more
than 'clichés and bromides', pious hopes at best. But when Blewett claims that
her film 'will change lives' she is on firmer ground – although perhaps the
changes are not quite what she had in mind.

    There can be no question that, consent or no, images affect lives – from Mag-
gie and Omerou to Maureen and Noeline the archive bulges with them. Again,
this power is not limited to documentary. For example, John Filo won a Pulitzer
for the celebrated photograph of a young girl kneeling in anguish beside the
fallen body of Jeffrey Miller, a student slain by the Ohio National Guard on Kent
State University campus in May 1960. Filo was a student photographer who
went on to be deputy photo-editor of *Sports Illustrated*. The girl, who was a
fourteen-year-old runaway at the time, tells of police harassment and her
mother of official accusations of communist agitation. 'It really destroyed my
life', the daughter said (AP, 1990: 32). It is when they are faced with this sort of
responsibility that documentarists doff their artistic beret and put on their

journalistic hat. Whether good or bad, life-changing outcomes for the participants are not, for the most part, the documentarists' concern. Instead they
claim for themselves a certain distance when it comes to assessing the effect of
the film on and their relationship with those they filmed.

Unless film-makers, in Cinéma Vérité mode, put themselves in the frame, it
is easy to leave aside consideration of their own moral standing and stature.
The tradition depends on self-effacing journalists and/or artists who for the
most part creatively treated actuality from behind the scenes. Unlike O'Rourke
in *The Good Woman of Bangkok*, Flaherty's sexual encounters on *Nanook*, for
example, involved the woman who played one of Nanook's two wives and produced a child, Joseph, whose daughter is a leader of the Inuit women's
movement and uses the Flaherty name. None of this is as important to the
ethics of *Nanook* as the fact that the film systematically misled us about the
reality of Inuit life in the early 1920s, recast Inuit family structures in inappro-
priate Western mode, proposed a Western exploitative relationship with the
land and did nothing to ease the burden of Allakariallak's short life. Flaherty's
personal morality is of no more (or no less) import to all this than that of other
artists to their work.

It is curious, though, to note that among the founding fathers of a film form
that claimed to represent the real honestly that a certain economical approach
to the truth was not unknown. In 1929, for instance, Grierson wrote of his first
film: 'I had spent a year or two of my life wandering about on the deep sea fishing boats, and that was an initial advantage' (Grierson, 1979: 19). The small
boats he really knew well, however, were the MTBs on which he had volun-
teered to serve in the First World War; and he had lied about his age, adding on
a year, in order to do this. As the child of the dominie in an inland Scottish village, his experience of drifters was likely much less.

In East Shotton in the Durham coalfield during the Great Depression, Grierson's colleague Paul Rotha recalls from his diaries that he misused his
Gaumont-British expenses to pay the rent of some miners and buy them a
drink or two: 'It gave me pleasure that the profits of Gaumont-British should
be so used. How I justified it in my accounts when I got back to London is
neither here nor there' (Rotha, 1973: 104). Here is the documentarist as ethically superior social activist, the cultural hero in the making.

The point is that personal behaviour, *per se*, is not at issue. This new documentary priesthood was – and is – held to no special moral standards. It is the
form, documentary, that makes a claim on the real and thereby raises particularly difficult moral issues. The mix of artistic and journalistic justifications for
such film-making is especially vexatious but until the current *kulturkampf*
about documentary scant attention was paid to it. Within the academic study
of the documentary, there is little talk of ethics prior to 1976 when the issue

first appears in the *Journal of the University Film Association* in America. This early focus was not made into a central concern but rather bubbled away on the margins of an interest that was itself rather marginal to cinema studies.[5] The academy had nothing to say to the professionals and they had only the 'myth' of consent and the unexamined 'right to know' as a guide to ethical behaviour. Because of the principle of free expression, including the right of investigation and the like, the ethicists (as in the case of the Nuremberg Protocols) are of little use, either. Only the journalists are left as a model of professional conduct. And the best journalism can offer are John Merrill's unsystematic ethical guidelines, voluntarily adopted, stressing authenticity and integrity as well as a respect for tried-and-tested moral principles and sensible flexibility in applying them.

This has the advantage of correctly focusing on the documentarist/participant relationship as the ethical key. As far as the audience is concerned, documentary promises insight and, given that a vision of unmediated image making is naïve and utopian, insight is what should be expected and demanded – not truth-telling defined as a species of impossibly mechanistic, strict observationalism. The assumption here is that in the market place of ideas the healthiest position for any reader of, or member of the audience for, mass communications' messages is an informed, sustained and profound scepticism. They should believe nothing, whether it is deemed to be 'a representation of reality and truth' or not (Directors Guild, 1999: 10). Readers and audience should not be nannied into this sceptical position; neither should they be protected from their own failure to adopt it – certainly not by the state or its agents. They either have legal protection because of actual or potential damage or are merely internally suffering from unactionable distress, spleen or bigotry. These last are the price of liberty and '*Caveat*', says the law; quite properly given the critical importance of free speech. The only constraint on expression, as 'Cato' wrote so long ago, should be grounded in an assessment of actual or potential damage and that constraint should be exercised through the law.

It will be objected that the common law especially is more than somewhat of an ass in this connection. The central action for damage, defamation, is a lottery (especially in the UK) and only the very rich can afford even to buy a ticket to that game. Judges sometimes (often?) display a tenuous grasp of the principle of free expression. There are already enough (too many?) legal restrictions and inhibitions. The answer to such proper complaints is not elaborate parcel-passing to non-governmental agencies to do what the law will not, but reform of the law itself.

This is not a libertarian position that opposes all forms of constraint. On the contrary, it acknowledges the need for control but disputes the way in which we are seeking to impose it. Accepting the test of (albeit restrictively defined) harmful consequences means there is no objection to content regulation by law as long as this is related to actual or potential damage. It also follows that the definition of what is actually or potentially damaging to the audience can change over time to reflect the concerns of society. Advertisements, for example, can and should be regulated; 'hate' speech can and should be controlled; even sedition and blasphemy can be made actionable, if they are carefully restricted in the light of what communications are 'necessary in a free society'. All that is required in this or any other case is that any constraints of free speech be subject to the direct rule of law and remain within the legal realm.

It goes without saying, though, that deliberate lying should be pilloried. It has nothing to do with documentary's project and is not sanctioned by documentary's complex vision of what truth-telling is. What is not acceptable is that such lying should also be subject to legal-style punishments in the name of a paternalistic responsibility to the audience, especially where the punishment is imposed by a government agency other than the court and the test for doing so fails to assess reasonably defined actual or potential damage.

Conclusion

I have argued that:

- Documentaries are a discrete form central to the idea of public service broadcasting and distinct from other factual programming including the news
- Documentaries, being both journalistic and artistic, are ethically vexed but the problems lie more with the way participants are treated than with responsibilities to the audience
- Documentaries require a more sophisticated view of truth-telling than is currently in play, one that embraces the reconstruction of prior witnessed events
- Regulation of infrastructure is confused with regulation of content and the later is not appropriate, if it ever was, in the contemporary world
- Regulation in particular to protect audiences from undamaging material is offensive to the principle of free speech
- The rule of law demands that the law (reformed if – or, as is – necessary) deals with these issues and does not hand them over to quasi-judicial bodies to do what it will not
- Mendacious documentarists should be vigorously exposed and denounced in the market place of ideas.

1. Documentarists

The difficulties involved in finding an ethical basis for documentarists is not in any way to suggest they have less need of morality. On the contrary, serving twin masters, one journalistic and the other artistic, makes their need greater. Documentarists require more than Merrill's generalities and the limited practicalities of the journalists' codes and the assertion of their own control over their material (as in the British Director's Guild Code of Practice); but they need these ethics not so much because of their presumed responsibilities to their audiences. That is to say, the documentarist's relationship to the audience is no more vexed than is the journalist's to readers. All the audience deserve is that documentary's difference from factual programming be re-established and the continuum of its procedures from observation through to the reconstruction of a witnessed past be readmitted as legitimate.

What is more difficult is the documentarist's relationship to participants where the need for unimpeachable ethical behaviour manifests itself far more clearly. The real contract, the release form, means far more ethically than does the legally mythic 'contract with the viewer'. The relationship between participants and documentarists is far more pregnant with ethical difficulties than is the connection of film-maker to audience. Unlike the audience, the vast majority of which remains usually unaffected (in measurable ways, at least) by any documentary it sees, participants are engaged in an exercise that could be life-changing.

First, though, it should be noted that, as with the audience, the relationship should be enforced by law and not by regulation, the law being changed if need be. For example, the common law notion of privacy, grounded in the pre-electronic world of physical trespass, could well be rethought in the light of the ECHR. Real respect for privacy could, and I would argue should, be made a legal responsibility but only wherever the right of free expression is also guaranteed by law (as it now is by UK law) – an ethical quid pro quo. This also applies to restrictions protective of participants: for example, the use of children or the reporting of rape victims' names – as long as these restrictions operate through the legal system.

But, if free speech rights are not to be abused, such legal considerations do not touch most of the interaction between documentarist and participant. There is still a pressing ethical need. As we have noted, a person's consent to participation is often ill-informed and they can poorly understand what it entails. This is where Merrill's injunctions and the professional codes become critical. It would seem to me that, on a voluntary basis, documentarists – exercising the power of the media and legally privileged by the right of free expression – should exercise maximum care in dealing with their collaborators and contributors.

Film-makers might undertake a form of ethical risk assessment to determine the extent of the difficulties or dangers involved in recruiting a person to their project. This assessment might turn on four heads:

- What sort of person is being filmed? (That is, how well-known or public a personality?)
- How socially deviant is the action being filmed?
- How public or private is the location of the action?
- How widely will the final documentary be seen?

All of these are grounded in legal concerns about persona, deviancy, domain and the channel of communication and, initially, before I grasped the full impact of the neo-liberal attack on broadcasting content, I argued in the 1980s that these could be made the basis of a legal duty of care to participants – a variant and extension, if you will, of the ethics lying behind the Nuremberg Protocols reformulated for the documentary and legally sanctioned (Winston, 1988: 54). I proposed this because, in the era of pure Direct Cinema, documentary had come to concentrate on society's victims and was so easily intrusive that the balance of power between film-maker and participant, always in favour of the former, had become woefully out of kilter. But now the emerging war on the documentary clearly means that such a position is risky since any moves, however ethically justifiable, would be extremely discouraging for free expression. I now understand that Merrill's domino theory is, unfortunately, entirely correct: extensions of the law, social responsibility and even, it must be admitted, the guidance of moral systems, will inevitably furnish the powerful with tools for abridgement of freedom of expression. The path to controlled media is paved with the best of ethical intentions and is very slippery.

I therefore reoffer the underlying principle of a duty of care as merely a refinement of Merrill's voluntary minimalist individual ethic. Such a quasi-duty of care is merited because it is still the case that documentary is fixated, albeit slightly less so these days in the UK, on the social victim. The taste for deviant proletarian youth is undiminished, however; and documentary is still intrusive, indeed more so with ultra-sensitive miniaturised camcorders and cheap videotape. The balance of power remains significantly tilted towards to the film-maker, despite trace elements of a slowly rising social awareness among participants of what being involved in a documentary means. But it is now clear to me that a legally enforced duty of care to redress this imbalance would have far too drastic a chilling effect on free expression which remains a paramount democratic need unchanged by the technologies of communication. So this duty of care might do no more (and no less) than inform the ethical behaviour of the individual documentarist on a voluntary basis.

Participants have different social positions, each person normally playing many roles in society. Many of these roles are played in private – mother, daughter, aunt, wife; many in public – secretary, nurse, CEO, MP/Congressperson. The courts have acknowledged this reality, drawing distinctions between public and private (e.g. in *Gertz*, 1974). Latterly, as we have seen, American law has begun to codify this concept at least in its provisions for the protection of the exploitation of celebrity. In a different legal field, the concept is emerging that a limited company can commit criminal offences such as manslaughter and its officers be held personally guilty for such actions. If different persona can exist for legal reasons, they can also be taken into account for ethical ones. Ethically, a person filmed in a public role is less protected than is the same person filmed in a private role. The ethical difficulty of intrusion is reduced the more public the role. It is also reduced, in contradistinction to the thrust of legal protections such as the Californian celebrity code, the more public the person. Legal personality can be of different kinds and the ethical documentarist can and does understand this and acts on it.

All this is without prejudice to the question of initial consent except to note that the more private the role, the greater need for the consent to be fully informed. The same is true of domain – the more private the place the greater the need for fully informed consent. And with domain in general the same public/private continuum is in place. Filming in public places is less intrusive than filming in private places and the ethical difficulties of doing so are, in general, reduced. The one exception to this is the problem of the bystander – that is the person outside, say, the drug-dealer's place of business who has nothing to do with drugs (the subject of the film) but just happens to be on the public street when filming takes place. Clearly, the documentarist has a duty of care to such a person not to misrepresent them by association inadvertently – although the bystander might also have a legal protection in an action in some jurisdictions based on this 'false light'. On the other hand, American courts have taken less interest in protecting people from distress who are re-exposed after, sometimes long after, the story that first forced 'fifteen minutes of fame' on them. The British regulatory codes have much to say on the ethics of the misuse of archival material which, if they were not mandatory, would be more ethically acceptable in this context.

It follows from 'false light' that the documentarist has no such duty to a person inadvertently filmed, say, canoodling his mistress in a public park. The film-maker has done nothing suspect; the 'light' shined on the couple is not false. This is because the relationship is illicit and that alone, not the public place, makes the action deviant.

Documentarists (and journalists) are much concerned with deviancy. It lies at the very heart of the traditional Anglo-American concept of news: 'Dog bites man, not news. Man bites dog, news', as Charles Dana of the *New York Sun* put it 130 years ago. Deviant behaviour, as we have just noted, is conditioned both by the people involved and the location. It is deviant to fight but not if one is a professional boxer. It is deviant to fight in the street, but not in the boxing ring. Given the current fad for docuglitz examinations of deviant sexual practice and the sloppiness of advertising for participants to reveal deviant sexual behaviour, greater sensitivity to the morality of filming deviance is in order – but in terms of participants rather than hyperventilating Whitehousean members of the public.

It is not good enough simply to muse, as Joanna Bailey does, on the short-sightedness of participants who forget that their 'Auntie Maud' might be watching their swinging lifestyle on the telly. But neither is it reasonable to ask for the sort of briefing the Stirling report envisages. Between these two positions, ethics does however tend towards Stirling. Better voluntary care in

informing participants about possible outcomes is clearly needed and acceptable if it becomes standard voluntary practice and even if it jeopardises
obtaining the contribution. The *aggie* should *not* come first.

The idea of deviancy can be, conversely, the basis of saying less to participants.
Are the persons being filmed acting in some illegal capacity? Have they a public
role that they are performing badly? Is the action being filmed deviant? (That is,
deviant to the point of misfeasance or criminality.) It is easy to justify filming
willing or unwilling participants whose misdeeds are being exposed on right-to-
know grounds, as even the regulatory codes acknowledge. The participants'
deviant lack of civic standards conditions the ethical justifications for using subterfuge and misrepresentation to gain access, or film without permission. The
documentarist relies on a 'public right to know' justification as does the journalist, even though the documentary is more personal than journalistic.

Which brings me to the last element, channel. This is largely moot since for
the most part we are concerned with television and film which normally means
large audiences with unfettered access. Nevertheless, the longevity of documentary as compared with, say, the more ephemeral nature of broadcast
journalism, as we have seen, has an ethical dimension. This is also true of the
timing of a transmission, which can affect content, as is the case with the British
concept of a 9 p.m. 'watershed' after which more adult and explicit material is
allowed by the broadcasting authorities' codes. Beyond this, normal channels
do not affect the ethics of a production, but they might. *Titticut Follies*, for
example, was banned from general exhibition but could be seen by legal experts
and mental health professionals. The rationale of the restriction was exactly
that ethical problems, such as invasion of privacy and the tenuous nature of
consent, were assuaged by the specialised nature of the audience.

This could happen in other cases. For instance, imagine a system for the
treatment of autism that involved considerable physical, apparently violent,
contact between the therapist and the autistic child. In an ordinary television
documentary, this might entail a public right to know which could perhaps ethically justify the intrusion into the autistic child's life, although the possibility
of encouraging, say, child abuse would have to be assessed. Such intrusion, however, would be more easily justified if the audience for the film was specialist –
other therapists or families with autistic children. Even the style can alter. Ethically acceptable close-ups, for example, for the specialised audience might be
considered as ethically unacceptable sensationalist images for the general audience, if the specialist film were, say, re-edited for general transmission or
release. It is in this way that the channel of communication, the distribution
context, can impact on the ethics of a documentary.

This sort of consideration could have affected Colin Low's Fogo films, which
were designed for a specific group of government workers and elected officials.

The content here was in no way ethically problematic, since it illuminated the islanders' case for the survival of their community and was made with their co-operation and editorial support; but it is easy to imagine how a targeted audience of this kind could impact on all questions of persona, domain and deviancy. This happens rarely but the possibility serves to highlight the flimsi-ness of the usual pious hope that the film will be seen by somebody somewhere who might perhaps make a difference. That everyday professional rhetoric fails to provide even an ethical fig-leaf.

In applying Merrill's situationist ethics, I am doing no more than calling for an ethical consciousness, appealing for responsible behaviour (especially a con-cern for others) and a sensitivity to the impact of transmission and distribution. This sensitivity is focused on participants. It encourages, but does not demand, renegotiation of the traditional balance of power between film-maker and participant. It assumes this relationship to be distinct from, and more ethically important than, the relationship between documentarist and audience. This is not only because there is a more direct contact with partici-pants but also because privileging (or even balancing) sensitivity to audience as the authorities' codes do, so that viewers are not misled, distressed, offended and so on, is far more worrying to freedom of expression than is an insistence that participants be dealt with ethically.

Obviously, the chances of changing the media's behaviour is extremely limited not so much because of the moral turpitude of documentarists but far more because of the structure of the industry. In its ruthless reduction of resources, its insatiable appetite for sensation and its casualised employment practices, the industry tends to make moral behaviour an unaffordable luxury. The media system as a whole has to demonstrate a commitment to ethical prac-tices and be willing to police it itself. It ought not to hide behind the shibboleth of a public right to know or the myth of informed consent. In the long term the 'consent defence' and vague appeals to the public interest are dangerous for documentarists. Such notions leave them primed to exploit the powerless but at the same time vulnerable to being manipulated by the powerful and the deviant. Worst of all, these facile concepts debase, in the name of free expression, both the right to speak and the right to hear. Their weakness encourages Hutchins-style calls for social responsibility. Such self-serving pro-fessional assumptions keep the glasses in the Last Chance Saloon topped up.

2. Regulators

Content regulators are the publicans in the Last Chance Saloon but there can be no question that, in a free society, ethical rules beyond the law's constraints must be self-imposed rather than imposed.

Regulation in the UK is justified because of inevitable market failure that can be seen in the media system no longer providing the quality and integrity PSB promises, if it ever did. The row about 'dumbing down' suggests that PSB is now but a shadow dimly seen behind current output. Given this situation, it is easy to agree that regulation is probably why programming is not even more inane than it is and good work would be even harder to find (or fund) without it. It is also true that many regulatory objectives are estimable – protecting bystanders from 'false light', attempting to limit distress. But, in my view, free expression cannot be threatened even in the name of these good intentions.

The problem lies in the method of achieving those regulatory objectives – in the UK, for example, public bodies empowered with sanctions and subject to the complexities and limitations of judicial review. This is simply unacceptable in a free society, whatever advantages can be highlighted. It might be 'off-message' to think so but these UK regulations as a whole, and the potential political thrust of 'due impartiality' in particular, clearly erect a powerful, nakedly ideological basis behind which the abridgement of free speech, if only by chilling effect, could go on. There is very good reason why the common law has elaborated the concept of free speech while not doing the same for the concepts of privacy or distress; or why it has not moderated *caveat emptor* for broadcasting's audience in connection with non-damaging expression. Simply, the liberty to communicate is 'necessary in a democratic society' and should not be casually abridged by the law.

The easy acceptance of the current environment is a measure of how insensitive British culture has become to this essential democratic need. It dismisses worriers about free speech by describing them with the damning epithet 'libertarian', thereby consigning them into the realm of loony extremism. But insulting pigeon-holing aside, fines for infringements of 3.7.i of the ITC Code (unlabelled reconstruction) could easily be precedents for fines for infringements of 2.5 ('unwarranted invasion of privacy') which would then be but a step away from fines for failing to maintain 'due impartiality'. It is not a sign of loony extremism to be concerned at this possibility. As I say, attempting to obtain a remedy in court for any of these probably would not succeed and certainly would be unlikely to do so without any demonstration of actual or potential legally recognisable damage; but what ITC licensee is going to risk the long-term consequences of trying to demonstrate that – even by the process of judicial review?

Content regulation, for all that it inhibits a measure of yellow-Press journalism and the worst aspects of sensationalism – albeit at the cost of threatening free speech – is actually also a thing of shreds and tatters by its own lights. This is probably one reason why it survives so unquestioned. In the UK, I can object to nudity and broadcasting regulators will leap to consider the objection; but these same regulators fall almost silent in the face of the issues currently causing real concern – 'dumbing down', production cost-cutting, 'de-skilling', insecurity. The unhappy result is a regulatory regime that is interventionist enough to be offensive to free expression but ultimately scarcely a guarantee of anything much beyond a knee-jerk response (however much formally encoded and backed by 'research') to the sex and violence obsessions of the bourgeoisie with its concomitant taste for control and repression. All this is in the name of 'balance' and/or non-damaging 'fairness'; but, as a font of precedents, regulation establishes a basis for far more dangerous unaccountable further exercises of power.

One does not have to be a loony 'libertarian' or even a more respectable American First Amendment absolutist, for whom any whiff of state or state-sanctioned interference with the principle of free expression is anathema, to query how the British codes come to have the force of law in a supposedly mature democracy. There can be no justification at all in a world of multiple TV channels for invasive content regulation, unless the right of free speech is given a secondary position. The quasi-legal codes should be consigned to the dustbin of history. The legal sleight of hand that establishes by statute an organisation which is required to produce a code that can then do what the law won't do is not acceptable.

The answer to all problems caused by mass communications in societies under the rule of law has to be the law, reformed as necessary. It is no good claming that as the codes are subject to judicial review they are within the law since the very idea of content regulation is what is in question. Judicial review is anyway a flawed remedy because in this situation its exercise involves parties (ITC contractors, for example) biting the hand that feeds them (i.e. the ITC). It is also unable to question the validity of the continued existence of codes. For this and many other reasons (the cost of defamation actions, for example), the plea for the supremacy of the law is not by any means a defence of media law as it stands. It is clearly in need of revision and indeed radical reform. My position is simply that content regulation is no substitute for such essential improvement. It is no more reasonable to offer the codes as an alternative to necessary law reform than it is to offer them as a way of controlling media moguls. Beyond the law, in a free society, the only acceptable and safe way to an ethics of expression is that such ethics be freely adopted by those 'speaking', not imposed by 'codes'.

The *Connection* mess and the media panic about documentary fakery it heralded arose from a climate in British broadcasting created in the 1980s. The vivid contradiction in Thatcherite policy was widely noticed at the time between a free market approach to reform of existing broadcasting structures (e.g. auctioning commercial broadcasting licences) or the introduction of new technologies (e.g. privately owned satellite channels or cable firms competing with telephone companies) and the imposition of new layers of content regulation and censorship (e.g. BSC). It is a measure of the comprehensive effectiveness of right-wing ideological domination that oppositional forces could make little or no progress exploiting such fundamental illogicalities.

Promised new legislation from the Labour Government in 2000 suggested 'a lighter touch' regulation but within the context of increased digital choice which would need continuing protection of viewers' interests and of children. This could, nevertheless, involve the removal of the Broadcasting Standards Commission. Despite this, any stirring against content regulation overall, even within the business, remained marginal, although the absurdity of the rules is a great as ever. 'As good almost as kill a man' as draw up a simplistic, un-nuanced code about broadcasting production that ignores the reality of such production, makes much of its paternalistic concern for the audience and seems unable to even spell 'free speech'. If this objection be old-fashioned – so be it. I am happy to stand behind Milton, 'Cato', Blackstone and the framers of the First Amendment in damning the content codes and insisting on the direct intervention of the law – reformed as is must be in the light of modern conditions (e.g. the Internet) and old deficiencies (e.g. defamation) – but of the law alone, when expression is being constrained.

To take this line is difficult not because it leads to libertarian anarchy (it does-n't) and not because it argues for the removal of the regulation of media infrastructure (again, it doesn't). What the abolition of extra-legal content regulation also does not in anyway sanction is the freeing of producers from their moral responsibilities. That they, for whatever good industrial reason, often display the ethical sensibilities of dead skunks almost, unfortunately, goes without saying. What I am questioning is whether or not such moral turpitude justifies regulation in general and the quasi-judicial imposition of fines by a statutory body following legal-style investigation in particular. In my view, without showing damage to the audience in a mature democratic society it simply does not. The media's ethical responsibilities (largely to those who participate) must either be a matter for the law or self-regulation.

So, for example, by all means castigate film-makers for misusing children, even if, say, a child was filmed actually soliciting without any prior contact with the film-makers. By all means sting broadcasters who lazily look for contributors through the 'Positions Vacant' columns (as it were) of the newspapers. Boycott the products of documentarists with sophomoric addictions to cheap outrage – even to the point of reducing them to silence. Their right to speak can be forfeited if they abuse it. Unethical film-making should most certainly be exposed and the film-makers should suffer the consequences of that exposure – the public destruction of their credibility. If TV professionals are stupid enough to debase the currency of their product by mendacity then by all means they should be denounced; but in a mature society that should be all.

Such a society should be far better informed about the limitations of the image's ability to represent reality. The camera can most assuredly lie. Indeed, it can do no more than tell *a* truth; *the* truth is beyond it. Whisper it not but Maureen of the *Driving School* documentary isn't 'real' (whatever her reality might be in 'real life'); nor is the 'mule' flying to London with or without heroin in his stomach; nor, come to that, is Buzz Lightyear. In the age of digital image manipulation, 'fakery' will become even more meaningless than it is at present. The current panic will seem quaint because the best and only defence against non-damaging media irresponsibility and mendacity in a free democratic society will be scepticism and scepticism alone.

Digital potential could be quite liberating for the realist image because it could free it of a burden it could never carry, that the image 'could not lie'. But, as the illusion of unproblematic truth fades, we need a new social understanding of the evidential status of the image. I do not want digitalisation, much less post-modern philosophy, to throw the realist baby out with the bath water. Despite the destruction of the ties between the image and the reality it represents, something of the realist project, the veracities of the Box Brownie (as it were), remains. We must be sophisticated enough not to believe a photographic image is like a window on the world, a window unmarked by the photographer's fingerprints; but to acknowledge the presence of the photographer is not necessarily to deny totally that one can still see something of the world. You can. I would describe this as making a weak claim for the photograph as evidence, adopting (as it were) 'a mild realist position'.

To take such a position, however, is to move a long way from the traditional view we have of image technologies. Such a move has considerable implications for how our audio-visual culture works. If we stop making strong claims on the real, in effect we transfer the onus of what remains from the image to the viewer. That is to say, we stop pretending that authenticity – truth, even – can be found within the frame. Instead we rely on 'inferential walks' (in Eco's term) in the mental landscape of our own experience and logic to test for authenticity and truth (Eco, 1984: 215–16). It is time to let go of the regulator's hand.

Robert Fairthorne, a radical film critic, implicitly understood Eco's concept when he wrote in 1933 that ' "actuality" is not a fundamental property' of the photographic image. He asked his readers to consider fast- or slow-motion. To understand *them* you need to have prior knowledge of speed in the real world (Fairthorne, 1980: 171). More generally then, to understand what is authentic in the image, a general knowledge of the real world – which, of course, we all have – is needed. If 'truth' is what we discover while making 'inferential walks', we would be moving the legitimacy of the realist image from *representation* (the screen – where nothing can be guaranteed) to *reception* (by the audience or the viewer – where nothing need be guaranteed, certainly not by nannying regulators).

The illusion that the photographic image provides simple, compelling evidence about the real world is ending. But it is only the illusion that photographic images are somehow *automatic* – scientific – reflections of the world that should be abandoned. In its place must come the idea that such images can provide evidence of the real world but in a way more akin to the evidence provided by painting or writing. We must finally acknowledge the photographer and the film-maker as subjective presences even while the science of their cameras allows us to continue to test, in Eco's sense, for authenticity. Documentarists would finally be left with the creative treatment of reality unfettered by the burdens laid on them by the undigitalised realist image.

The burdens are to be found most clearly in the assumptions of Direct Cinema. These have become so imbedded in general understanding that now broadcasters reap the consequences. As a result of Direct Cinema's rhetoric, content regulators and journalists (and, for all I know, the general public as well) appear to hold quite primitive 'camera cannot lie' views about documentaries with absurd expectations as to what truths of the real world are really on offer. The deal that created this situation now cannot be easily undone so that proper distinctions between different types of factual programmes and different levels of intervention cannot be made. Hence 'fakery'.

The industry's silence when facing 'fakery' has an ideologically, and ethically suspect, consequence in that it leaves most factual programming with its claim on objectivity and truth and so on firmly in place. Why else are the mass of programmes not investigated and punished? After all, those programme-makers haven't been fined £2 million for a 'breach of public trust'. A cynic might well assert that this in itself is a breach of public trust itself at least as heinous as any of those about which the documentary film-makers have been accused. It perpetrates a fraud on the public – that the telly is to be trusted – every bit as damaging as the putative fraud perpetrated by the 'faked' shows. Just as the audience must let the regulator's hand go, so the documentarist must forfeit Direct Cinema's strong claim on the real. This is anyway bound to happen because of digitalisation.

If our common-sense, everyday understanding of the documentarists' ability to illuminate our understanding of the world is to be maintained in the age of digital image manipulation, then a weak realist position that throws the onus of evaluating the images' authenticity on to the viewer might just be sustainable. Jejune assumptions about 'fakery' are utterly beside the point. Content regulation is also irrelevant and not just because the principle of *caveat emptor* is enhanced by Eco's inferential walks. It is also untenable because, to work with digital media, it will have to become even more intrusive if it is to guard against being digitally hoodwinked. And if it does interfere in this way, why would we, the audience, not see this as the work of Milton's 'oligarch of engrossers' returned 'to bring a famine upon our minds again'?

In media terms, personal ethics do not necessarily produce social responsibility, fairness or truth but any other basis for seeking such ends in a democratic society is worse. 'Democracy', said Churchill in the Houses of Parliament in 1947, 'is the worst form of government except all those other forms that have been tried from time to time.' The documentary 'fakery' scandals suggest that much the same can be said of freedom of expression under the law without further regulation. The best we can do is guarantee free expression and encourage (not censure or chill) its exercise by individuals who have freely adopted ethical standards of behaviour.

The price we pay for doing this is the occasional misleading image and the even rarer deliberate fake.

With no damage proved, so what?

High Barnet
July 2000

Notes

Chapter One

1. The Carlton investigation concluded that: 'Although the whistle-stopping references in the statement were obscure, they should nevertheless have been scrutinised' (Carlton, 1998: 36). The document in question, 'Adriana's statement', is signed 'Adriana Quintana' who is described as 'specialist researcher' by the Carlton investigation panel (Carlton, 1998: 45). (She received no screen credit.) It is clearly not the work of someone overly familiar with English and the first six pages concentrate on the issue of the dangers that had been endured and various money matters. There are five references to the mule not questioning his status. On pages seven and eight (of nine), one then reads:

   > Next of this, offer Me a new travel to Colombia with a new salary of £600,oo a week plus £5000,oo for my part in the new work, and from this amount I must pay my expences [*sic*] and must make contact with a man named Gustavo, who must feing [*sic*] coming with a drug in his stomach to England with a false passport, document that I paid with the money of the expenses … he [de Beaufort] told Me that I must stay in Colombia while he travel with the drug'sman [*sic*] to London, waiting for new orders but the fake 'mule' (Gustavo), said that he don't travel without Me because I was his garantee [*sic*] that nothing happen to Him once are in Englad [*sic*], and Mr de beaufort must bring Me again to London. Once In London, the immigration stop Gustavo saying to him that them know Him travel with a fake passport, detained and deporting him to Colombia.

2. These two terms are used interchangeably with the latter coming more into popular usage to describe all documentaries made with the new equipment whether transparent or reflexive. Cinéma Vérité is here reserved for the reflexive mode where the film-making process is made apparent to the audience; Direct Cinema is where it remains hidden in the 'fly-on-the-wall' style (Winston, 1995: 148).

3. Take the *Undercover Macintyre* story, for example. Were one less sensitive than I to the need not to argue with those who buy their ink by the barrel, one could draw easy attention to the guilt-by-association quality of raising the issue of faked scenes in the context of a row about a documentary nobody is accusing of fakery. I hasten to add that the *Guardian* made op-ed space

available to the series senior editor (Homes, 2000: 17). (Nevertheless, were one extremely foolish, one could also ponder the role of the leading liberal organ on all issues of Press freedom, freedom of information and the like being so gung-ho for any sort of media content regulation even if it was limited to a rival medium. But, not being so foolish, I would do no such thing, not even in the decent obscurity of a footnote.)

Chapter Two

1. The simple sense of 'public service' – as a service for the public without the public ownership spin – was reasserted by the 1981 Thatcherite Broadcasting Act, which required that commercial broadcasting should be 'conducted as a public service conducted by a public authority' (Tracey, 1998: 20–1). The Reithian opposition of public quality and private profit was cast out, curiously, by dint of pretending that the ITC, the regulators, were in fact the public owners; but such double talk was merely a disguise for the final abandonment of the Reithian non-commercial 'trade-basis' for broadcasting. As far as Reith was concerned (or indeed successors like Hugh Carlton Greene who was still arguing a passionate case against commercial ownership in the 1960s) commercial public service in broadcasting was an oxymoron; but, thanks to Thatcher, it was no longer (Tracey, 1998: 88–9).

2. The network share of audiences, we are often told, has been decimated, falling from over 90 per cent in the early 1970s to some 60 per cent in the mid-1990s. Wilfully sacrificing audience numbers on the altar of public service, especially in the absence of a requirement by the regulator, was no longer possible, it was claimed. This rationale can be easily disputed. Given the rise in population over this same period and the establishment of 20 million new US homes, the fall in the actual numbers of people watching the networks is far less than the fall in share. In 1975 there were 71 million homes with television sets in the US. In prime time the networks reached 37 million of them. In 1995, there were 95.5 million and the networks reached about 34 million of them. The networks' advertising take was still in the order of $32 thousand million a year (Russell *et al.*, 1996: 92, 104–5).

3. Carroll does not give details of this production and the title is not unique since it is shared by series, narrated by Charlton Heston, called *Wings of the Luftwaffe: Fighter Attack, Wings of the Luftwaffe: Blitzkrieg, Wings of the Luftwaffe: Vengeance*. One of these at least was transmitted on the Discovery Channel in 1996, after the date of Carroll's essay although video cassettes of the series were published before that year.

4. This is not quite the whole story. Rarest of all were films on straightforward documentary subjects such as Peter Davis's study of the war in Vietnam *Hearts and Minds*, which achieved a specialised theatrical release in 1974.

5. Sarah Boston revealed to the 1999 Sheffield International Documentary
    Festival that in his unpublished autobiography Donnellan has preserved an
    exchange of letters that perfectly encapsulates the problems of television's
    supposed 'golden age'. In 1973 the BBC Director General, Charles Curran,
    wrote to Philip on the occasion of his twenty-five years with the Corporation:

    > Over the years, mainly in Birmingham but also for a time in London, you have
    > made some first-rate programmes which have brought credit to the Corporation as
    > well as yourself. It would be disingenuous of me not to add that it is evident on a
    > number of occasions you have acted with a disregard for normal disciplines … As a
    > brother ex-officer of the former Indian Army you will certainly understand the
    > demands of corporate obligation.

Philip replied:

> The point you raise about corporate obligation is an interesting one: I was never
> actually in the Indian Army but in a very individualistic raiding force (5
> Commando) in which tactical imagination had to be combined with a high level of
> independent action – so one's obligation was to the common end rather than to a
> formal unity.

It is a fine point whether or not the army officers were more or less hostile to
creativity and relevance than the management consultants currently in
charge.

Chapter Three

1. The International Covenant on Civil and Political Rights that came into force
    in 1976 confirmed this (Article 19, General Assembly Resolution 2200 A
    (XXI) 1966 (in force 1976) in Anon., 1992: 41).
2. David Elstein: 'The production team did not know whether to be gratified (by
    apparent public support) or dismayed (by the alternative interpretation,
    public indifference) that the ratings for the blank screen were no different
    from the average for the series.' Personal communication, May 2000.
3. Following the Berne Convention, authors *et al.* in the UK cannot, as yet,
    claim an uncontracted percentage of subsequent sales revenues as they can
    elsewhere but still have to witness exponential increases in the value of their
    works going to others. The British Act protects authors (including film
    directors) only from the 'derogatory treatment' or 'false attribution' of their
    work (Copyright, Designs and Patents Act 1988 4: 80, 84) and puts a
    limitation on the use which can be made of photographs taken in specific
    circumstances of a commissioned shoot (4: 85). This might be hard for them
    but, for example, these restrictions are pointed to by the London auction
    houses as a primary factor in maintaining the pre-eminence of the UK in the

international high art market. Nevertheless, the UK government agreed to a European Commission decision of March 2000 to require an economic *droit de suite* within the Union but, in the British case, it was to come into force only in 2015.

4. The New Zealand national film archive has agreed that any footage of Maori life it holds cannot be released for use without the approval of tribal authorities in place at the time of the request, irrespective of the fact that the individuals filmed might not be the individuals granting permission for use. This is a restriction in perpetuity and acknowledges, in contradistinction to common law traditions, a collective, inextinguishable measure of image ownership (Barry Barclay: personal communication, October 1996).

5. Although, it must be said, some observers have suggested that the Court is becoming more pro-government in its rulings which, in this context, means slightly altering the balance in favour of privacy considerations and other constraints. This is not least because other countries have been following the British practice of appointing 'government lawyers, rather than distinguished and independent jurists, to its bench' (Robertson and Nicol, 1992: 9).

6. Wiseman, after this experience with written consent forms but burdened by the legal requirement for some sort of record, went on routinely to ask participants to assent into his microphone: 'We just took your picture and it's going to be for a movie, it's going be shown on television and maybe in theatres … Do you have any objections?' (Pryluck, 1976: 256). Much thought was given by Wiseman and his colleagues during the earliest phase of the *Titticut Follies* affair to the contract law requirement that a 'consideration' be offered. They thought that perhaps a dollar ought to be given to participants as consideration in return for a signed release form, but this procedure was never implemented.

Chapter Four

1. It is no accident that the Europeans began only with broadcasting networks that as often as not incorporated the state's name – the British Broadcasting Corporation, Radio-Television Française, Radio-audizioni Italiane – just as the Americans until 1943 enjoyed only the National Broadcasting Company and the Colombia Broadcasting System. (The American Broadcasting Company was created, Eve-like, from the second network of NBC, in 1943.) The USA Cable channel is even later, having been founded in 1980. Germany is exceptional in that the Reichsrundfunkgesellschaft (RRG) spoke of a state broadcasting entity without mentioning the state's name.

2. To accept the reality of multi-channels and the need for new standards does not also mean making naïve assumptions about the proliferation of channels or the supposed uncontrollability of system because of its technology. Take

the myth of Internet freedom. In essence, it ignores the reality of the structure of the system, where the spines can be monitored, because it envisages multiple nodal point networks as lacking control, which they do not (Winston, 2000).

Any Internet move towards TV will involve the production conventions of television, Hollywood grammar and so on. As cable and satellite broadcasters have already discovered, these have established expensive tastes in the audience. In fact, the history of the development of the conventions is best understood as a series of decisions about technology and institutional arrangements designed to limit competition by raising the cost of entry. This results in an audience expectation that programming will be at a technical and artistic level it can recognise *as* programming – call it the $1.5 million-an-hour rule. ($1.5+ million is the 2000 price for a 52-minute episode of a US drama. Other programme genres are cheaper, say $300,000 for the documentary hour or even £65,000 for a docusoap episode.)

Accountants are well pleased with the audience response to yet cheaper studio programming (talk/confession, lifestyle, home videos) but these have yet to oust the expensive staples of the prime-time network. In the face of the $1.5 million rule, arguments about whether or not Internet-based channels can be regulated or not are beside the point. Free or controlled, they are subject to the same production economics.

Given that people have to eat, sleep and work, multiple channels of all kinds potentially fragment audience and revenues to the point where expectations cannot be met. This is why in fifty years, American cable TV, however effectively it has exploited niches (e.g. The Weather Channel which does only weather reports or Court TV which just lurks in courtrooms), has failed to produce its own general entertainment channel, although this was promised by the early rhetoric (as soon as the audience reached 20 per cent!) and discussed extensively thereafter until the early 1980s. The proposition that programming, revenues and audience expand to fill the channels, however many there are, is simple minded and has been proved so a number of times.

The *locus classicus* is the 100-plus interactive cable channels of the Warner Qube system in Colombia, Ohio begun in 1977 and ending in mid-1980s, killed by audience confusion in the face of abundance and a paucity of programming. There is no reason to believe that we have advanced much with digital, satellites or Internet. One can remain moderately cynical about all claims of the revolutionary impact of 100 or 500 or more channel systems. The concept of 'video-on-demand' currently touted as a major attraction of such platforms is nothing but an admission that showing the same film/programme on ten, twenty or more channels with slightly different starting times means there is plenty of space to fill.

However delivered, it could well be that no system is viable beyond the thirty to fifty channels range of cable, yet that still is a much greater number than was provided by the analogue TV transmitters in the market-led US, never mind in statist Europe. Five hundred channels or Internet infinities of provision might well be a delusion but this does not affect the basic point that current availabilities wipe out scarcity as it has been traditionally understood and that with it goes that legitimisation for content regulation.

3.   The annual report from which these figures are derived is visually arresting but rather opaque. Complaints received are given as whole numbers, complaints upheld as percentages. These last do not yield whole numbers. I could have got this wrong so confused is the presentation. The BSC Press Office explanation is that the percentages have been 'rounded up'. Anyway, even if the highest figure of 4,992 is taken, the number is still derisory and the cost per complaint large.

4.   The single instant they bothered to report that glancingly deals with this crucial matter reveals that 55 per cent of their respondents saw no need to seek consent for CCTV footage being used in an investigative programme, specifically for 'combating crime through exposure' (2000: 9, 41).

5.   Personal communication, February 2000.

Chapter Five

1. The SPJ formulation in Section III can be seen as a more or less standard summary of such codes. For example, 'TV News 2000 and Beyond', a seminar including journalists from the Balkans, the Baltic states and other parts of the old Soviet empire, Egypt, Western Europe and the USA held in the summer of 1999 at the European Journalism Centre, Maastricht, produced the following:

   1. Journalists have a responsibility to society

   2. The role of the journalist is essential to the functioning of democracy and a diverse multi-cultural society

   3. Journalists must fight to full freedom of expression regardless of censorship, sponsors, owners, management, politicians and commercial interests

   4. Journalists should resist political and economic influence or pressure

   5. Pressure of time should not affect the depth of journalistic investigation

   6. In television news, the pursuit of ratings should not affect the standard of journalism

   7. Journalists must report fairly, accurately and objectively

   8. Journalists must behave at all time in an ethical way

   9. Journalists must protect sources of information at all times

10. Journalists must act as a watchdog of government and society

11. Journalists must respect individual privacy and rights

12. Journalists must speak up for people who do not have a voice

13. Journalists should protect their sources, but at the same time be cautious of them

14. New technology may change the way a journalist works but cannot and must not ever change a journalist's professional behaviour and adherence to standards of the kind listed here

15. Information is more important than entertainment!

This, the product of a few days' work, contains terms as ill-defined as any in the British regulatory codes but it also clearly illustrates, despite over-lapping areas, a very different overall emphasis from such 'top-down' articulations.

2. On the other hand, also consider the quite extraordinary publication of a fourteen-page supplement in the *Los Angeles Times* late in 1999 attacking its own parent company's CEO and the paper's publisher for producing a special magazine boosting the development of a sports arena in which the company had interests without revealing those connections. This rare overt display of journalistic power over its own Press barons, however, was occasioned by the intervention of 72-year-old Otis Chandler, the fourth generation of that family to publish the paper which he did from 1960 to 1980. His intervention, dictating a statement to the newsroom condemning his successors for their lack of integrity, started the ball rolling (Lyman, 2000: 6–24). Times-Mirror has now been taken over.

3. Personal communication, February 2000.

4. Curiously, although coded insistence on detachment and truth run counter to a concept of social responsibility that encourages involvement with community organisations and permits the suppression of divisive information in the name of community good, nevertheless civic journalism broadly supports the codes.

Chapter Six

1. The Weaver Brothers were also at work on the Gettysburg battlefield moving corpses around a boulder for two views called 'Dead soldiers in Devil's Den' (Collins, 1985: fig. 13).

2. Although those appearing on the minicams must be classed as actors, Bill Nichols has drawn attention to the documentary element generally to be found in the porn film (Nichols, 1994: 74–75). Ejaculation becomes an earnest of documentary veracity. European broadcasters have been ploughing the same furrow of arranged encounters. The most elaborate has been an RTL German language series, *Big Brother*, shot in a specially built house. The output is permanently on the Net but footage is also shown on prime-time

television. Every two weeks, the audience can vote to drop one of the ten denizens until only one survives to 'win'. The Federal Interior Minister Otto Schilly has been quoted as saying, 'Those who still cherish feeling for human dignity should boycott the show' (Anon., 2000c). *Big Brother* is based on a Dutch original and now has copies in the pipeline in Scandinavia, Portugal and the US. In Britain 45,000 people applied to be in the show, which became a summer ratings sensation in 2000. In Spain, the participants made a pact not to vote each other out of the house and to donate the prize money to help the handicapped daughter of one of their number (Karacs, Nash and Jury, 2000: 25).

3. This repetitiveness is perhaps less surprising when the realities of the production process are considered. No production office is without some record of the contacts it has made and the participants it has used over time. This database constitutes the first port of call for programme researchers and if, as is too often the case, there is little or no time for further research, the established names become the next invitees. This is probably truer of continuous series such as talk shows than of one-off documentaries but, although the Stirling research divided the forty participants interviewed by age, sex, class and region, it failed, not insignificantly, to acknowledge any difference in the programming types involved. The finding was not analysed along these lines.

4. Linda Lovelace claimed that she appeared in the pioneering porn feature *Deep Throat* because of coercion including physical threats, an exception that clearly proves the rule.

5. In that year, 1976, James Linton first considered 'The moral dimension in documentary' and Calvin Pryluk 'The ethics of documentary film-making'. In 1977, Vivian Sobchack first addressed ethics in her consideration of the faked documentary *No Lies* (Mitchell Block, 1973) which purports to be an account of a rape. That same year Richard Blumberg raised the whole issue of participant rights and Seth Feldman discussed the ethical implications of allowing participants to share directorial and editorial decision making (Henderson, 1988: 276–379). Two conferences in 1984 and 1985 at the Annenberg School of Communications at the University of Pennsylvania produced a slew of papers and the volume *Image Ethics*; but, again, the issue remained at the periphery (Gross *et al.*, 1988).

References

AFL-CIO v. *FCC* 1991, 11 F. 3d 1480.

Ahmed, Kamal, 'What next? A piece about how to construct a gas chamber?', *Media Guardian*, 10 January 2000.

Anderson, Carolyn and Thomas Benson, *Documentary Dilemmas: Frederick Wiseman's Titticut Follies* (Carbondale, Illinois: Southern Illinois University Press, 1991).

Anon., 'Composographs', *Life*, 2 January 1950.

Anon., 'A man of mercy', *Life*, 5 November 1954.

Anon., *BBC Handbook 1960* (London: BBC, 1960).

Anon., *BBC Handbook 1966* (London: BBC, 1966) (1966a).

Anon., *Observer*, 1 September 1966 (1966b).

Anon., *BBC Handbook 1976* (London: BBC, 1976).

Anon., *BBC Handbook 1986* (London: BBC, 1986).

Anon. (Directorate of Human Rights), *Human Rights in International Law* (n/a: Council of Europe Press, 1992).

Anon., 'BSkyB changes contract', *inside-cable.co.uk/n97qsky.htm* (1997).

Anon., 'ITC fines Carlton £2 million for faked drugs documentary', *mediatel.co.uk/1998/12dec/18/itc.htm* (1998a).

Anon., 'A betrayal of viewers', *Guardian*, 19 December 1998 (1998b).

Anon., 'Film report complaint is rejected', *Guardian*, 8 March 2000 (2000a).

Anon., www.rbs2.com/privacy.htm (2000b).

Anon., *MediaNews*, European Media Centre, 2 March 2000 (2000c).

Anon., *Human Rights in International Law* (Netherlands: Council of Europe Publishing, n.d.).

AP, 'Kneeling with death haunted a life', *New York Times*, National Section, 6 May 1990.

Atiyah, P. S., *An Introduction to the Law of Contract* (Oxford: Oxford University Press, 1989).

Autonic AG judgment, European Court of Human Rights, 22 May 1990, Series A no. 61.

Bainbridge, David, *Intellectual Property* (London: Pitman Publishing, 1994).

Bailey, Joanna, 'Faking it for the cameras', *Guardian*, Media section, 1 February 1999.

Barendt, Eric, *Freedom of Speech* (Oxford: Oxford University Press, 1985).

Barnett, Steven and Emily Seymour, 'An Iceberg travelling south ...': Changing trends in British Television* (London: Campaign for Quality Television September, 1999).

Barsam, Richard, *Nonfiction Film* (New York: E. P. Dutton, 1973).

BBC, *Producers' Guidelines*, February 2000.

Belsey, Andrew, 'Privacy, publicity and politics', in Belsey and Chadwick (eds.) (1992).

Belsey, Andrew and Ruth Chadwick, 'Ethics and politics of the media', in Belsey and Chadwick (eds.) (1992).

Belsey, Andrew and Ruth Chadwick, (eds.), *Ethical Issues in Journalism and the Media* (London: Routledge, 1992).

Benson, Thomas and Carolyn Anderson, *(Reality Fictions: The Films of Frederick Wiseman* (Carbondale, Illinois: University of Southern Illinois Press, 1989).

Berne Convention (1928) for the Protection of Literary and Artistic Works, 9 September 1886 as revised Rome, 2 June 1928.

Berry Chris, 'Dennis O'Rourke's original sin', in Berry *et al.* (1997).

Berry, Chris, Annette Hamilton and Laleen Jayamanne(eds.), *The Film-maker and the Prostitute: Dennis O'Rourke's 'The Good Woman of Bangkok'* (Sydney: Power Publications, 1997).

Bethell, Andrew, 'Pleasure plus principle', *Guardian*, Media section, 2 February 1998.

Blackstone, W., *Commentaries on the Laws of England* (1765).

Blewett, Kate, 'We see, but so what?', *Independent on Sunday*, 5 September 1999.

Bluem, William, *Documentary in American Television* (New York: Hastings House, 1968).

Briggs, Asa, *The Birth of Broadcasting* (Oxford: Oxford University Press, 1961).

Brooks, Richard, 'Squirming under the documentary microscope', *Observer*, 5 November 1995.

Brooks, Tim and Earle Marsh, *The Complete Directory to Prime Time Network TV Shows 1946 to the Present* (New York: Ballantine, 1976).

BSC, *Codes of Guidance* (June 1998).

BSC, *Annual Review 1998–99* (1999).

Capro Industries v. *Dickman* 1990, 1 All ER 568.

Carlton Communications, *'The Connection': Report of the Investigation Panel appointed by Carlton Communications Plc* (London: Carlton Communications, December 1998).

Carroll, Noel, 'Nonfiction film and postmodernist skepticism', in Bordwell, David and Noel Carroll (eds.), *Post-Theory: Reconstructing Film Studies* (Madison, WI: University of Wisconsin Press, 1995).

Cartwright, John, *Unequal Bargaining: A Study of the Vitiating Factors in the Formation of Contracts* (Oxford: Oxford University Press, 1991).

Case-law concerning Article 10 of the European Convention on Human Rights (Strasbourg: Directorate of Human Rights, 1997).

Castells judgment, European Court of Human Rights, 23 April 1992, Series A no. 236.

'Cato' (John Trenchard and Thomas Gordon), Letter 15: 'Of freedom of speech: that the same is inseparable from publick liberty' (1720).

Cawston, Richard and Stephen Hearst, Robert Reid, Anthony de Lotbiniere, Christopher Ralling, Anthony Jay and Roger Cary, *Principles and Practice in Documentary Programmes* (London: BBC Television Service, April 1972, issued internally).

Christians, Clifford and Kim Rotzoll, ('Ethical issues in the film industry', in Bruce Austin (ed.), *Current Research in Films* (Norwood, New Jersey: Ablex, 1985).

Christians, Clifford, Kim Rotzoll and Mark Flaker, *Media Ethics: Cases and Moral Reasoning* (New York: Longman, 1983).

Collins, Kathleen, *The Camera as an Instrument of Persuasion: Studies of Nineteenth-Century Propaganda Photography* (Pennsylvania State University PhD, Ann Arbor: University Microfilms International, 1985).

Corner, John, 'Documentary voices', in John Corner (ed.), *Popular Television in Britain* (London: BFI, 1991).

—— *The Art of Record* (Manchester: Manchester University Press, 1996).

Cooley, T. M., *A Treatise on the Law of Torts* (1888).

Couprie, Elaine and Henry Olsson (eds.), 'Author's rights etc. 1985: Articles 23, 32, 28, 51', *Freedom of Communication under the Law* (n/a: European Institute for the Media, 1987).

Coward, Ros, 'Too many flies on the wall, all wanting a story', *Guardian,* 11 November 1996.

Darbo (David John) v. *DPP* 1991, *The Times,* 11 July

Directors Guild of Great Britain, *Code of Practice for Directors in Film and Television: Documentaries* (London: DGGB, 1999).

Dodd, Vikram, 'BBC film ends in deaths tragedy', *Guardian,* 5 July 1999.

Donaher, Noeline, *The Sylvania Waters Diary* (London: Orion, 1993).

Dovey, Jon, 'Freakshows: the political economy of cheating', *Journal of Media Practice* 1:1, 2000.

Durgom v. *CBS* , 1961, 214 NYS 2nd 1008.

Duval Smith, Alex, 'How the hacks stole the aid circus limelight', *Independent on Sunday,* 12 March 2000.

Eaton, Mike (ed.), *Anthropology-Reality-Cinema: The Films of Jean Rouch* (London: BFI, 1979).

ECHR (European Convention on Human Rights), *European Issues: European Convention on Human Rights Collected Texts* (Strasbourg: Council of Europe Press, 1995).

Eco, Umberto, *The Role of the Reader: Explorations in the Semiotics of Texts* (Bloomington: Indiana University Press, 1984).

Edelman, Bernard, *Ownership of the Image: Elements for a Marxist Theory of Law* (trans. E. Kingdom) (London: Routledge and Kegan Paul, 1974).

Fairthorne, Robert, 'The principles of the film', in Don Macpherson (ed.), *Traditions of Independence* (London: BFI, 1980).

Feldman, D., *Civil Liberties and Human Rights in England and Wales* (Oxford: Oxford University Press, 1993).

Fowler, Roger, *Language and Discourse in the News: Discourse and Ideology in the Press* (London: Routledge, 1991).

Freely, Maureen, 'The honeymoon's over', *Observer,* 2 April 2000.

Fry and Lane 1888: 40 Ch. D.

Fulton, Marianne, *Eyes of Time: Photojournalism in America* (New York: New York Graphical Society, 1988).

Gaines, Jane, *Contested Culture: The Image, the Voice and the Law* (London: British Film Institute, 1992).

Garnham, Nicholas, *Emancipation, the Media and Modernity* (Oxford: Oxford University Press, 2000).

Glasgow Media Group, *Bad News* (London: Routledge and Kegan Paul, 1976).

Gertz v. Robert Welch, Inc. 1974, 418 U.S. 323.

Goldberg, Marcy, 'Touring the world of the dispossessed', *Dox* no. 22, April 1999.

Goodwin, Peter, *Television under Thatcher* (London: BFI, 1998).

Gordon Kaye v. *Andrew Roberston and Sport Newspapers* 1991, FSR 62 CA.

Graef, Roger, 'A tricky business', *Television*, April 1999.

Green, Michael, *Independent*, 30 March, quoted in Tracey (1998).

Grierson, John, (ed. Forsyth Hardy), *Grierson on Documentary* (London: Faber and Faber, 1979).

Groppera AG judgment, European Court of Human Rights, 28 March 1990, series A no. 173.

Gross, Larry, John Katz and Jay Ruby (eds.), *Image Ethics: The Moral Rights of Subjects in Photographs, Film, and Television* (Oxford: Oxford University Press, 1988).

Haelan Laboratories, Inc. v. *Topps Chewing Gum, Inc.* 1953, 202 F, 2d 866 (2d Cir.).

Halliwell, Leslie, *The Filmgoer's Companion* (New York: Avon, 1975).

Hammond Jr., Charles, *The Image Decade: Television Documentary 1965–1975* (New York: Hastings House, 1981).

Handyside judgment, European Court of Human Rights, 7 December 1976, Series A no. 24.

Hansard, 30 March 1994.

Hansard, 16 February 1998.

Harris v. *Wye Forest District Council* 1989, 2 All ER 514.

Hazelwood School District et al. v. *Kuhlmeier et al.* 1988, 484 US 260 no. 86–836.

Hedley Byrne v. *Heller* 1963, 2 All ER 575.

Henderson, Lisa, 'Selected annotated bibliography', in Gross *et al.* (1988).

Hepple, B. and M. Matthews, *Tort: Cases and Materials* (London: Butterworth, 1991).

Hessey, Ruth, 'Bad sex', reprinted from *Rolling Stone* no. 496, April 1992, in Berry *et al.* (1997).

Hill, Annette, 'Fearful and safe: audience response to British reality programming', *Television and New Media 1*, 2 May 2000.

Homes, Alex, 'The police take sides', *Guardian*, 27 June 2000.

Horowitz, David and Lawrence Jarvik, *Public Broadcasting and the Public Trust* (Los Angeles: Second Thought Books, 1995).

Hoyt, Mike, 'Are you now or will you ever be, a civic journalist?', *Colombia Journalism Review*, September/October 1995.

Hugill, Barry and Graham Moory, 'Mounting scandal: hardline regime of Durham children's home', *Observer*, 9 August 1992.

Hunnings, Neville, *Film Censors and the Law* (London: Allen and Unwin, 1967).

ITC, *The Programme Code* (London, 1998).

ITC, 'Human Rights Act and the ITC programme code consultation', *News Release*, 40/00, 12 May 2000.

Ivens, Joris, *The Camera and I* (New York: International Publishers, 1969).

Jacobson, H., 'Michael and me', *Film Comment*, 25:6 1989.

Jones, Stephen, *The British Labour Movement and Film 1918–1939* (London: Routledge and Kegan Paul, 1987).

Karacs, Imre, Elizabeth Nash and Louise Jury, 'Broadcaster's sensation is captivating audiences across Europe', *Independent on Sunday*, 7 May 2000.

Katz, John (ed.), *Autobiography: Film/Video/Photography* (Toronto: Art Gallery of Ontario, 1978).

Katz, John and Judith Milstein Katz, 'Ethics in the autobiographical documentary', in Gross *et al.* (1988).

Kerr, Simon, 'New voices – or just new prices', *Whistleblower* (2000) (www.mediachannel.org/whistleblower/index.html).

Kilborn, Richard, 'New contexts for documentary production in Britain', *Media, Culture and Society*, vol. 18 no. 1, January 1996.

Klaidman, Stephen and Tom Beauchamp, *The Virtuous Journalist* (New York: Oxford University Press, 1987).

Knowlton, Stephen and Patrick Parsons (eds.), *The Journalist's Moral Compass. Basic*

Principles (Westport, Connecticut: Praeger, 1995).

Lawson, Mark, 'The real connection', *Guardian*, 19 December 1998.

Lennon, Peter, , 'It started with a kiss', *Guardian*, 26 January 1993.

— 'Whatever happened to all these heroes?', *Guardian*, Media section, 30 December 1998.

Levy, Leonard, *Emergence of a Free Press* (New York: Oxford University Press, 1985).

Liebling, A. J., *The Press* (New York: Ballantine, 1964).

Lingens judgment, European Court of Human Rights, 8 July 1986, Series A no. 103.

Lister, David, 'He talks a good game. But is MacKenzie's plan for a radio empire on the ropes?', *Independent*, 23 March 2000.

Lyman, Rick, 'Otis Regrets', *New York Times*, 23 January 2000.

Mapplebeck, Victoria, 'The tabloid formula', *Dox* no. 13, October 1997.

Meridith Corp. v. *FCC* 1987, 809 F. 2nd 863 D. C. Cir.

Merrill, John, *The Dialectic in Journalism: Towards a Responsible Use of Press Freedom* (Baton Rouge: Louisiana State University Press, 1989).

Merrill, John, Peter Gade and Frederick Blevens, *Twilight of Press Freedom: The Rise of People's Journalism* (Mahwah, NJ: Lawrence Erlbaum Associates, 2000).

Milton, J., *Areopagitica: A Speech for the Liberty of Unlicensed Printing* (1644).

Morin, Edgar, 'Chronicles of a film' (trans. S. Feld and A. Ewing), *Studies in Visual Communication* vol. 11 no.1, Winter 1985.

Munro, David, 'Death of the documentary', *Stage Screen and Radio*, July/August 1994.

Murdock, Graham, 'Citizens, consumers and public culture', in Michael Skovmand and Kim Christian Schrøder (eds.), *Media Cultures: Reappraising Transnational Media* (London: Routledge, 1992).

Nichols, Bill, *Blurred Boundaries* (Bloomington: Indiana University Press, 1994).

New York Times v. *Sullivan* 1964, 376 S 254.

Observer and Guardian Newspapers Ltd judgment, European Court of Human Rights, 26 November 1991, Series A no. 216.

O'Neill, John, 'Journalism in the market place', in Belsey and Chadwick (eds.), 1992.

Paget, Derek, *No Other Way To Tell It: Dramadoc/docudrama on television* (Manchester: Manchester University Press, 1998).

PCC (Press Complaints Commission), *Code of Practice* (n/d).

Pember, Don, *Privacy and the Press* (Seattle: University of Washington Press, 1972).

Phillips, William, 'Hit or miss?', *Television* vol. 30 no. 7, December/January1994 (1994a).

— 'Top of the Box', *Television* vol. 31 no. 1, February/March 1994 (1994b).

— 'The Fourfront [*sic*] of programming?', *Television* vol. 31 no. 7, November/December 1994 (1994c).

Pool, Ithiel de Sola, *Technologies of Freedom* (Cambridge, Massachusetts: Harvard University Press, 1983).

Prager judgment, European Court of Human Rights, 26 April 1995 Series A no. 313

Preta, Auguston, Maria De Angelis and Marcella Mazzotti, *The Quest for Quality: Survey on Television Scheduling Worldwide* (Rome: RAI, General Secretariat of Prix Italia, June 1996).

Prince Albert v. *Strange* 1848, 2 De G and Sm. 652.

Pryluck, Calvin, 'Ultimately we are all outsiders: the ethics of documentary filming', *Journal of the University Film Association* vol. 28 no. 1, Winter 1976.

Purser, Philip, 'Jack Le Vien', *The Guardian*, 31 December 1999.

R. v. *IBA ex parte Whitehouse* 1985, *The Times*, 4 April CA, in Robertson and Nicol, 1992: 31.

Red Lion Broadcasting Co. v. *FCC* 1969, 359 U.S. 367.

Reith, John, *Broadcast over Britain* (London: Hodder and Stoughton, 1924).

Reynolds, P. D., *Ethics and Social Science Research* (Englewood Cliffs, New Jersey: Prentice Hall, 1982).

Roberts, Tom, 'The truth debate', *Guardian*, Media section, 24 August 1998.

— 'Who do these kids belong to?', *Observer*, Review, 2 May 1999.

Robertson, Geoffrey and Andrew Nicol, *Media Law* (Harmondsworth, Middlesex: Penguin, 1992).

Rosenthal, Alan, *The Documentary Conscience* (Berkeley: University of California Press, 1980).

Rotha, Paul, *Documentary Diary: An Informal History of the British Documentary Film, 1928–1939* (New York: Hill and Wang, 1973).

Ruby, Jay, 'The aggie will come first', *Studies in Visual Communication* vol. 6 no. 2, Summer 1980.

Russell, Christopher, Scott Peters, David Wilkofsky, Arthur Gruen and Joe Chung, *The Veronis, Suhler and Associates Communication Industry Forecast* (New York: VSA, 1996).

Scannell, Paddy, 'The stuff of radio', in John Corner (ed.), *Documentary and the Mass Media* (London: Edward Arnold, 1986).

Schechner, Richard, 'Restoration of behaviour', *Studies in Visual Communication* vol. 7 no. 3, Summer 1981.

Schering Chemicals Ltd. v, Falkman Ltd 1981, 2 All ER 321.

Schoots, Hans, *Living Dangerously: A Biography of Joris Ivens* (Amsterdam: Amsterdam University Press, 2000).

Sekula, Allan, 'The body and the archive', *October* no. 39, Winter 1986.

Seymour-Ure, Colin, *The British Press and Broadcasting* (Oxford: Blackwell, 1992).

Shachtman, Thomas, 'The exploitation factor', *Media and Methods*, January 1977.

Siebert, Fred, Theodore Peterson and Wilbur Schramm, *Four Theories of the Press* (Urbana, Illinois: University of Illinois Press, 1956).

Smith v. *Bush* 1989, 2 All ER 514.

Solomon-Godeau, Abigail, *Photography at the Dock: Essays on Photographic History, Institutions, and Practices* (Minneapolis: University of Minnesota Press, 1991).

Stirling Media Research Institute, *Consenting Adults* (London: Broadcasting Standards Commission, 2000).

Stoney, George, 'Must the film-maker leave his mark?' (unpublished paper, 1978).

Street, H., *The Law of Torts* (London: Butterworth, 1959).

Sunday Times judgment, European Court of Human Rights, 26 April 1979, Series A no. 30.

Sunday Times Ltd and Neil (no.2) judgment, European Court of Human Rights, 26 November 1991, Series A no. 217.

Sussex, Elizabeth, *The Rise and Fall of British Documentary* (Berkeley: University of California Press, 1975).

Swallow, Norman, 'Rotha and television' in Paul Marris (ed.), *BFI Dossier 16: Paul Rotha* (London: BFI, 1982).

Telecommunications Research and Action Centre v. *FCC* 1987, 801 F. 2nd 501.

Thorgeir Thorgeirson judgment, European Court of Human Rights, 25 June 1992, Series A no. 239.

Time Inc. v. *Bernard Geis Associates* 1968, 293 F. Supp. 130.

Tracey, Michael, *The Decline and Fall of Public Service Broadcasting* (Oxford: Oxford University Press, 1998).

Vihimagi, Tise, *British Television: An Illustrated Guide* (Oxford: Oxford University Press, for the BFI, 1994).

Welsh, Tom and Walter Greenwood, (*McNae's Essential Law for Journalists* (London: Butterworth, 1990).

Williams, Linda, 'The ethics of documentary intervention', in Berry *et al.*, 1997.

Warren, E. and L. Brandeis, , 'The right to privacy', 4 Harv. LR, 1890.

Wells, Matt and Jamie Wilson, ('Undercover reporter a hit with viewers and executives', *Guardian*, 26 June 2000.

Williams, Raymond, (*Culture and Society 1780–1950* (New York: Colombia University Press, 1983).

Willumson, Glenn, (*W. Eugene Smith and the Photographic Essay* (Cambridge, Mass.: Cambridge University Press, 1992).

Winston, Brian, 'The tradition of the victim in Griersonian documentary', in Gross *et al.*, 1988.

— *Claiming the Real* (London: BFI, 1995).

— *Technologies of Seeing* (London: BFI, 1996).

— *'Fires were started –'* (London: BFI, 1999a).

— ('"Honest, straightforward re-enactment": the staging of reality', in Kees Bakker (ed.), *Joris Ivens and the Documentary Context*) (Amsterdam: University of Amsterdam Press, 1999b).

— ('Smell the tulips: the Internet, neoliberalism and millenarian hype', in Stephen Lax (ed.), *Access Denied* (London: Macmillan, 2000).

Zimmermann, Patricia, *States of Emergency: Documentaries, Wars, Democracies* (Minneapolis: University of Minnesota Press, 2000).

Index